The Francophone Caribbean Today

Literature, Language, Culture

The Francophone Caribbean Today

Literature, Language, Culture

edited by
Gertrud Aub-Buscher
and
Beverley Ormerod Noakes

Studies in Memory of Bridget Jones

The University of the West Indies Press
Barbados ● Jamaica ● Trinidad and Tobago

University of the West Indies Press
1A Aqueduct Flats   Mona
Kingston 7   Jamaica

© 2003 by The University of the West Indies Press
All rights reserved. Published 2003

07 06 05 04 03   5 4 3 2 1

CATALOGUING IN PUBLICATION DATA

The francophone Caribbean today: literature, language, culture:
studies in memory of Bridget Jones / edited by Gertrud Aub-
Buscher and Beverley Ormerod Noakes.
p. cm.
Includes bibliographical references.
ISBN: 976-640-130-6

1. West Indian literature (French) – History and criticism. 2.
West Indies, French – Intellectual life – 20th century. 3. Jones,
Bridget, 1935–2000. I. Aub-Buscher, Gertrud. II. Noakes,
Beverley Ormerod. III. Jones, Bridget, 1935–2000. IV. Title.

PQ3940.F83 2003   840.9/92729'21

Cover illustration: Colin Garland, *Higgler* (pen and ink), *c.*1975.

Book and cover design by ProDesign Ltd, Red Gal Ring, Jamaica.

Printed in Canada.

CONTENTS

VI **Contents**

Introduction

Beverley Ormerod Noakes
and **Gertrud Aub-Buscher**

The essays in this volume consider various literary and linguistic aspects of fran-cophone Caribbean writing at the beginning of the twenty-first century, after eight or nine decades that have brought rich growth and astonishing change. Following its tentative beginnings as a colonial literature experimenting with European genres and representing diverse social groups in terms of European perceptions, francophone Caribbean writing acquired a distinctive voice in the first half of the twentieth century through authors inspired by the African her-itage of the region's majority population. Using the tools of Negritude or *indigénisme,* the great writers of this era – Aimé Césaire of Martinique, Jacques Roumain of Haiti – ensured that the racial and cultural legacy of Africa, long denied or overlooked by the educated middle class, could no longer be excluded from any literary portrayal of modern Caribbean society.

At stake was the issue of cultural identity – an issue inevitably bound up with racial identity and social class. This was a time less than a hundred years away from the end of slavery, when the interests of a disparate population were often in conflict. Césaire's emphasis on blackness and affiliation with Africa was an inevitable and long-awaited counterbalance to the decades when white or light-skinned West Indian writers presented a view of reality limited by the outlook of their circle, ignoring or condescendingly romanticizing the life of the non-white poor. Césairean Negritude was in effect a rehabilitation of the African-descended peasantry and working class. It introduced a new type of romanticization, in which Africa became the great mother country of the black

Caribbean intellectual: racial pride was now a dynamic force in poetry, drama and fiction. Negritude was also a call for social revolution from a political leader keenly aware of the need for economic reform, as well as psychological healing, in Martinican society. Self-limiting in its erudite references, its enigmatic surrealism, and its racial exclusivity, Negritude nonetheless opened up new ways of thinking about cultural identity, and it is impossible to underestimate its significance in the development of francophone Caribbean literature.

However, in his focus on the African-descended majority, Césaire simplified the complexities of Caribbean society, critically inclusive of the economic oppressor – *béké, métropolitain, grand mulâtre* – but bypassing the diversity of the working or lower middle class: descendants of Indian and Chinese indentured labourers, of early French seamen and Syrian pedlars, and the mixed-race population which had been growing from slave days onwards. In turning away from Europe towards Africa, he also ignored the historical links between the francophone islands and the rest of the Caribbean. Later twentieth-century writers, living in a different sociopolitical situation, would abandon his race-driven definition of Caribbean identity and his vision of a single vertical root linking his country with a historically distant Africa. Edouard Glissant's concept of *Antillanité* replaces Césaire's image of the fixed tree root with that of the laterally moving roots of the rhizome, and moves away from the unrealizable dream of union with a lost Africa. In Glissant's positive vision, Caribbean culture is a diverse yet unifying phenomenon born of the common experience of slave societies in countries throughout the region. The more recent founders of the *Créolité* school explicitly reject Césaire's emphasis on Africa alone, stressing the racial melting pot of their society as the key to its Creole identity. For Patrick Chamoiseau, Raphaël Confiant and Jean Bernabé, Caribbean culture is a complex of language and customs springing from the cultural fusion of the several races that have been brought or have found their way to the Caribbean in past centuries. Where *Antillanité* suggests a regional network of relationships, *Créolité* looks as far as the Indian Ocean islands in its inclusive definition of Creole culture.

The present collection of essays examines contemporary francophone Caribbean writers in the light of these major twentieth-century preoccupations, and points to the trends that are emerging as these writers make the transition into the twenty-first century. Cultural identity, although no longer addressed through race alone, remains the most important issue in the literature. It is explored through linguistic and stylistic considerations; through narratives of childhood, of injustice, and of exile; through a reassessment of the notion of revolution. An important change in the region has been the emergence of women writers in the late twentieth century: the voice of francophone Caribbean writing is no longer almost exclusively male, as it was half a century ago.

Marie-José N'Zengou-Tayo's essay (chapter 9) reviews the changing relationship between francophone Caribbean writers and history, contrasting Césaire's invention of a mythical past with the ways in which the novelists of *Créolité* have sought to represent collective folk memory in their works. Indebted to Glissant for elaborating the concept of collective memory, Chamoiseau and Confiant have recreated past Caribbean society in idiosyncratic ways but with similar goals. In dealing with history, both have faced the challenge of devising strategies for bypassing traditional narrative techniques – linear chronology, the traditional omniscient narrator – which are deemed inappropriate to Caribbean concepts of time. The influence of postmodernism is evident in the self-conscious intrusions of the authors into their fictions. According a privileged place to individual histories rather than to History, they foster the presence of uncertainty, ambiguity and contradiction in their evocations of the speech and lifestyles of obscure and uncelebrated communities.

Another aspect of the project of collective memory is the increasing use of autobiography by *Créolité* writers to address the question of cultural identity. Within this genre, the deceptively simple childhood narratives of Chamoiseau and Confiant are in fact sophisticated representations of Caribbean society in transition during the late twentieth century. The interplay of race, colour and language at school, for example, shapes the child's awareness of the class and identity codes of the adult world. Mary Gallagher (chapter 4) contrasts one of these recent memoirs of childhood, Chamoiseau's *Antan d'enfance* (1990), with Saint-John Perse's *Eloges,* published near the start of the twentieth century. These two texts set out to recapture a Caribbean childhood from very different social perspectives, yet they are linked by their joint approach to memory. Chamoiseau's work proves to be rich in intertextual references to *Eloges,* with which it also shares a poetic and celebratory tone and certain patterns of orality. However, essential differences are perceived in the area of cultural agenda, differences which highlight the importance, for Chamoiseau and other writers entering the twenty-first century, of ethnic allegiance and communication with the Caribbean collectivity.

Bridget Jones's essay (chapter 7) on *La Rue Cases-Nègres,* the first appearance in print of a paper presented to an Institute of Commonwealth Studies

Caribbean Societies seminar in 1993, indicates the extent to which some key issues gained or lost popularity as the second half of the twentieth century distanced itself from the first. This is illustrated by the ways in which the same subject matter was differently presented in a well-known Negritude novel by Joseph Zobel (set in the colonial Caribbean society of the 1930s) and in a 1983 film version of the novel. The novel's emphasis was on the plantation, social wrongs, alienation, the folk oral tradition, poverty, the slave heritage of Martinique's peasantry and its spirit of endurance. The film significantly restructures the novel in the interests of a later generation's notion of postcolonial identity and in the light of historical change. The decline of sugar production, the greater accessibility of education and increased social mobility make some of the novel's concerns outdated, while other aspects are given greater prominence in accordance with the interests of the 1980s. Thus, Creole is used as a mark of authenticity; there is more emphasis on links with Africa, on black militancy and resistance to white oppression, and on the ambiguity of the mulatto role. Although shot in the early 1980s, the film's praise of diversity seems to anticipate the principles of *Créolité*.

Reassessing the notion of revolution in Caribbean literature, J. Michael Dash (chapter 3) holds that *fin de siècle* authors have had to recognize the impossibility, or even the irrelevance, of the passionate rhetoric that characterized Negritude and the militant writing of the mid-twentieth century: the era of apocalyptic discourse has been overtaken by realism and the detachment of postcolonialism. Yet paradoxically, he sees the current promotion of the Creole language as a new type of essentialist claim in the politics of identity, whereby members of the *Créolité* school are setting out to establish Creole as the true source of cultural authenticity and the first language of the Caribbean. Contrasting this essentialism with the detached, deconstructive approach of Glissant, Dash considers the effects of politics on language and society – the influence of the French consumer society in the Départements d'Outre-Mer (DOM), the impact of US aid in Haiti – and implicitly questions the future role of Creole in Guadeloupe, Martinique and Guyane, while foreseeing the possibility of Haiti's national languages becoming English and Creole. These linguistic and cultural uncertainties are complicating factors in the search for a final definition of francophone Caribbean identity.

The question of Creole cultural authenticity and the use of language is one that spans the fields of linguistics and literature, and goes beyond the boundaries of the French DOM. Pauline Christie (chapter 2) reminds us both of the linguistic and cultural ties which link these islands to their "anglophone" neighbour, Dominica, and of the differences resulting from their different political histories. Although Dominica was a French colony for only a brief period in the eighteenth century, French settlers played a prominent part in its economic and cultural development during the colonial period, and its rapport with Martinique and Guadeloupe has remained close, not least because they share a common language. If the varieties of French-lexifier Creole spoken in each of the three islands are not identical, such differences as there are do not impede communication, and the problems of their relationship with the official language – French in the DOM, English in Dominica – exercise the minds of those concerned with local culture in all three. Concentrating on the DOM, Gertrud Aub-Buscher (chapter 1) discusses the changing dynamics of that relationship. While universal education, the desire for social mobility and the modern media revolution have favoured the spread of French, increased awareness of the part played by Creole in the Antillean cultural consciousness has led to movements for the preservation and propagation of the language, which at the close of the century seemed likely to be successful in some areas.

Marie-Christine Hazaël-Massieux (chapter 6), however, examining the use of Creole in French Caribbean novels of the 1990s, points out that after an initial burst of publication in Creole between 1975 and 1990, and despite much discussion of the role of Creole in spoken communication over the last thirty years, there has been a decline in the production of such texts in Martinique and Guadeloupe. Distinguishing between various forms of non-standard, regional and creolized French, and bearing in mind that Creole was well-represented in poetry and drama throughout the twentieth century, Hazaël-Massieux links the relative absence of Creole in the fiction of the DOM with the fact that the novel is the genre most removed from orality. Drawing on parallels with Haitian fiction, she explores the literary difficulties of exploiting (or, with more subtlety, representing) Creole in a conventional novel, pointing to the frequent literary marginalization of Creole by its confinement to sexual, aggressive or exclamatory contexts, and touching on the paradox of *Créolité*'s ambition to promote an oral language through the written word.

Créolité, the most prominent literary movement in the French Caribbean at the turn of the century, has proposed other cultural ideals which owe much to its mentor Edouard Glissant such as that of diversity of identity and of narrative voice. Yet some of these notions are also celebrated by writers working independently of Glissant's influence and of the *Créolité* school. Maryse Condé, for one, has established her own successful rival mainstream in Caribbean fiction. Carol Sanders's analysis (chapter 11) of polyphony in Condé's *La Migration des cœurs* (1995) shows this novelist's exploitation of linguistic and cultural diversity through a variety of devices: multidimensional time; shifts in narrative perspective; multiple narrative voices dominated by those of servants, traditional healers, dispossessed black males – representatives of minority cultures within Caribbean society; and underlying all this, the presence of a collective consciousness. In this novel, which covers four generations of a Guadeloupean family, Creole itself is a marker of identity or of implicit social conflict, but more important cultural references are race, colour, folklore and journeys bridging the distance between Caribbean islands.

While Gisèle Pineau has drawn on the elements of *Créolité* in some of her work, her view of Caribbean cultural identity is more closely focused on the legacy of the past and its effects on individual aspiration. Beverley Ormerod Noakes (chapter 10) discusses the motif of the dysfunctional family in Pineau's writing, where the direction of narrative emphasizes the links between childhood experience and adult behavioural patterns. By implication, the harmonious development of Caribbean society is associated with family stability and the capacity to triumph over the negative aspects of personal and social history.

The notion of francophone cultural unity is relevant not only to the DOM but also to Haiti, once the focal point of black revolt in the Caribbean, whose proud beginnings have been tragically obscured by its tumultuous history since independence. In the closing years of the twentieth century, in the francophone Caribbean as well as the United States, Haitian refugees from political and economic oppression have been at best patronized, at worst relegated to a status of unquestioned inferiority. Anthea Morrison (chapter 8) sets Simone Schwarz-Bart's *Ton beau capitaine* (1987) in the context of West Indian ambivalence towards Haiti in the Duvalier and post-Duvalier years, and sees the playwright's sympathy and sense of kinship with Haiti as a subversion of the assimilationist discourse of French neo-colonialism. Wilnor, the Haitian outsider in Guadeloupe, is an emblem of exile and loss, representative of the uprootings of the Caribbean diaspora that characterized the twentieth century and the effects of which – as we are reminded by the reference to Edwidge Danticat – continue to be felt today. Through her innovative use of a cassette recorder as an integral part of the dramatic action, Schwarz-Bart also proposes an intriguing technical solution to the problem of valorizing orality, a problem that continues to exercise the writers of the early twenty-first century.

Emigration may be experienced not only as nostalgic exile but also as challenge and opportunity. Sam Haigh (chapter 5) presents Dany Laferrière as a Haitian-born Canadian who feels "plutôt Américain", and aligns him with other francophone writers who have made of *errance* a positive concept. Examining some contemporary manifestations of *errance* – Chamoiseau's *drive,* Depestre's banyan identity, Glissant's rhizome – Haigh shows Laferrière as a writer who refuses to be preoccupied with his birthplace. Issues of racial, sexual and cultural identity are dealt with playfully and provocatively in much of his work. In his tongue-in-cheek world, remote from the *errance* of *Tout-monde* (which appeared in 1993, the same year as Laferrière's *Cette grenade dans la main du jeune Nègre est-elle une arme ou un fruit?*), *errance* is about physical and erotic freedom; mobility and travel across North America are means of shaping identity. Yet here is no traditional search for identity, since any fixed identity is to be avoided as a form of limitation and exclusion which is contrary to the spirit of *errance.*

The short story by critic and writer Priska Degras, which ends the collection, encapsulates the difficulties of the relationship with others. The appendix, Betty Wilson's select bibliography of francophone Caribbean fiction published between 1980 and 2000, highlights the contribution made by Haitian writers to the rich output of that period.

There is one DOM which does not figure prominently in the present volume. Bridget Jones, one of the few scholars actively engaged in research on writing from Guyane, was mapping recent developments in the life of that fascinating though rather neglected country when her sudden death cut short her project and so deprived the collection of a key contribution. "French Guiana Revisited" was to have traced social movements of the 1990s – notably the role of the young and of women in events of that decade – as well as developments in literature, especially in the theatre. The partial draft she left behind contains many perceptive insights but is far from the perfection which she demanded of herself before she would entrust anything to a printer, and the editors have therefore reluctantly decided not to include it.

The volume, which was originally planned as a festschrift in her honour, is now dedicated to the memory of a scholar who, as the sections below show, explored most of the areas covered by the book and encouraged and helped others to do the same.

Bridget Jones

Bridget Jones was born in London on 20 November 1935, the first child of Ernest and Kathleen Wheeler. She and her younger brother grew up in wartime London. After attending Hazelwood Primary, she went on to Minchenden Grammar School, where she obviously made her mark, for a half-century later a former classmate still remembers her as the sort of formidable person who excelled in every academic subject as well as on the sports field. She repeated that performance at university: having won a state scholarship to Newnham College, Cambridge, she was awarded a not-unexpected First in the Medieval and Modern Languages Tripos (French and Spanish) as well as a half-blue for hockey. It was in Cambridge that she met her husband. Donald Jones was a Jamaica Scholar reading for a degree in Chemical Engineering. In 1959, on her return from a year spent as an *assistante* in Douai, they married and moved to London, where Donald had got a job. She registered to do postgraduate work at King's College, London, under the supervision of J.M. Cocking, and was awarded her PhD in 1967. The thesis, entitled "Antonin Artaud, His Work and Literary Situation", was a pioneering work, written before Artaud became an academic industry, and it is a great loss to scholarship that it was never published.

In 1963, she and Donald moved to Jamaica to allow Donald to take up a position at the new oil refinery in Kingston. Bridget quickly made Jamaica her home. She gave much of what she had brought with her – a rigorously trained mind, her love and knowledge of the arts – but in return Jamaica also gave her a great deal. She had a deep understanding of the way Jamaica was developing – in the sense not of the know-it-all expatriate expert but of someone who had come to love the place and was growing with it. Aided and abetted by Donald, she became an important part of the Kingston cultural scene. Together with a small group of equally enthusiastic cinephiles, they founded and ran the first successful film society since the 1950s, they gathered friends and colleagues at their house for play readings, and between 1967 and 1973, Bridget could be heard or read all over the island when she took part in a weekly arts programme on JBC radio or wrote film reviews in the *Sunday Gleaner*. The Jones's parties were legendary: Bridget produced cauldrons of pumpkin soup and mountains of rice and peas and stamp-an'-go, and with Donald's rum punch and his aficionado's selection of reggae and the latest calypsos, guests were kept happy and dancing until the early hours of the morning.

But she had not just become a hausfrau or socialite. On her arrival in Jamaica, she took a job teaching Spanish at a boys' secondary school, and the following year she was appointed to the Mona (Jamaica) campus of the University, first teaching languages to students in the History Department and then as a member of the Department of French.

The University College of the West Indies, established in 1947 as a college of the University of London, had recently become the independent University of the West Indies, just as many of the territories it served were becoming independent nations (notably, both Jamaica and Trinidad in 1962). The climate in the institution was therefore very favourable to young academics eager to innovate and rethink both teaching syllabuses and their research in order to reflect the environment in which they were working. The hallowed exercise in prose translation began to include extracts from West Indian writers, frequently involving vocabulary unknown to the authors of traditional bilingual dictionaries, and it had to share its place on the programme with more imaginative approaches to language teaching. In literature, though the canon of metropolitan writing from the middle ages to the twentieth century still structured the basic syllabus, new options in francophone Caribbean and African writing were chosen by enthusiastic cohorts of students. While Bridget continued to teach nineteenth- and twentieth-century French literature and to interest Jamaican, Kittitian, Barbadian and Trinidadian students in Baudelaire, Sartre and Ionesco, she participated enthusiastically in the revamping of language teaching and was a key member of the team creating syllabuses for the new options in francophone African and Caribbean literature. She supervised one of the first English-language PhD theses on French Caribbean literature (the student concerned is now a professor in New York).

Her own research interests also began to focus on writers of the French Overseas Departments in the Caribbean. She published on Damas, Depestre and Schwarz-Bart, among others, and in particular developed an interest in the little-researched areas of writing in Guyane and the francophone theatre of the Caribbean. A project for publishing a much-needed anthology of five francophone Caribbean poets, developed with colleague and writer Merle Hodge in the mid-1970s, was much admired by the publishers to whom it was submitted, but was returned with regrets, no doubt because it was ahead of its time. She also developed her interest in folklore, served on the faculty's committee on folklore studies, and edited and contributed to its *Folklore Bulletin*. At the same time, she furthered the cause of teaching French in the general Jamaican community as an active member of the Alliance Française de la Jamaïque and the Jamaican Association of Teachers of French, serving on the committees of both.

Bridget gave her all to her teaching, and not just in the classroom: the students' engagement with set authors continued at play readings she organized at her home and in very professional productions of French and Caribbean plays in the University's theatre, which are still alive in the memories of those who took part in them. She was an exacting teacher, demanding the same high standards of her students as she did of herself: sloppy thinking was totally alien to her. Some found that a little daunting, but those who realized how lucky they were found that they were capable of making "the intellectual leap", as one of them recently put it, and remained forever grateful to her. She had a unique gift for drawing out the best in people, revealing talents that they never suspected they had, not only in students but also in her fellow academics. She was the most stimulating of colleagues, full of good ideas that sparked off good ideas in others and gave them the impression that they had thought of them in the first place.

It was her research on both francophone and English-language writing from the Caribbean, as well as the poetry which she wrote throughout her life, that helped to keep her going during a difficult period in the early 1980s. Since the late 1970s, the Jamaican economy and its politics had been going through turbulent times, and in 1982 Donald went to take up a job in Saudi Arabia to ensure a secure future for the family and a good education for their two sons, Daniel and Matthew. Bridget and the boys moved to Reading, so as to be a little nearer to Donald. The return to England meant that Bridget could see more of her English relatives, but it was not a good time to find a university job in the United Kingdom: the 1981 cuts meant that universities were shedding staff rather than recruiting. Between school runs and trips to Saudi Arabia during the school holidays, she used her time to gain a master of arts in applied linguistics, but her heart was not really in it: she missed Jamaica and her academic work at Mona. She continued her research and publications as well as her work for the Caribbean Examinations Council, which she had started in 1981. In 1985 and 1986 she had temporary contracts at the University of Reading, where she had the opportunity to teach some French Caribbean literature, but it was not until 1988 that she was appointed to a post at the Roehampton Institute, where she was to work until her retirement.

At Roehampton, she was as active as she had been at the University of the West Indies. She continued lively language classes and innovative approaches to the teaching of literature, especially in the area of francophone studies; she took over the job of admissions officer for the department and enjoyed and promoted the international contacts made possible by European mobility programmes; she was one of the moving spirits in the organization of study days on *Francophonie: mythes, masques et réalités* in 1994 and on *Surréalisme et francophonie* in 1997. Staff and students came to appreciate all the qualities which had made her such a valued teacher and colleague at the University of the West Indies. She was never too busy or too tired to help research students who had got into a rut, even when they were not her own supervisees, or to cast a critical eye over a colleague's inaugural lecture or latest article. If she did not have the brilliant career that could have been hers, it is partly because she always put the needs of others before her own.

Roehampton was not alone in benefiting from her presence in Britain. She regularly attended conferences at the Institute for Commonwealth Studies of the University of London, organized a section on African and Caribbean francophone literature at the 1994 annual meeting of the Society for French Studies, served on the committee of the Society for Caribbean Studies, was co-organizer of *Language Contact, Cultural Contact,* a symposium held at the Institute of Germanic Studies, London, in April 1995, was responsible for the French Caribbean section of *The Year's Work in Modern Languages* for four years and acted as consultant for various publishers. Above all, she devoted her energies to ensuring a place for francophone Caribbean literature on syllabuses and in research agendas in higher education. In 1989 she joined a group of colleagues from all over the country to found the Association for the Study of Caribbean and African Literature in French (ASCALF), a lively society with annual conferences and publications, which has fostered the teaching of African and Caribbean literature in higher education in Britain as well as in Ireland. The importance of her contribution to ASCALF was recognized by her colleagues when they elected her to the chair for 1994–95 and when the association made a presentation to thank her at its annual conference in November 1999. The latter occasion, which many feared (rightly, as it turned out) might be their farewell from her, only encouraged her to continue – she was busy planning future activities with a colleague just a few weeks before she died. The success of ASCALF is one of the best monuments to Bridget Jones's career: there are now a good twenty institutions in the United Kingdom and Ireland where students have the opportunity to study francophone Caribbean and African literature, and papers on Caribbean authors are no longer a rarity at conferences of the Society for French Studies. Her work lives on in that of the younger specialists in the area, who acknowledge her support in the books they are publishing and who will ensure that her legacy will be passed on to their students.

She continued to work and help others well after ill health forced her to retire in 1995. It was hoped that the cancer diagnosed in 1992 had been arrested, but in the summer of 1995 she was told that the pain in her back of which she had been complaining for several months signalled a recurrence. Initially, she was mainly angry, but that anger was transformed into a couple of stiff letters, an angry poem and a determination to get the most out of the time she had left. She went on research trips to Martinique and Guyane; she attended conferences and gave papers; she wrote articles (her publications list is particularly rich from that time onwards); she and Sita Dickson-Littlewood finished and published *Paradoxes of Caribbean Theatre* (their "Little Red Book", as it came to be called), a checklist of all the plays, in French and Creole (about four hundred of them), written or produced from 1900 onwards; she moved to Oxford and laid out and tended a beautiful new garden; she was a gracious hostess to numerous visiting friends and to guests at parties; she made sure to see all the plays worth seeing in Oxford, London and Stratford; she and Donald discovered Tuscany and the Czech Republic, celebrated their fortieth wedding anniversary and in March 2000 were part of the crowd on the Savannah in Port of Spain watching Carnival, an experience which seemed to have given her renewed courage and vitality. The sudden deterioration in her condition on their return came as a shock to all who knew her. She died on 4 April 2000, leaving unfinished projects ranging from a return to her work on Artaud and an article on Beckett in Jamaica to the publication of her own poems.

The loss of her incisive mind, her lively imagination, her subtle humour and her boundless concern for others was felt by the academic community on both sides of the Atlantic. Her memory will be kept alive by the work of those she helped and influenced, and by the publications dedicated to her – the *ASCALF Year Book* for 2000; *Les Théâtres des Antilles et de la Guyane: perspectives nouvelles,* a special number of the *Annuaire théâtral,* the journal of the Société Québécoise d'études théâtrales (no. 28, November 2000); *Les Théâtres francophones et créolophones de la Caraïbe: Haïti, Guadeloupe, Guyane, Martinique, Sainte-Lucie,* to be published by L'Harmattan; *Ici-là: Place and Displacement in Contemporary Caribbean Writing in French*, papers from a conference in Dublin which she attended a few months before she died (Rodopi, forthcoming); as well as the present volume.

Publications of Bridget Jones

1965
"Saint Artaud". Letter to *Times Literary Supplement*, 6 May.

1967
Review of Errol John, *Screenplays: Force majeure, The Dispossessed, Hasta Luego. Caribbean Quarterly* 13, no. 3: 57–59.

1970–71
Weekly contributions to a programme of arts criticism of the Jamaica Broadcasting Corporation.
Weekly film criticism for the *Sunday Gleaner*.

1974
"Léon Damas as Storyteller: 'Sur un air de guitare'". *Black Images* 3, no. 3: 19–23.

1975
"Serge Patient et 'Le Mal du pays'". *Black Images* 4, no. 3–4: 71–76.
"Some French Influences in the Fiction of Orlando Patterson". *Savacou* 11–12: 27–38.
"Léon Damas". In *A Celebration of Black and African Writing*, edited by Bruce King and Kolawole Ogungbesan, 60–73. Zaria, Nigeria: Ahmadu Bello University Press with Oxford University Press.

1977
"Two Short Stories". *Arts Review* (Creative Arts Centre, University of the West Indies, Mona) 2, no. 1–2: 38.
"Love Poems" ("Test at the Oval", "To a Tune by Jimmy Cliff", "Woman Say . . . Man Say"). *Arts Review* (Creative Arts Centre, University of the West Indies, Mona) 2, no. 1–2: 62.

1979
"Léon Damas and His 'Riding Horse'". In *Léon-Gontran Damas 1912–1978, Founder of Negritude: A Memorial Casebook*, edited by Daniel L. Racine, 227–32. Washington, DC: University Press of America.
Review of Jacques Roumain, *Masters of the Dew*, translated by Langston Hughes and Mercer Cook. *Caribbean Quarterly* 25, no. 4: 75–76.

1980

Seven poems ("Naming the Work", "Study fe Teacher", "Chores and Worse", "For Madame Camille M.", "Thermo-static", "Knucklebone Soup", "To a Tune by Jimmy Cliff"). In *Jamaica Woman: An Anthology of Poems*, edited by Pamela Mordecai and Mervyn Morris, 45–48. Kingston, Jamaica: Heinemann Educational Books (Caribbean).

Two poems ("Faculty of Arts", "Switched to Record in the Music Room"). *Caribbean Quarterly* 26, no. 3: 52.

1981

"Comrade Eros: The Erotic Vein in the Writing of René Depestre". *Caribbean Quarterly* 27, no. 4: 21–30.

1982

Introduction to Simone Schwarz-Bart, *The Bridge of Beyond*, translated by Barbara Bray, iv–xviii. London: Heinemann Educational Books.

1985

With J. Michael Dash (eds.), *Perspectives on Language and Literature: Essays in Honour of William Mailer*. Mona, Jamaica: University of the West Indies.

1986

"Theatre in the French West Indies". *Carib*, no. 4: 35–54.

"Orlando Patterson". In *Fifty Caribbean Writers*, edited by Daryl Cumber Dance, 368–76. New York: Greenwood.

1987

Translation of Pierre Clitandre, *Cathédrale du mois d'août* (Paris: Editions Syros, 1982), as *Cathedral of the August Heat*. London: Readers International.

1988

Two articles ("Léon Damas as Storyteller: 'Sur un air de guitare'" and "Léon Damas") republished in *Critical Perspectives on Léon-Gontran Damas*, edited by Keith Q. Warner, 31–42, 161–66. Washington, DC: Three Continents.

1989

Translation of a Haitian folktale, Alex-Louise Tessonneau, "The Little Girl Saved by Her Father". In *Under the Story Teller's Spell*, edited by Faustin Charles, 117–27. Harmondsworth, UK: Viking Kestrel. Republished in 1990, London: Puffin.

1990

"Two Plays by Ina Césaire: *Mémoires d'Isles* and *L'Enfant des passages*". *Theatre Research International* 15, no. 3: 223–33.

1992

"With *Banjo* by My Bed: Black French Writers Reading Claude McKay". *Caribbean Quarterly* 38, no. 1: 32–39.

"The Prospects for Literature in French Guiana". In *Protée noir: essais sur la littérature francophone africaine et antillaise,* edited by P. Hawkins and Annette Lavers, 88–97. Paris: L'Harmattan/ACCT.

Poem ("Thermo-static"). In *The Virago Book of Wicked Verse,* edited by Jill Dawson, 45. London: Virago.

Obituary of Vincent Placoly. *Guardian,* 15 February.

1993

"French Studies: Caribbean Literature (1991/92)". In Modern Languages Research Association, *The Year's Work in Modern Languages* 54: 252–55.

Review of Simone Schwarz-Bart, *Between Two Worlds. Wasafiri* 17 (Spring): 57–58.

1994

"Ti-Jean and Other Brothers". *Verse* 11, no. 2 (special issue on Walcott/Gaelic poets): 130–38.

With E. Stephenson, "Politique et société à la Guyane". In *Les Antilles-Guyane au rendez-vous de l'Europe: le grand tournant?* edited by Richard D.E. Burton and Fred Reno, 101–21. Paris: Economica.

"French Guiana". In *A History of Literature in the Caribbean,* vol. 1, edited by A. James Arnold, 389–98. Amsterdam: Benjamins.

"Duppies and Other Revenants: With Particular Reference to the Use of the Supernatural in Jean D'Costa's Work". In *"Return" in Post-Colonial Writing: A Cultural Labyrinth,* edited by Vera Mihailovich-Dickman, 23–32. Amsterdam: Rodopi.

Entry on Orlando Patterson (and others?). In *Encyclopedia of Post-Colonial Literatures in English,* edited by Eugene Benson and L.W. Conolly. London: Routledge.

"French Studies: Caribbean Literature (1993)". In Modern Languages Research Association, *The Year's Work in Modern Languages* 55: 280–82.

1995

"'The Unity Is Submarine': Aspects of a Pan-Caribbean Consciousness in the Work of Kamau Brathwaite". In *The Art of Kamau Brathwaite,* edited by Stewart Brown, 86–100. Bridgend, Wales: Seren Books.

"Quelques perspectives d'Outre-Manche sur l'étude des littératures francophones". *Etudes créoles* 18, no. 2: 39–48.

With E. Stephenson, "Society, Culture and Politics in French Guiana". In *French and West Indian: Martinique, Guadeloupe and French Guiana Today,* edited by Richard D.E. Burton and Fred Reno, 56–74. London: Macmillan.

Fourteen entries on Caribbean literature (Joby Bernabé, D. Boukman, Ina Césaire,

P. Clitandre, M. Condé, L. Damas, M. Jeanne, B. Juminer, J. Manicom, D. Maximin, S. Patient, E. Stephenson, *Tropiques*, M. Warner-Viyera). In *The New Oxford Companion to Literature in French*, edited by Peter France. Oxford: Clarendon.

"French Studies: Caribbean Literature (1994)". In Modern Languages Research Association, *The Year's Work in Modern Language* 56: 262–64.

Review of Marie-Christine Hazaël-Massieux, *Ecrire en créole: oralité et écriture aux Antilles*. *Journal of French Language Studies* 5, no. 1: 126–27.

1996

"French Caribbean Theatre (Overview)". In *World Encyclopedia of Contemporary Theatre*, vol. 2, *The Americas*, edited by Don Rubin, 276–84. London: Routledge.

With Arnaud Miguet and Patrick Corcoran (eds.), *Francophonie: mythes, masques et réalités*. Paris: Publisud.

"'With Crusoe the slave and Friday the boss': Derek Walcott's *Pantomime*". In *Robinson Crusoe: Myths and Metamorphoses*, edited by Lieve Spaas and Brian Stimpson, 225–38. London: Macmillan.

"French Studies: Caribbean Literature (1995)". In Modern Languages Research Association, *The Year's Work in Modern Languages* 57: 229–32.

1997

With Sita Dickson Littlewood, *Paradoxes of French Caribbean Theatre: An Annotated Checklist of Dramatic Works – Guadeloupe, Guyane, Martinique – from 1900*. London: Roehampton Institute.

"Quelques choix de langue dans le théâtre antillais (1970–1995)". In *Black Accents: Writing in French from Africa, Mauritius and the Caribbean*, edited by J.P. Little and Roger Little, 17–29. Proceedings of the ASCALF conference, Dublin, 8–10 April. London: Grant and Cutler.

"French Studies: Caribbean Literature (1996)". In Modern Languages Research Association, *The Year's Work in Modern Languages* 58: 249–52.

Review of Christiane P. Makward and Judith G. Miller (eds. and trans.), *Plays by French and Francophone Women: A Critical Anthology*. *French Studies* 51, no. 3: 362.

Review of Belinda Jack, *Francophone Literatures: An Introductory Survey*. *Wasfiri* 25 (Spring): 100–101.

1998

"Telling the Story of King Béhanzin". In *ASCALF Year Book 1998*, edited by Sam Haigh, 13–22. Warwick, UK: ASCALF.

Review of Evelyne Accad, *Wounding Words*, translated by Cynthia T. Hahn. *Bulletin of Francophone Africa* 12–13: 149–50.

1999

" 'We were going to found a nation . . .': Dramatic Representations of Haitian History by Three Martinican Writers". In *The Colonial Caribbean in Transition: Essays on Postemancipation Social and Cultural History,* edited by Bridget Brereton and Kevin A. Yelvington, 247–60. Kingston, Jamaica: University of the West Indies Press; Gainesville: University Press of Florida.

"Theatre and Resistance? An Introduction to Some French Caribbean Plays". In *An Introduction to Caribbean Francophone Writing,* edited by Sam Haigh, 83–100. Oxford: Berg.

"Approaches to Political Theatre in the French Caribbean". *International Journal of Francophone Studies* 2, no. 1: 36–44.

2000 (posthumously)

With S. Dickson Littlewood, entries on Jenny Alpha, José Alpha, Joby Bernabé, D. Boukman, I. Césaire, M. Césaire, M. Condé, A. Dalmat, G. Dambury, J. Exélis, J. Florentiny, G. Greg, Ho-You-Fat, Joël Jerdinier, José Jerdinier, A. Justin-Joseph, H. Kancel, J.A. Laou, A. Lérus, R. Liensol, J.-M. Martial, M. Mathéus, G. Mauvois, O. Pedro Leal, E. Pennont, J. Régina, E. Rézaire, L. Saint-Eloi, L. Salibur, E. Stephenson, F. Zobda. In *Who's Who in Contemporary World Theatre,* edited by Daniel Meyer-Dinkgräfe. London: Routledge.

Four entries (on J. D'Costa, C. McKay, V. Placoly, SERMAC). In *Encyclopedia of Contemporary Latin American and Caribbean Cultures,* edited by Dan Balderston, Mike González and Ana M. López. London: Routledge.

Four poems ("The Hurricane Veered North", "Long Mountain Close", "Yo Lorna G!", "Craigton Churchyard [for Shirley]"). In *Pathways* 16 (April): 12–16.

2001

Review of Micheline Rice-Maximin, *Karukéra: présence littéraire de la Guadeloupe. Modern and Contemporary France* 9, no. 2: 254–55.

Conference and Seminar Papers Not Published

"Léon Damas: A Poem and a Folktale". Caribbean Seminar series, University of the West Indies, Mona, 1975.

"Writing in French Guiana: Myths and Realities". Faculty Seminar in Caribbean Literature, University of the West Indies, Mona, 1977.

"Theatre in the French West Indies". Caribbean Studies Seminar, University of the West Indies, Mona, 1982.

"Written and Spoken Literature in the Francophone Caribbean". Institute of Commonwealth Studies, University of London, 1987.

"Why the Theatre Matters in the Caribbean". Caribbean Societies Seminar, Institute of Commonwealth Studies, University of London, 1989.

"Problems of Identity in French Guianese Writing". Centre for Caribbean Studies,

University of Warwick, 1989.

"Ti-Jean from Voice to Page and on to Stage". ACLALS Conference, University of
Kent, 1989.

"Questions of Identity in French Guiana". Centre for Caribbean Studies, University
of Warwick, 1989.

"Tortue et Tigre dans le ventre d'un bœuf: commentaire sur un conte créole
guyanais". Colloque des études créoles, Cayenne, French Guiana, 1989.

"Inside Cow Belly: Images of Dependency in the French Caribbean". Centre for
Caribbean Studies, University of Warwick, 1990.

"'Toi là-bas et moi ici': Schwarz-Bart's *Ton beau capitaine*". ASCALF Caribbean
Seminar, University of London, 1990.

"'Woy-o, a-how you come over?' Notes on a Scene from *The Hills Were Joyful
Together* by Roger Mais". ACLALS Conference, Mona, Jamaica, 1992.

"*La Rue Cases-Nègres:* From Novel to Film". Institute of Commonwealth Studies,
London, 1993.

"Une Parole insaisissable: le langage du théâtre antillais". Universität Bayreuth, 1995.

"Voyage vers l'impossible: Antonin Artaud au Mexique". Surréalisme et
Francophonie, Roehampton Institute, London, 1997.

"Staging French Caribbean History: Some Plays Dealing with the 19th Century".
Society for Caribbean Studies annual conference, Hull, UK, 1997.

"Comment identifier une pièce de théâtre de la Caraïbe?" Les Théâtres francophones
et créolophones de la Caraïbe: pratiques textuelles, scéniques et transculturelles,
CALIFA (Centre d'analyse des littératures francophones des Amériques), Carleton
University, Ottawa, Canada, 15–18 October 1997. To be published posthumously
in *Les Théâtres francophones et créolophones de la Caraïbe: Haïti, Guadeloupe,
Guyane, Martinique, Sainte-Lucie,* edited by Alvina Ruprecht (Paris: L'Harmattan,
coll. *Univers Théâtral,* forthcoming).

"Approaches to Political Theatre in the French Caribbean". Francophone Theatre,
Leeds, UK, 1998.

"A Prophet at Home: Aimé Césaire's Plays in the Caribbean". University of
Warwick, 1998.

Unpublished Manuscript

"Quelques aspects de la créativité créole (orale et écrite) de la Guyane française".

1

Linguistic Paradoxes
French and Creole in the West Indian
DOM at the Turn of the Century

Gertrud Aub-Buscher
University of Hull

Seldom have questions of language choice been a more central preoccupation
of the writer than in the closing years of the twentieth century in the French
islands of the Caribbean. Whereas most creative literature written in Martinique
and Guadeloupe in earlier periods, however "exotic" its subjects, bore little trace
of the linguistic mosaic of the countries depicted, the parallel existence of
French and Creole in the lives of authors writing in last four decades or so has
been a pivotal, if not always explicit, issue. Marie-Christine Hazaël-Massieux
writes eloquently in this volume on some of the paradoxes inherent in the subject,
and the purpose of what follows is simply to outline some aspects of the sociolinguistic landscape which forms the backdrop for contemporary writers in
Martinique and Guadeloupe.

At least two languages have been in common use in the islands since the eighteenth century: a form of French (not necessarily that of Paris), and the French-
lexifier Creole which arose as a result of the contact between French colonizers
and African slaves coming from a variety of linguistic backgrounds. French has
functioned as the official language, the language of the elite, of administration and
education, while Creole has been the mother tongue of most, the only language
of much of the rural population and known by all except recent arrivals from France.
The great majority (well over 90 per cent) of Creole vocabulary derives from Gallo-
Romance sources, in particular the non-standardized, colloquial language of the

seventeenth- and eighteenth-century settlers, who came from the provinces of the north and west as well as from Paris. Its grammar, though it shares features with spoken French, is very different; for example, it generally does not mark number or gender, and it uses particles, rather than flexions, to express tense and aspect. (For an overview of the theories concerning the origin and development of Creole, see Corne 1999.)

Although there is some evidence that in the early stages white planters were involved in the development of Creole (Bernabé 1983, 38 ff.), as a language without a written code, the language of African slaves and the poor, it has spent a large part of its history at the bottom of the status ladder, even among its native speakers – the *créolophones créolophobes* described by sociolinguists and wickedly ridiculed by Daniel Boukman in *Délivrans!* (1995). "Baragouin sauvage", "jargon (nègre)", "français corrompu/abâtardi/ imparfait/négrifié", "patois", and "patoiserie" (Prudent 1980, 27–30 and passim) are some of the terms used to describe it. It has been compared to child language, as by Jean Raspail in *Punch Caraïbes,* who speaks of its "simili-grammaire" and its infantilism, and pronounces that "Quelqu'un qui dit «fini parler» pour «j'avais parlé», «tigoute» pour «un peu», «piti piti» pour «très petit», «un zouézo» et «un zanimo» pour «un oiseau» et «un animal», «gadé» pour «regarder», «bitasion» pour «habitation», etc., créole ou pas créole, celui-là est bon pour le pédiatre" (1970, quoted in Valdman 1978, 330).

No less offensively, Elodie Jourdain, a *béké* and Creole speaker, set out in her Sorbonne thesis to show "ce que devient une langue de grande civilisation . . . en passant par des cerveaux et des gosiers noirs" (1956, xxii). Such attitudes betray little awareness that an essentially oral language is being compared with a notion of "beau français" which is written and very much more complex morphologically and syntactically than colloquial spoken French. It would appear that whereas linguists have recognized Creole as a separate language since the nineteenth century, its very resemblance at the lexical level to the colonizers' language has made for a fraught relationship with French.

Several models have been used to describe that relationship. The creolophone islands of the Caribbean were for a long time cited as classic examples of diglossia, the coexistence of two varieties of a language in a sort of complementary distribution. The model is hierarchical: one of the varieties has high status (H), the other low (L), with each attributed a well-defined role. In the essay which launched the term, Charles Ferguson ([1959] 1972) lists situations and the variety of language which is typically used in them (see Table 1.1).

Table 1.1: Charles Ferguson's High-Status and Low-Status Situations

	High-Status (H)	Low-Status (L)
Sermon in church or mosque	X	
Instructions to servants, etc.		X
Personal letter	X	
Speech in parliament, political speech	X	
University lecture	X	
Conversation with family, friends, colleagues		X
News broadcast	X	
Radio soap opera		X
Newspaper editorial, news story, caption on picture	X	
Caption on political cartoon		X
Poetry	X	
Folk literature		X

Adapted from Ferguson [1959] 1972.

In the DOM, French is assumed to occupy the H position, with Creole the L variety. Whether the classic model ever in fact applied has been debated over the years (see, for example, Prudent 1980 and Hazaël-Massieux 1996). If it did, there have certainly been shifts in the functions of the two languages, especially in the last half-century, with major gains made by Creole. Paradoxically, however, there has been a parallel strengthening of the position of French in the consciousness of many DOMiens, and at the beginning of the twenty-first century either language could be used in most of the contexts listed (with the possible exception of Creole in a letter or a university lecture, and even that is set to change). The model has hence lost much of the usefulness it may have had.

A quadripartite system consisting of French, creolized French, French-influenced Creole, and Creole, sometimes suggested as a better description of the situation in the DOM (see Bernabé 1983, 71), is no more satisfactory, in that it implies the existence of four discrete entities, which is supported neither by linguistic facts nor by the perception of speakers. More recent discussion has instead centred on the notion of the continuum, a model which sees not opposition between two languages but a system in which the practice of speakers varies depending on their own competence, the topic, the context, their interlocutors, and so on, along a notional line stretching from the basilect, the purest rural Creole, to the acrolect, the system nearest to the standard language, that is, French (see Figure 1.1).

Figure 1.1: Continuum from Basilect to Acrolect

basilect
form of language furthest
removed from SL
(rural Creole)

acrolect
standard language
(French)

While this more dynamic view certainly gives a more informative account, it is based on a simplification which implies that there is no stylistic variation within Creole, and it fails to reflect the complex nature of the linguistic situation. Hazaël-Massieux (1996, 138) has therefore suggested a double model with two parallel continua, one ranging from *français soutenu* to *français populaire* and the other from *créole soutenu* to *gros créole*, speakers operating on varying sections of both. To complicate matters, while each of the two continua has a range of registers, each language may also serve to mark a change of register in the other. Other linguists have further refined the description by insisting on the importance of the mesolect, or *interlecte* as Prudent calls it, the particularly Antillean French which differs from both metropolitan French and Creole, especially at the phonological and lexical levels, though it also shares features with both: "en Martinique, on parle martiniquais" (Prudent, quoted in Cichon 1999, 74). It has still not been adequately described (for a not altogether satisfactory description of the lexicon, see Telchid 1997), and many of its speakers are not aware that they are speaking a non-standard variety, though Prudent maintains that a growing number consciously play on it "comme si c'était une langue en gestation" (in Cichon 1999, 75).

No theoretical construct seems capable of adequately describing the etiquette that governs language choice. The use of Creole in the wrong context, especially by an outsider, may be perceived as an insult, implying that the person addressed does not know French, while French may give an air of distance or coldness. Even within the *créolophone* community, patterns of usage are very delicate. A survey carried out in the Martinican commune of Rivière Pilote in 1988 found, for example, that older people used Creole more than the young; the young spoke it more with their friends than to older people (to whom they replied in French even when addressed in Creole); hardly anyone used it when speaking to someone in authority; it was found more often at home than outside, even while being the only language for transactions in the market; men readily spoke in

Creole to their male friends but less so to women; women reciprocated but were undecided about how to address other women; and men between twenty and thirty had rules all their own (Coadou 1990). All these represent merely tendencies: there was much hesitation, especially in non-hierarchical exchanges, and often French and Creole were used in similar circumstances and even within the same conversation. Although Creole plays a more prominent part in Guadeloupe, comparable patterns can no doubt be found in both islands but are subject to constant change as a number of social and political developments alter the linguistic power relationships.

In recent decades, the position of French, traditionally the language of administration, education and high culture, has been extended and consolidated thanks to a number of factors. These include the greater penetration of the French electronic media – technological developments mean that Martinicans and Guadeloupeans can watch the same soaps as the couch potatoes of Bordeaux or Lille – and the increasing influence of returnees from a period spent living in France: whereas in the sixties and seventies, there was mainly an outward flow of those looking for work in the *métropole,* increasing numbers have returned in the last two decades with their Gallicized linguistic habits (Prudent, interviewed in Cichon 1999, 72). Most important, however, are the influences of parents and the school. Both involve some degree of paradox. Mothers who themselves had Creole as their first language discourage their children from using that language because they see that a good command of French paves the way to a successful future (March 1990), and they view the promotion of Creole as a game played by the privileged, as shown by this quotation from a Guadeloupean: "Sé moun ki ja konnèt pale fwansé ki ka di lézot pa bizouen-i" ("It's people who already know French who tell others that they don't need it"; Bebel-Gisler 1985, 243).

The advent of universal education, which has ensured that all children come into contact with the language of the Republic at an early age and that there are now no longer any truly monolingual speakers of Creole, was strongly supported by the left, who in other circumstances might be expected to want to ensure the survival of the local heritage, of which Creole is such an important component.

There has hence been much pessimism among those for whom Creole is an essential expression of their West Indian identity (and its use a political act of opposition to the growing encroachment of French). And yet, while French has undoubtedly made gains, the status of Creole has also been enhanced, sometimes in the same areas. Much of this is the result of the work of younger West Indian intellectuals. Where the previous generation – Fanon, Césaire, especially Césaire the politician – spoke of the critical role of Creole in the West Indian psyche but wrote in standard French, the generation of the seventies and later has actively studied Creole and promoted its use in all spheres of life.

It was probably the perceived relationship with French which delayed serious study of Creole by native speakers in the French West Indies until relatively recently. While Creoles began to interest European linguists in the nineteenth century and the earliest systematic description of a French-lexifier Creole (that of Trinidad, a British colony at the time) appeared in 1869 (Thomas [1869] 1969), and while a steady flow of studies of Haitian Creole by Haitians began in the 1930s, the West Indian DOM had to wait until much later in the century for the establishment of a school of local linguists examining Creole in its own right. Earlier theses, such as those of Poyen-Bellisle (1894) and Jourdain (1956) were the work of *békés* and more than a little coloured by racist attitudes. The generation of DOMiens who set about applying the tools of general and sociolinguistics to their native language became active in the closing decades of the twentieth century, notably with the doctoral theses of Guy Hazaël-Massieux (1972) on the phonology of Guadeloupean Creole; of Dany Bebel-Gisler, whose 1974 thesis, turned into a book two years later (Bebel-Gisler 1976), placed the question of language at the forefront of the anti-colonial struggle; and of Jean Bernabé (1983), the first large-scale study of an Antillean French-lexifier Creole by a native speaker.

Bernabé has been the moving spirit in the GEREC (Groupe d'Etudes et de Recherches en Espace Créolophone; more recently, and significantly, GEREC-F, Groupe d'Etudes et de Recherches en Espaces Créolophone et Francophone), the group of linguists and writers centred on the Université des Antilles et de la Guyane which has done more than any other to bring the question of language to the forefront, fighting for the recognition and protection of Creole and all that it stands for. It has fostered descriptive studies of Creole, sponsored publications such as the *Charte culturelle créole* (1982) and *Eloge de la créolité* (Bernabé, Chamoiseau and Confiant 1989) and the journals *Espace créole* and *Mofwaz,* and has taken active steps in a process of instrumentalization. Most important of these steps is the development of a standard orthography, since in the modern text-oriented world the lack of an established written tradition is a serious handicap in the attempt to raise the status of a language. The spelling of Creoles has always been an emotive subject: systems reflecting that of the lexifier language have the advantage of being easy to read for those who are already literate in that language but perpetuate the illogicalities of its system and get in the way of seeing Creole as a language in its own right, while a codification of the phonemic system of Creole is deemed to be difficult to read and poses the problem of which phonetic system, for example, that of Martinique or or that of Guadeloupe, underlies it. The alphabet proposed by the GEREC-F (in its latest form in Bernabé 2001) represents the phonemic system of Creole through a combination of phonetic symbols (for example, ò to indicate open [O]), with some of the conventions of French spelling (for example, the use of the digraph *ch,* or *n* to indicate a nasal vowel); despite some opposition (see, for example, Hazaël-Massieux 1996), it appears to be now generally accepted and features in many of the new uses of Creole which have developed in the last two decades.

For there is no doubt that the use of Creole has spread in many domains. While the metropolitan media are ever more available, there is no genre of mass communication which does not also feature Creole. Whereas earlier those who wanted to listen to Creole on the radio had to tune in to St Lucian or Dominican stations, they now have a choice of *radios libres* broadcasting from the French islands – RLDM and Radio-Apal in Martinique, Radio-Tanbou and Radio Inité in Guadeloupe (Confiant 2001, 17). There is local television using Creole and films with dialogue in Creole, notably in Palcy's adaptation of Zobel's *La Rue Cases-Nègres* (see Jones in this volume). Creole e-mail discussion lists flourish, and Creole can be found on a number of Web sites (Pierozak 2000), both as the medium of communication and its subject (see, for example, the site at www.potomitan.fr.st and Bernabé and Confiant's exhortation to use the Web as a means of spreading Creole [2001]). However, although Creole has been used in advertisements and cartoons for many years, it has been less successful in the print media. Articles in Creole continue to appear in the local press, and there are publications entirely in Creole, such as *Antilla-Kréyol,* but the wholly Creole *Grif en tè* only lasted from 1978 to 1982, and the one Creole edition of the *UNESCO Courier* published in 1987, while Edouard Glissant was editor-in-chief, failed to add Creole to the twenty-six languages in which that newsletter regularly appears. The problem is almost certainly that Creole still lacks a sufficiently large number of skilled readers: the process of codifying and generalizing a written system for an essentially oral language is a long one, fraught with problems (for a full discussion of these, see Hazaël-Massieux 1993).

The same factor has largely determined the role played by Creole in literature. Marie-Christine Hazaël-Massieux, in this volume, discusses some of the
paradoxes inherent in its place in prose fiction, and if Sonny Rupaire, Hector
Poullet and Joby Bernabé (see, for example, Rupaire 1973) have shown that Creole
can be used for serious poetry (and not only for popular songs, or translations
of the fables of La Fontaine, a fashionable pastime in the Indian Ocean as well
as the Caribbean in the nineteenth century), there is as yet no substantial
school of poets writing in Creole in the DOM. The problems surrounding the
accessibility of written texts are less acute for drama, the literary form most closely
allied to orality, as is shown in Jones and Dickson Littlewood's checklist of plays
performed in the Caribbean DOM (including Guyane) from 1900 onwards
(1997). As expected during a period when Creole was gaining ground in many
fields, an upsurge in plays entirely in Creole or using both Creole and French
began in the 1970s: from a total of 5 plays in Creole or using some Creole in the
three preceding decades, to 19 in Creole and 12 using both French and Creole
out of a total of 55 written or produced in the 1970s, to 44 and 45 respectively
out of 139 (a total of 64 per cent of total dramatic production) in the 1980s.
However, despite the progress made by Creole in other areas, that momentum
does not seem to have been maintained in the 1990s: only 23 plays were written
in Creole and 40 combined French and Creole (together just over 52 per cent)
out of the total of 121 listed for the period up to the end of 1996.

The area in which the role of Creole seems poised to be enhanced most effectively in the early years of the new millennium is education, traditionally the
greatest stronghold of French. Calls for the introduction of Creole into the
schools have come, especially since the 1970s, from those, like the GEREC, who
want to protect the West Indian cultural heritage, supported by practitioners
who have seen the damage caused to children required to learn and operate in
a language not their own (see, for example, Chevry-Ezelin 1999). It is also clear
that Creole has not been entirely absent from the classroom: one-third of
respondents in Kremnitz's 1975 survey of primary school teachers in Martinique
admitted that they used Creole at times to facilitate comprehension (Kremnitz
1983, 148–50), and over 70 per cent answered in the positive when the question
was refined to elicit responses on the use of Creole "pour expliquer certaines
choses" (Kremenitz 1983, 256–60). However, regulations continued to make the
use of Creole by teachers a serious breach of rules, which could lead to disciplinary
procedures and even dismissal. The concept of Creole as a means of instruction

has been a taboo not only for administrators but also for teachers, the general public and parents: surveys have consistently indicated opposition. For example, a poll carried out in Guadeloupe in June 1983 showed that 53.1 per cent of those questioned were still against the introduction of Creole into schools (Comité international des études créoles 1984, 189). Creole was (and to some extent still is) seen as a problem, distracting pupils from the proper acquisition of the national language: there were schemes for teaching Creole to teachers from metropolitan France, not so they could communicate with their pupils but so they could fight more effectively against "créolismes" (Kremnitz 1983, 61).

Many are the tales of punishments meted out to little Martinicans or Guadeloupeans caught speaking Creole in the school playground. Children in the Basque Country or Brittany shared the same fate, but for them the climate began to change in 1951 with the *loi Deixonne,* which provided for the possibility of some teaching in Basque, Breton, Catalan and Occitan. Other *langues régionales* (Corsican, even Tahitian) were added to the list over the years, but such recognition was very long in coming for Creole. René Haby's circular of 1976 acknowledged the need to take into account local culture but did not extend the range of recognized regional languages, and a further circular of 1982, which allowed for the inclusion of regional languages and cultures throughout the French educational system, left the choice of what was to be taught to the relevant *recteur d'Académie* (Chaudenson 1989, 187). The response of the rector of the Académie des Antilles-Guyane, Bertène Juminer, was first made public not in the DOM themselves, but at the fourth conference of the Comité international des études créoles held in Lafayette, Louisiana, in May 1983 (Orville 1983); a week later the declaration had still not been officially promulgated in the departments concerned (I.CAR 1983).

The declaration made it clear that changes would not be made overnight. In 1982, Juminer had declared himself a partisan of "la politique des petits pas" (I.CAR 1982) and his "softly, softly" approach was very comprehensible in view of the uncertain and often hostile attitude of the population. The proposal was to introduce Creole first in the early years of schooling, when the Creole-speaking background of most of the pupils was most likely to cause problems. The document speaks of "l'enseignement du créole et en créole" (Orville 1984, 52) and is equally vague about the training to be given to the teachers participating in the early stages: teacher training was envisaged as coming on stream later. Whereas written Creole was to be taught from the *cours préparatoire* onwards, the full codification of writing was also seen as a task for a later stage in higher education.

The evolution since 1983 has been slow. The pioneering work of Hector Poullet and Sylviane Telchid at the college in Capesterre-Belle-Eau in Guadeloupe and similar experimentation with optional classes at Basse-Pointe in Martinique from 1984 were the subject of workshops organized for the benefit of teachers and also for parents (see, for example, I.CAR 1985), but schemes were still far from universal: figures from the French Ministry of Education for regional languages taught in secondary schools in 1996–97 still make no mention of Creole (Ministère de l'éducation nationale, de la recherche et de la technologie 1998). There are several reasons for that delay, among them a dearth of appropriate teaching materials (though see, for example, Damoiseau 1999) and, most crucially, the lack of trained and recognized teachers of Creole. By 1985 the official French statistics on secondary school posts for the teaching of regional languages still did not include a single post for Creole among the fifty-nine listed (Institut d'Etudes Créoles 1985). Those who, led by the GEREC-F, campaigned for the creation of a CAPES (Certificat d'aptitude au professorat de l'enseignement secondaire) in Creole had to wait until October 2000 for a positive response from Paris.

Paradoxically, it was the European Union which gave the impetus for change in the West Indies: documents concerning the French response to the *Charte européenne des langues régionales ou minoritaires* include references to Creole (see, for example, Bernard Poignant's 1998 report to Lionel Jospin), and special measures – such as the recruitment of teachers qualified to teach regional languages, including Creole, and to use them as a medium of instruction – were announced in April 2001 (Lang 2001). Beginning in 2002, Creole will be heard regularly in the classroom, both as a taught language and as the medium of instruction for certain subjects, while French will continue to play an important part in education – even strong defenders of Creole have never suggested that French should be eliminated.

Developments in higher education began a good deal earlier. Research on Creole was part of the agenda of the Centre Universitaire (later Université) des Antilles-Guyane from the 1970s on. The first undergraduate course in Creole language was available to students in 1979, a *licence de langues et cultures régionales – option créole* in 1994, but in the absence of a teaching qualification, students who successfully completed that degree or the equivalent *maîtrise* could not go on to teach Creole in schools. Teams of researchers were, however, set to run training courses for teachers and prepare materials for the *CAPES de langues et cultures régionales (option créole)* once it was agreed, and an impressive list of guides for prospective candidates prepared by eminent Creolists and writers such as Raphaël Confiant and Daniel Boukman, is in place (GEREC-F 2001). The syllabus, a judicious combination of language study and language use, is effective from 2002 and applicable to Réunion as well as the Caribbean (while recognizing the difference between Atlantic and Indian Ocean Creole); the oral tests are being held in Paris for the time being.

With trained teachers officially allowed to teach the language and to use it as a medium of instruction for subjects related to the local context, the future for Creole seems bright, and one might hope that there will soon be a generation of French West Indians for whom reading in Creole will seem a normal activity. The paradox here lies in the timing of the new dispensations: because of developments outlined above, few, if any, of the pupils coming into education for the first time will be monolingual speakers of Creole, and a large number of them, children of those castigated for their French tainted with *créolismes,* will speak a Creole heavily influenced by French.

The process of decreolization, which has affected all aspects of the language, including the phonetic system, is well under way in both islands, and is only partially the result of the increasing mastery of French by all sectors of the population. Paradoxically, some of the threats to the purity of Creole derive from its own success. As it has assumed functions until recently reserved for French, it has had to expand linguistically from being a mainly oral language used in everyday contexts to an instrument able to cover in speech and writing the whole of modern life, with a full range of registers, including formal writing. (The syllabus for the *CAPES créole* includes a four-hour essay on a literary or cultural topic, in the best French tradition but written in Creole.) The most obvious and readily available means of plugging gaps is French. There has hence not only been large-scale lexical borrowing, especially of abstract and scientific terms and much of the vocabulary of modern life, but Creole syntax is also affected, with, for example, the creation of complex constructions in written Creole unknown (and not needed) in the spoken language. Although lexical items are adapted to the Creole phonetic structure, there is no doubt that the character of the language is profoundly altered by the newcomers.

Though accepted as inevitable by some defenders of Creole, such as Prudent, the resultant dilution of language is much regretted by many of those engaged in the struggle to raise its status, notably members of the GEREC-F. Their aim has always been to preserve and further Creole in its purest, most basilectal form, the form most different from French. Faced with the possibility of a massive influx of Gallicisms, they have reacted by proposing "true Creole" neologisms, most recently through the publication of the first volume of a *Dictionnaire des néologismes créoles* (Confiant 2001). Instead of transfers from French, it is suggested that old Creole terms should be resuscitated, or borrowed from neighbouring Creoles, and new ones coined using the mechanisms proper to Creole – derivation (however rare that may be in Creole), composition and the lexicalization of metaphors (Confiant 2001, 23). So for example, *konstriksyonnaj* is recommended instead of a creolized form of *architecture, mizirè lapli* for *pluviomètre,* and *palapenn,* from the old Martinican *biyé palapenn* (notice of dismissal), instead of *licenciement.* Whether Creole speakers will take to these terms designed to be true to their language but in fact created by intellectuals or whether they will continue to borrow from the lexifier language (as French speakers did from Latin in the late middle ages) remains to be seen.

The latest developments in the educational system make it difficult to predict what the future holds. Claude Hagège, in a recent volume entitled *Halte à la mort des langues* (2000, 35 ff.), discusses Creoles only as a means of linguistic renewal, whereas the inclusion of a volume on Creoles in the series Langues en peril (Hazaël-Massieux 1999) seems to presage something more sinister. Will Creole gradually disappear, ousted by the inexorable advance of French in the personal lives of French West Indians or, paradoxically, rotted from the inside through its own success and the consequent need for linguistic expansion? Or will the introduction of teaching of and in Creole, including written Creole, in schools ensure that the next generation of Martinicans and Guadeloupeans will feel comfortable in all aspects of Creole and view their ability to operate in two languages (three if we add to Creole and West Indian French, the "français français" of the school) as an enrichment of which they can be proud? Linguists, and especially sociolinguists, have an interesting time ahead.

References

Bebel-Gisler, Dany. 1976. *La Langue créole, force jugulée.* Paris: L'Harmattan.
———. 1985. *Léonora: l'histoire enfouie de la Guadeloupe.* Paris: Seghers.
Bernabé, Jean. 1983. *Fondal-natal: grammaire basilectale approchée des créoles guadeloupéen et martiniquais.* 3 vols. Paris: L'Harmattan.

———. 2001. *Guide de la graphie créole*. Petit Bourg, Guadeloupe: Ibis Rouge.

Bernabé, Jean, Patrick Chamoiseau and Raphaël Confiant. [1989] 1993. *Eloge de la créolité. In Praise of Creoleness*. Bilingual edition. Translated by M.B. Taleb-Khyar. Paris: Gallimard.

Bernabé, Jean, and Raphaël Confiant. 2001. *Le Créole à travers les âges de l'oral à l'internet, en passant par l'écrit* [online]. Available at: http://kapeskreol.online.fr/creole_ages.htm [accessed 9 July 2001; available in 2002 at kapeskreol.online.fr/creole_ages, with aditional author Daniel Barreteau].

Boukman, Daniel. 1995. *Délivrans!* Paris: L'Harmattan.

Chaudenson, Robert. 1989. *Créoles et enseignement du français*. Paris: L'Harmattan.

Chevry-Ezelin, Ellène. 1999. "Créole et inhibition verbale: évolution de l'inhibition verbale chez des enfants guadeloupéens de 4–7 ans". *Espace créole* 9: 93–105.

Cichon, Peter. 1999. "Témoignages sur la situation sociolinguistique à la Martinique en 1998". *Quo vadis Romania?* 12–13 (1998–99): *Martinique: Sprachen und Gesellschaft / Martinique: langues et société*. Special issue: 70–91.

Coadou, Martine. 1990. "A la recherche des règles d'étiquette sociolinguistique: une enquête de terrain en Martinique". *Nouvelle revue des Antilles* 3: 37–51.

Comité international des études créoles. 1984. Special issue: *Créole et Education. Etudes Créoles* 8, nos. 1–2.

Confiant, Raphaël. 2001. *Dictionnaire des néologismes créoles*. Vol. 1. Petit-Bourg, Guadeloupe: Ibis Rouge.

Corne, Chris. 1999. *From French to Creole: The Development of New Vernaculars in the French Colonial World*. Westminster Creolistics Series 5. London: University of Westminster Press.

Damoiseau, Robert. 1999. *Eléments de grammaire comparée français-créole*. Petit-Bourg, Guadeloupe: Ibis Rouge.

Ferguson, Charles A. [1959] 1972. "Diglossia". In *Language and Social Context*, edited by Pier Paulo Giglioli, 232–51. Harmondsworth, UK: Penguin.

GEREC. 1982. *Charte culturelle créole*. Martinique: Centre Universitaire Antilles-Guyane

GEREC-F. 2001. *Liste des guides de préparation aux épreuves du C.A.P.E.S. de langues et cultures régionales – option créole* [online]. Available at: http://www.kapeskreol. online.fr/concours/guides.htm [accessed 29 November 2002].

Hagège, Claude. 2000. *Halte à la mort des langues*. Paris: Odile Jacob.

Hazaël-Massieux, Guy. 1972. "Phonologie et Phonétique du Créole de la Guadeloupe", thèse de 3e cycle, Université de Paris III, Sorbonne Nouvelle.

Hazaël-Massieux, Marie-Christine. 1993. *Ecrire en créole: oralité et écriture aux Antilles*. Paris: L'Harmattan.

———. 1996. "Du français, du créole et de quelques situations plurilingues: données linguistiques et sociolinguistiques". In *Francophonie: mythes, masques et réalités: enjeux politiques et culturels*, edited by Bridget Jones, Arnaud Miguet et Patrick

Corcoran, 127–57. Paris: Publisud.

———. 1999. *Les Créoles, l'indispensable survie*. Langues en péril. Paris: Editions Entente.

I.CAR (Information Caraïbe). 1982. "Le recteur Juminer sur le créole à l'école." I.CAR 429: 2.

———. 1983. "La déclaration de Louisiane sur le créole." I.CAR 463: 2.

———. 1985. "La créole à l'école: la la marche se prouve en marchant." I.CAR 556: 1.

Institut d'Etudes Créoles. 1985. "Informations." *Gazet sifon blé / Lavwa ka bay*, 6: 3. Aix-en-Provence, France: Institut d'Etudes Créoles.

Jones, Bridget, and Sita E. Dickson Littlewood. 1997. *Paradoxes of French Caribbean Theatre: An Annotated Checklist of Dramatic Works – Guadeloupe, Guyane, Martinique – from 1900*. London: Roehampton Institute.

Jourdain, Elodie. 1956. *Du français aux parlers créoles*. Paris: Klincksieck.

Kremnitz, Georg. 1983. *Français et créole: ce qu'en pensent les enseignants: le conflit linguistique à la Martinique*. Hamburg, Germany: Buske.

Lang, Jack. 2001. "Les Nouvelles orientations pour le développement de l'enseigne-ment des langues régionales". Speech given 25 April 2001 [online]. Available at: http://kapeskreol.online.fr/textes/lang_25avril.htm [accessed 09 July 2001].

March, Christian. 1990. "L'Attitude des mères martiniquaises dans le processus de minoration linguistique". *Nouvelle revue des Antilles* 3: 53–63.

Ministère de l'éducation nationale, de la recherche et de la technologie. Direction de l'enseignement scolaire. 1998. *Enseignement des langues et cultures régionales au collège et au lycée, 1996–1997*. Quoted in *Les Langues régionales. II. La politique de l'Etat en faveur des langues régionales et d'Outre-mer* [online]. Available at: http://www.culture.fr/culture/dglf/lang-reg/lang-reg9.htm [accessed 21 February 2001].

Orville, Xavier. 1984. "Déclaration de M. B. Juminaire [*sic*], recteur de l'Académie des Antilles-Guyane". *Etudes créoles* 7, no. 1–2, 51–53.

Pierozak, Isabelle. 2000. "Essai d'analyse semio-sociolinguistique des créoles sur Internet". *Etudes créoles* 23, no. 1: 88–109.

Poignant, Bernard. 1998. *Langues et cultures régionales: rapport de Monsieur Bernard Poignant, Maire de Quimper, à Monsieur Lionel Jospin, Premier Ministre* [online]. Available at: www.ladocfrancaise.gouv.fr/cgi-bi [accessed 23 February 2001; available in 2002 at http://bzh.com/identité-bretonne/chante/fr-poignant.html].

Poyen-Bellisle, René de. 1894. *Les Sons et les formes du créole dans les Antilles*. Baltimore and Chicago: John Murphy.

Prudent, Lambert-Félix. 1980. *Des baragouins à la langue antillaise*. Paris: Editions Caribbéennes.

Rupaire, Sonny. 1973. . . . *cette igname briseé qu'est ma terre natale, ou grande parde, ti cou-baton*. Paris: Parabole.

Telchid, Sylviane. 1997. *Dictionnaire du français régional des Antilles, Guadeloupe,*

Martinique. Paris: Éditions Bonneton.

Thomas, J.J. [1869] 1969. *The Theory and Practice of Creole Grammar.* Introduction by Gertrud Aub-Buscher. London; Port of Spain, Trinidad: New Beacon.

Valdman, Albert. 1978. *Le Créole: structure, statut et origine.* Paris: Klincksieck.

2

Dominica and the French Caribbean

So Far and Yet So Near

Pauline Christie

University of the West Indies, Mona

The labels generally used to distinguish between groups of islands in the Caribbean reflect only their ultimate colonial affiliations. In other words, designations such as "the French Caribbean", "the Dutch Antilles" and "the former British West Indies" do not tell the whole story, as throughout the centuries many of these islands moved back and forth between the jurisdictions of one European power and another. Subgroups which cross the boundaries the labels indicate are sometimes clearly recognizable. One such, based on earlier historical associations together with geographical proximity, comprises Dominica, St Lucia, Martinique and Guadeloupe. It is the long-standing relationship between Dominica and its French neighbours, despite its membership in the "anglophone" group, which is the subject of this paper.

Current Links between Dominica and the "Anglophone" Caribbean

The ties that bind Dominica to the rest of the former British Caribbean are well established. Like the other members of this group, it inherited from the British its official language, English, its political and judicial institutions, its education system, its popular sports, and other aspects of its culture. In relatively recent times, especially since the achievement of political independence by nearly all the states in question, a wide range of associations linking them still further has been established, some primarily political, others relating to trade, education, sports and culture.

Specific administrative ties with neighbouring British-ruled islands characterized much of Dominica's history. The island was governed from Grenada between 1764 and 1770, but subsequently became a Crown colony. Later, between 1871 and 1939, it formed part of the Leeward Islands colony administered from Antigua, then rejoined Grenada with St Lucia and St Vincent as a member of the Windward Islands group, an affiliation which lasted until 1960. Currently, the members of this last group, along with Antigua, Barbuda, St Kitts and Nevis, constitute the Organisation of Eastern Caribbean States (OECS), a relatively loose arrangement of small politically independent territories which was formed in 1981.

In the wider sphere, Dominica was part of the short-lived West Indies Federation of the late 1950s, which brought together the British West Indian territories. It is also a founding member of the Caribbean Community (CARICOM), an organization established in 1968 to promote trade within the region. Indeed, a former prime minister of Dominica, Dame Eugenia Charles, played a significant leadership role in this body during the 1980s.

Educational institutions, originally set up in accordance with British tradition, also reflect recent developments within the "anglophone" territories of the region. For example, Dominican students take examinations set by the Caribbean Examinations Council after five years of secondary school, and some go on to tertiary education at one of the three campuses of the University of the West Indies in Jamaica, Barbados and Trinidad. Dominicans also participate with the other islands in regional cricket – the sport most closely associated with British heritage – and some have served on the West Indies team in international competitions. Some Dominican Creole words of French origin have been given a place, along with their counterparts of French origin from Trinidad and Grenada, in the *Dictionary of Caribbean English Usage* (Allsopp 1996). Last but not least, Dominica's currency, the Eastern Caribbean dollar, is shared with other members of the OECS.

Dominica and the French: The Historical Background

Dominica is sandwiched between the French islands. It lies 48 kilometres north of Martinique and 40 kilometres south of Guadeloupe. The tiny islands of Marie Galante and the Saintes group, dependencies of Guadeloupe, are in fact its closest neighbours, but in this paper they are lumped together with Guadeloupe. Despite the different European affiliations of Dominica, Martinique and Guadeloupe in recent times, their colonial histories were constantly intertwined. Indeed, for much of the seventeenth and eighteenth centuries all the islands in the Lesser Antillean arc were pawns in the struggle for power between the English and the French. Dominica's position between the French colonies made it particularly valuable, but although both European nations had staked their claims to it as early as 1627, owing to the ruggedness of the terrain and the hostility of the native Caribs the island did not officially become a colony of either until 1763, when it was ceded to the British. It remained under their jurisdiction for the next two hundred years, except for five years (1778–83) during the War of American Independence when it was in French hands. In contrast, official French colonies had been set up in Martinique and Guadeloupe in 1635 and they have remained French except for a short period of wartime British occupation each experienced during the second half of the eighteenth century. Their institutions, their official language and much of their culture are French, and they are still officially linked to France as Départements d'Outre-Mer. Their inhabitants are French citizens.

Despite the lack of official ties to France, Dominica too has had a long-standing relationship with the French. Both British and French settlers were to be found there as early as 1632, in which year it was reported that there were 349 French persons on the island, possessing Negro slaves (Baker 1994, 44). These settlers had presumably come from St Christopher (modern St Kitts), where a French colony had been established seven years earlier. French missionaries visited early on from Guadeloupe and Martinique. A Carib-French dictionary and grammar by one of these, Fr. Breton, was published in 1665. Later, settlers came from Martinique and Guadeloupe after colonies had been established on these islands. Many white indentured servants from France, no longer needed after the establishment of large sugar estates on Martinique and Guadeloupe and the large-scale importation of African slaves in the second half of the seventeenth century, were among these. The settlers were not men bent on conquest, but were, for the most part, woodcutters and small farmers living peaceably among the Caribs and producing cotton, cacao, bananas and garden produce for sale to the neighbouring French colonies. Some officials were later appointed from Martinique to promote law and order, and later to collect revenue (Honychurch 1984, 35). Between 1730 and 1763, the population of Dominica grew from 776 to 7,890 (Baker 1994, 47), of whom the majority were Frenchmen and their slaves. During the Seven Years' War between England and France (1756–63), the strategic position of all the islands of the Lesser Antilles was important, but none was more so than Dominica, which lay between two French territories. Though not officially French, it was seen as a threat by the British because of the loyalty of its mainly French inhabitants to the French cause. Being poorly defended, it fell to an attacking force in 1759 and was officially granted to Britain at the end of the war.

The French inhabitants remained numerically and economically influential long after the island was ceded to Britain in 1763. Immediately after this event, leases of not less than seven years in the first instance were issued to those French inhabitants who consented to take the oath of allegiance to the King of England. Indeed, at this time they were not allowed to dispose of their land without the governor's permission. There was some emigration then, and even more when the island was returned to Britain after the period of French rule between 1779 and 1783, but their ranks were strengthened again immediately after the French Revolution by large numbers of refugees. According to Cecil Goodridge (1972, 155), in the summer of 1793 between five and six thousand refugees came from Martinique alone. The presence of so many French residents was a source of anxiety for the British administrators. Their fears were well founded: some French inhabitants actively supported two abortive invasions of Dominica during the wars which followed.

French planters owned most of the rich coffee estates until well into the nineteenth century. English efforts to establish sugar, on the other hand, had only short-lived success. Many would-be settlers from Britain, surprised by the rugged nature of the terrain they had expected to cultivate and by Maroon raids, soon migrated, leaving their estates in the hands of managers. Many were eventually taken over by mulattos from Martinique and Guadeloupe who came in search of the relative social freedom that existed on Dominica.

Africans also contributed to the perpetuation of French influence on Dominica. As early as 1632, French inhabitants were reported to have 338 Negro slaves. Since Martinique and Guadeloupe were only then being colonized, these first slaves had most likely come either from St Christopher, the first colony to be established, or through capture or shipwreck. Some Africans also lived among the Caribs, having been seized during raids on European settlements on neighbouring islands. By 1753, there were reportedly 5,872 slaves on Dominica (Boromé 1972, 94). Some of these must have been descendants of those who had accompanied their masters from Martinique and Guadeloupe, where sugar production was already well established by 1664. There had also been runaways from the plantations of these neighbouring islands, and some slaves had been acquired in illicit trading. Since Dominica had no sugar estates before it became a British colony, it is likely that few slaves, if any, would have been directly imported from Africa at this stage. The relationships between masters and slaves on Dominica were closer at this time than those which existed on the large sugar plantations of the other islands. Ex-slaves loyal to their French owners participated in the capture of the island by the French during the War of American Independence and were particularly active in French attempts to take the island during the Revolutionary and Napoleonic Wars at the turn of the nineteenth century.

However, new members of the slave population had less reason to show loyalty to the French after the British takeover. Many of them had been brought to Dominica by settlers migrating from colonies established earlier, such as Antigua. There were also newcomers from Africa, purchased in the usual way. According to a Report on the State of His Majesty's Island of Dominica (CO 71–72), the number of Negroes, which in July 1772 had been 15,753, increased in the following year by nearly three thousand "by the Sales of many Guinea Cargoes since sold the planters". Roseau had become a free port soon after the cession and dealt in slaves as well as other merchandise. Later the number of slaves actually decreased, as many died and others ran away from the plantations. Settlements of Maroons had existed on the island even before 1763, but their populations increased significantly after the arrival of the British. As the British attempted to strengthen their position on the island, Maroon raids on their estates became frequent. The severe punishments meted out to the perpetrators of revolts between 1812 and 1814 finally put an end to their resistance.

Later Relationships

The early nineteenth century saw the end of the rivalry between the European powers for the possession of the islands and the establishment of new, less turbulent relationships. After the abolition of slavery in Dominica in 1834, the black population of the island was increased by the arrival of runaway slaves from Martinique and Guadeloupe, where emancipation did not take place until 1848.

In the contemporary era, kinship ties, already established from the earliest contacts, have continued to grow, mainly as a result of Dominicans emigrating to the more prosperous French islands in search of work. Trade between the islands, another important factor throughout the centuries, still plays an important role. Nowadays, planes have joined the traditional sea-going vessels in providing the means of transport for the large numbers of hucksters involved in taking goods from one island to another. Indeed, Dominica's most direct air links are with Martinique and Guadeloupe, through daily flights provided by Leeward Islands Air Transport (LIAT) flying out of Antigua to the southern Caribbean. Dominicans are also within reach of radio programmes from the French islands and vice versa.

Relationships between Dominica and continental France have also survived and been strengthened during the twentieth century. In World War II, Free French forces were based on the island. Since then, the developments which have taken place have been directed towards providing socioeconomic assistance to the island while at the same time fostering French cultural interests. Dominica is a member of the Agence de coopération culturelle et technique (ACCT), founded in 1970 with the aim of promoting co-operation in the domains of education, culture, science and technology. In recent years the French government has actively promoted the teaching of French in Dominican schools. It has also helped to extend the airport near Roseau, the capital, and to improve the roads. There have been formal commercial links as well, such as the opening of the Banque Française Commerciale in the late 1970s. The continued association between the French islands and continental France has also helped Dominica's tourism, as French visitors often take trips from Martinique and Guadeloupe to visit the island.

The French Legacy

The new developments have, of course, been encouraged and facilitated by Dominica's French heritage. Although this legacy is most noticeable in the lexically French Creole traditionally spoken by most Dominicans, it is also evident in the areas of religion, folk tales, proverbs and sayings, music, dance, traditional costumes and cuisine. Language is important for all of these even if, in some cases, it merely provides descriptive labels.

Where religion is concerned, from the earliest contact, French missionaries had worked among the Caribs. Later their successors established themselves among the settlers and slaves. The churches they established remain striking landmarks in towns and villages throughout the island. Although the British introduced Anglicanism and, more significantly in this case, Methodism, these remained confined to specific areas of the island. The majority of Dominicans, a proportion estimated at 90 per cent in the 1960s, are still at least nominally Roman Catholics (see the report on the 1960 census). Until quite recently, it was normal for priests to be sent from Martinique and Guadeloupe and therefore to be francophone. Some use has always been made of Creole in religious worship, at least informally. This may not have been confined to the Roman Catholics; a Creole version of the Gospel of St Mark, translated by J. Numa Rat, a physician, was published by the British and Foreign Bible Society in London in 1894. Recently, a project for a Creole Bible which would be used in all the franco-creolophone Caribbean territories has been sponsored by the US-based Summer Institute for Linguistics.

Before discussing the lexically French Creole for which the island is best known and its relationship with the vernaculars of Martinique and Guadeloupe, it is worth commenting on the position of the French language in the context of efforts to anglicize Dominica. English became the official language as soon as the British assumed political power in 1763. There followed, in 1771, a proclamation (Melvill 1771) designed to change certain place names from French to English, but this move was largely unsuccessful; many of the places listed retain their original names to this day. French surnames still predominate among the population.

The survival of French culture even under British rule is underlined by a number of observations. For example, early in the nineteenth century "A Resident" wrote, "In Dominica which was settled by the French, many of the coffee planters are still Frenchmen or their descendants, speaking the French language and being French in manner and habits, as are also their slaves, though living in a British colony" (1828, 222–23). Much later in the century, it was not unusual to find in newspapers articles, notices, poems and even letters to the editor written in French. Some of these were accompanied by English translations, but there is evidence that French was still generally understood. For example, accompanying a physician's letter which appeared in French in the Roseau *New Chronicle* of 6 December 1895 was this comment: "As the generality of our readers read and understand French, we make no apologies for not having translated it." That this may not simply have been the editor's personal opinion is suggested by statements from officials and visitors to the island. For example, one inspector of schools commented in his 1869 report on the continued use of French alongside English for the conduct of business and in the law courts.

The lexically French Creole, referred to locally as *patwa,* which has traditionally been the first language of the non-European members of the population, was first brought to Dominica from Martinique and Guadeloupe by slaves when the early European settlements on the island were established. It was adopted by the Caribs over the centuries, to the extent that they eventually abandoned their own language in favour of it. As recently as approximately fifty-five years ago, monolingual and bilingual speakers of this variety were estimated to form 93 per cent of the total population (Census Report 1946).

The widespread use of such Creoles in Dominica and St Lucia, more or less two centuries after English became these islands' official language, reflects the relatively slow development of education and is itself a cause of this slow development. Since schools were first established, English has been the official medium of education, but as one nineteenth-century writer commented with regard to Dominica, "In Dominica, English education meets with a special difficulty, for a century and a quarter of British occupation has not removed the traces of French settlement" (Lucas 1890, 166). A similar comment could justifiably be made today. The phenomenon is all the more striking when one considers the virtual disappearance of the lexically French Creoles from Trinidad and Grenada, where they were also widely spoken.

Causal factors in the Dominican situation include poor internal communications within the island. This not only hampered the spread of education, but over the years made communication by boat with the French islands easier for many residents than communication with other parts of Dominica. Other causal factors are the role of Creole as the vehicle of traditional folklore and the sentimentality attached by some Dominicans to Creole as a symbol of French heritage. These were summed up in an editorial in the *Dominica Herald*:

> No constituent of this heritage has resisted the erosive march of time or the rivalry of other contesting elements such as those associated with one hundred and sixty years of British Rule more than the composite Patois dialect. None has proved more evocative of our historic association with the French, or to a lesser degree the Caribs whom Christopher Columbus found here and to whom we owe most of our geographical names. In no other element has so much of our folklore, so rich in wit and humour, been enshrined as in patois. (23 October 1965)

It is unlikely that such a statement would appear in the public media now, but the sentiment it expresses has not altogether disappeared. Moreover, proverbs and traditional songs and stories remain associated with Creole.

The varieties of Creole spoken in Dominica, St Lucia and the French islands are structurally very close to each other. A few differences are nevertheless observable. Both similarities and differences are illustrated in the following extracts:

Dominican Creole[1]

On fwa, on chyen volé on mòso vyann évé i té ka kouwi pou alé jwenn met-li. Kon i ka kouwi, i wè on pon. I té ka pasé anlé pon-a lè i wè on lot mòso vyann ki pli gwo, ki pasé sa'y-la. I lajé sa'y-la évé i alé an glo-a. . . .

One day, a dog stole a piece of meat and he was running to meet his master. As he was running, he saw a bridge. So he passed on to the bridge when he saw another piece of meat which was bigger, bigger than his. He let go of his and he went into the water. . . .

Martinican Creole[2]

An tan-ta-la, Bon Dyé té ka désann tou lonng an lé latè. I té ka vini wè la Sint-Vyej ki té ka resté la. Péson pa té sav i té la, paské i té ka sanm lézot moun-lan.

I té ka mété mem rad ki yo é an chapo bakwa. I té ni osi an "baton makak" ki té ka palé. Sé béké-a té ni labitid-ta-la. Lè yo té lé sav an bagay, yo té ka mété baton-an bò zorey-yo, yo té ka mandé'y an bagay, baton-a té ka réponn.

At that time, God often came down on the earth. He came to see the Virgin Mary who lived there. No one knew he was there, because he looked like the other people.

He wore the same clothes as they did and a "bakwa" hat. He also had a monkey stick that could speak. Those white people had this habit. When they wanted to know something, they would put the stick to their ear. They would ask it for something, the stick would reply.

Guadeloupean Creole

On jou, konpè Lapin té ka pasé owa kaz a konpè Tig. Tupannan i té ka pasé, on kalité bon lodè rantré an né a'y. I mété'y ka lonviyé andidan kaz-la. I vwè inki bon biten I té tini manjé la kon tilili.

One day, Brer Rabbit was passing by Brer Tiger's house. As he was passing, a nice smell reached his nostrils. He began to examine the inside of the house. There he saw only nice things. There was food galore.

The past marker *té,* the progressive aspect marker *ka,* the third-person singular subject pronoun *i* and the definite determiner *la* (with their morphophonological variants) are among the grammatical features appearing in all three extracts. One of these, *ka,* the marker of progressive and habitual aspects, distinguishes the group to which all three varieties belong from other lexically French Creoles, including Haitian and Louisiana Creoles.

The most significant grammatical difference concerns the expression of possession. The possessive phrases *zorey-yo* "their ear" (Martinican) and *met-li* "his master" (Dominican), in which the form denoting the possessor immediately follows the one referring to the entity possessed, contrast with the Guadeloupean *ne-a'y* "his nose", with an intervening particle *a.* This contrast applies whether the possessor is represented by a noun or by a pronoun.

Some of the forms occurring in one or another of the extracts are also worth noting as they are associated with one rather than other varieties. These include the Martinican demonstrative *ta,* which corresponds to the Dominican and Guadeloupean *sa,* and the Guadeloupean *biten* "thing", which contrasts with the Martinican and Dominican *bagay.*

Where Martinican and Guadeloupean usages differ, it is usual to find both variants in Dominica – the Guadeloupean form particularly in the north of the island, which is geographically closer to Guadeloupe and its dependencies, the

Martinican form in the south. The forms most widely used in Dominica, however, are those associated with Martinique. At the same time, some forms which have disappeared or are disappearing from Martinique, such as *tini* "have" (vs *ni*), have so far been retained or are relatively frequent in Dominican and Guadeloupean usage.

For the most part, however, there is a common vocabulary. While statistics must always be treated with some degree of caution, it is useful to note that a survey carried out by McVey Graham Jr. (1986) on behalf of the Summer Institute of Linguistics led him to the conclusion that 92 per cent of the 200 words on Morris Swadesh's word list (Swadesh 1966) were identical in St Lucian and Martinican, and 91 per cent in St Lucian and Guadeloupean. Although Graham did not directly compare Dominican with the Creole varieties spoken in the French islands, the further fact that the extent of identity between St Lucian and Dominican was put at 92 per cent gives some indication of the closeness of all four varieties.

One other feature shared by all three varieties is the influence of the official languages with which they coexist, English in the case of Dominica, French in the cases of Martinique and Guadeloupe. For Dominica, the effect of English is particularly evident in the areas of vocabulary and phonology. Words of English origin have been introduced to refer to institutions associated with administration or with relatively recent inventions, for example, *stechan* "(police) station", *tayprayt* "typewrite". Sometimes these are used alongside forms of French origin, especially where it is necessary to distinguish between two related entities. For example, *stov* "stove" refers to a modern stove (gas or electric), whereas the older term, *wecho,* refers to a coal pot. The influence of English is also observable on other parts of speech, for example, *bikòz* "because" alongside *pis, so* "so", *help* "help" and *tchray* "try" are the usual forms. The influence of English on the phonology of Dominican *patwa* is most obvious with regard to the occurrence of the word-final consonants *tch* and *dj* and the initial *r* in words of English origin, as well as the increasing absence of nasalized vowels in the variety as a whole in contexts where they would once have been expected. The grammatical structure of Dominican, however, has not been affected by English.

In Martinique and Guadeloupe, of course, the parallel influence has been from French. However, a few words of English origin have found their way there too. Some of these, such as *braf,* from the English "broth", used for a local stew, have been part of the Creole for centuries; others, such as *hamburger* and *snack (bar)* reflect the relatively recent spread of US influence and may justifiably still be regarded as loans in the local variety of French as well as in Creole.

One consequence of the introduction of Western education in the colonies was the threat it posed to the survival or development of an indigenous culture. After all, one underlying aim of colonialist education policy, whether instituted by church or by state, was to promote the language of the Europeans along with other aspects of their culture. Deliberate efforts were often made to eradicate local vernaculars, which were seen as obstacles to the achievement of that aim. The culture with which these vernaculars were often associated was also stifled.

The Caribbean colonies were particularly affected by this kind of experience since they were peopled to a large extent by ex-slaves whose speech was considered merely a corruption of their masters' and was therefore particularly stigmatized. European values came to be idealized, non-European ones to be associated with illiteracy and backwardness as well as with slavery; these were therefore denied, or at best ignored, in the pursuit of what was considered the sole means of access to civilization. The slave ancestors had lost their own languages, and with them much of their original culture – or so it was thought. In the latter half of the twentieth century, however, there was increasing appreciation of the indige-nous cultures and with this a re-evaluation of the languages in which all agree that these cultures are best expressed. While sentiments in support of the tra-ditional status quo are still to be heard in many circles, they are rarely unac-companied by ambivalence.

In all the territories with which this paper is concerned, recognition of the value of Creole was a natural correlate of the awakening consciousness of a national identity. Creole, as the vehicle of Martinican or Guadeloupean or Dominican folk culture, was now seen as an important symbol of that identity. Not surprisingly, however, the course of events was affected by other factors. For example, the fact that Dominica had been an independent state since 1978, while Martinique and Guadeloupe were still answerable to a government in France, played a role. Differences in the social structures of the two French territories also accounted for different responses to what was taking place. Martinique had a relatively significant industrial sector with clear ties to France, and European influence was very evident. Guadeloupe, on the other hand, was still a pre-dominantly agrarian society, and it had preserved much of the African culture of the forbears. In these respects, Guadeloupe is not unlike Dominica. As Ellen Schnepel put it, in Guadeloupe "Creole's distribution and frequency of usage among different social strata contrasts sharply with language norms in Martinique where assimilation to and penetration of French culture is more pronounced" (1993, 119). It is not surprising, therefore, that protest against the dominance of metropolitan France has been more evident in Guadeloupe and that Creole has been more strongly identified there as a symbol of that protest.

The presence in Martinique and Guadeloupe of a number of academics with a particular interest in standardizing and codifying Creole is another significant factor. Much of the impetus for the promotion of Creole in both Martinique and Guadeloupe came from academics attached to the Université des Antilles et de la Guyane (formerly the Centre Universitaire Antilles-Guyane). The year 1976 saw the formation of a research unit, the Groupe d'Etudes et de Recherches en Espace Créolophone (GEREC), by scholars from both French territories, led by Jean Bernabé. The group's activities resulted in, among other things, the design of a script for writing Creole and the publication of a number of pamphlets written exclusively in Creole. A more indirect result was the establisment of new radio stations which relied heavily on the use of Creole in their programming. This prompted pre-existing government-controlled radio stations to follow their example by making limited use of Creole in their own programmes.

The University of the West Indies, which serves the "anglophone" Caribbean territories, had no campus in Dominica and there were no resident intellectuals whose status could match those of its neighbours. Interest in Dominican Creole was mainly confined to its role as a vehicle of culture. Not many Dominicans were even aware that Dominican Creole had been described as a language in its own right in several articles dating as early as the late 1940s, by Douglas Taylor, an English-born resident, at a time when in the French territories Creole was still viewed only in relation to French.

Moves to promote the instrumentalization of Creole in Dominica started in the early 1980s. These moves were largely influenced by what was taking place in the neighbouring French islands. Thus, in 1981 and 1982, a group referred to as the Standing Committee on Creole Studies met in St Lucia to work out a common orthography for Dominican and St Lucian, one that would also be acceptable to GEREC. Out of that enterprise came the Konmité pou Etid Kwéyòl (KEK), a subcommittee of the Dominican National Cultural Council, a government-sponsored entity. The Creole Desk, which was established to implement the aims of the *konmité*, promoted the new orthography through courses for interested learners and through publications in Creole, including a dictionary and a manual; was responsible for setting up a Memory Bank to preserve data collected from senior citizens in the form of personal recollections or stories; and sponsored and planned Creole-related events. As in the French islands, radio programmes in *patwa* were increasingly accepted. These included news broadcasts and information on health and agriculture as well as storytelling and commercial advertising.

Programmes designed to make exclusive use of Creole face the problem of having to deal with concepts for which there is no word in the language. This is especially the case when technical subjects are being discussed. Ad hoc borrowings from English are quite frequent in such programmes. Although code switching in everyday discourse among bilinguals normally passes unnoticed, it is considered somewhat unnatural in programmes designed to promote the use of Creole. A similar problem exists in the French islands, where the gaps are often filled by ad hoc borrowings from French, a sore point for those nationalists who want to stress the independence of Creole from French.

The formal launching of Bannzil, a pan-Creole movement, at an international conference held in the Seychelles in 1982 was both a consequence of changing attitudes to the Creoles and a call to further action. It became a victim of its own idealism, but one lasting reminder of this attempt to promote *créolophone* solidarity on a global scale is the annual Simenn Kwéyòl (Creole Week) characterized by focus on local culture, which includes a Creole Day on which everyone is encouraged to speak only Creole. This day continues to be observed on the last Friday in October in Dominica, as well as in Martinique and Guadeloupe and other parts of the franco-creolophone world.

Conclusion

One might justifiably conclude that the long-standing links between Dominica and the French islands in particular – the more or less shared vernaculars, the Catholic religion, the folklore (*contes,* proverbs, sayings), the music – are relics of a past era, all slowly disappearing. Indeed, the recent efforts to promote *patwa* have been spurred on by the fact that a growing number of Dominicans, especially in urban areas, no longer speak it as their first language or even at all. Although no figures are available, casual observation even in rural areas suggests that this traditional Creole is not as extensively used as it was even thirty years ago. It is worth recalling that during the past century, other "anglophone" islands, notably Trinidad and Grenada, have all but lost the lexically French Creoles which had been bequeathed to them, too, by the French. In Dominica, already many of the younger generation speak only a lexically English Creole which has much in common with the Creoles spoken in the other territories that have a long history of British colonialism. Even if *patwa* were to survive in Dominica, Creole-dominant speakers would become more and more marginalized in practice, despite the sentimentality attached to the language by intellectuals or nationalists.

The factors that delayed the dissemination of English, and consequently the development of the related vernacular, are not as evident as they once were. Dominica now has a relatively well-developed network of roads, communication by telephone is no longer confined to a few privileged individuals and television programmes in English, originating in the United States, are available to those Dominicans who can afford to pay for them. Educational opportunities have improved, especially at the secondary level. English is the only officially sanctioned language in schools and is likely to remain so as the use of Creole in education is still a highly sensitive issue. While many Dominicans still emigrate to the French islands in search of work or to join relatives already settled there, at least as many have emigrated to Britain and North America. These considerations, together with increasing contact with the other formerly British colonies, indicate that in the future Dominica is likely to move further from its francophone neighbours, that other considerations will override geographical proximity. The fact that Martinique and Guadeloupe are considered part of France – with consequences for economic development, for migration to mainland France and for the strengthening of French institutions and culture within their bounds – also serves to emphasize the distance between them and their autonomous island neighbour.

Where religion is concerned, the Catholic hegemony, another long-standing bond between the islands, is being weakened by a recent influx of non-traditional religious groups from the United States, a development which has also reached the French islands along with other North American influences but is restricted by the more serious language barrier in these territories.

For the present, though, ordinary Dominicans remain very conscious of their kinship with the islanders who live just across the way. For them, at least, it is still a case of "so far and yet so near".

Notes

1. The orthography used for these extracts is that of Louisy and Turnel-John 1983. The extract from Dominican Creole was recorded in Roseau. The speaker was a thirteen-year-old schoolboy.
2. The extracts from Martinican and Guadeloupean Creole are adapted from Bricault 1976, 41, 56.

References

Allsopp, Richard. 1996. *Dictionary of Caribbean English Usage*. Oxford: Oxford University Press.

Baker, Patrick L. 1994. *Chaos, Order and the Ethnohistory of Dominica*. Kingston, Jamaica: University of the West Indies Press.

Boromé, J. 1972. "The French and Dominica, 1699–1763". In *Aspects of Dominican History*, 80–102. Roseau, Dominica: Government Printing Division.

Bricault, M., ed. 1976. *Contes créoles illustrés*. Paris: Agence de Coopération Culturelle et Technique.

Goodridge, Cecil. 1972. "Dominica: The French Connexion". In *Aspects of Dominican History*, 151–62. Roseau, Dominica: Government Printing Division.

Graham, McVey, Jr. 1986. *Caribbean French Creole Survey*. (Occasional Paper 19). Mona, Jamaica: Society for Caribbean Linguistics, University of the West Indies.

Honychurch, Lennox. 1984. *The Dominica Story*. 2nd ed. Roseau, Dominica: The Dominica Institute.

Jamaica Central Bureau of Statistics. 1950. *West Indies Census 1946*. 2 vols., 1958–1950. 1H: *Census of the Windward Islands: Dominica, Grenada, St Lucia, St Vincent, 9th April, 1946*. Kingston, Jamaica: Government Printer.

Louisy, Perlete, and Paule Turnel-John. 1983. *A Handbook for Writing Creole*. Castries, St Lucia: Research St Lucia Publications.

Lucas, C.P. 1890. *A Historical Geography of the British Colonies*. Oxford: Oxford University Press.

Melvill, Robert [Governor of Dominica]. 1771. *Proclamation Concerning the Change of Place-names in Dominica*.

Rat, J. Numa. 1894. *St Mark's Gospel in Dominican Creole*. London: British and Foreign Bible Society.

"Report of the Inspector of Schools, Dominica". 1869.

"Report on the State of His Majesty's Island of Dominica". Colonial Office Papers, 1764–99. C/O 71/72.

"A Resident". 1828. *Sketches and Recollections of the West Indies*. London.

Schnepel, Ellen. 1993. "The Creole Movement in Guadeloupe". *International Journal of the Society of Language* 102: 117–34.

Swadesh, Morris. 1966. *El lenguaje y la vida humana.* Mexico City: Fondo de Cultura Económica.

Trinidad and Tobago. Central Statistical Office. 1963. *East Caribbean Population Census of 1960.* 4 vols., 1963–1970. 1–2WD: *Windward Islands: Summary Tables.* Port of Spain, Trinidad: Central Statistical Office.

3

Postcolonial Eccentricities
Francophone Caribbean Literature
and the *fin de siècle*

J. Michael Dash
New York University

L'explosion n'aura pas lieu aujourd'hui. Il est trop tôt . . .
Ou trop tard.
Je n'arrive point armé de vérités décisives.
Ma conscience n'est pas traversée de fulgurances essentielles.

(Fanon 1952, 25)

Les vérités de l'humain n'éclatent pas aujourd'hui dans la fulguration
crispée, mais s'évaluent par la redite, l'approximation difficile, chaque fois
recommencée, d'une théorie d'évidences (à peu près, de banalités) dont
la conscience refuserait ici et là les leçons. La fulguration est l'art de
bloquer l'obscur dans sa lumière révélée; l'accumulation, celui de con-
sacrer l'évident dans sa durée enfin perçue. (Glissant 1969, 48)

The notion of the apocalypse is not important within the culture of the
Caribbean. The choices of all or nothing, for or against, honor or blood
have little to do with the culture of the Caribbean. These are ideological propositions articulated in Europe which the Caribbean shares only
in declamatory terms, or better, in terms of a first reading. (Benítez-Rojo
1992, 10)

The single most important issue that has been raised in francophone Caribbean
literature at the end of the twentieth century is arguably the conceptualization

of the Caribbean region as a site for romantic fantasies of liberation or more precisely of redemptive or revolutionary apocalypse. As we can see from these three quotations, the problem of apocalyptic thought and the longing for "vérités décisives" has been a preoccupation among French Caribbean writers for almost half a century. Frantz Fanon in his Janus-like reading of francophone Caribbean identity politics in *Peau noire, masques blancs* (1952) is able in a moment of penetrating lucidity to look critically at the reality of the absent volcano and the possibility that there may not be decisive truths on which to predicate future eruptions. Nevertheless, the power of his longing for a consciousness exploding with "fulgurances essentielles" has such a hold on him that eight years later he gives in to his dream of transgressive explosiveness and in *Les Damnés de la terre* visualizes the agressivity of the colonized in terms of purifying violence: "Tout est permis car, en réalité, l'on ne se réunit que pour laisser la libido accumulée, l'agressivité empêchée, sourdre volcaniquement" (Fanon 1968, 22) With the coming of true revolutionary activity, Fanon envisages violence as the apocalyptic force that is an all-encompassing ideal:

> Cette praxis violente est totalisante, puisque chacun se fait maillon violent de la grande chaîne, du grand organisme violent surgi comme réaction à la violence première du colonialiste. . . . Au niveau des individus, la violence désintoxique. Elle débarrasse le colonisé de son complexe d'infériorité, de ses attitudes contemplatives ou désespérées. Elle le rend intrépide, le réhabilite à ses propres yeux. (Fanon 1968, 51)

Eight years after Fanon's dream of fiery apocalypse, Edouard Glissant, in *L'Intention poétique,* takes us back to the hesitancy of Fanon's unexploded volcano and suggests that human truths do not explode today "dans la fulguration crispée" (1969, 48). Instead, he proposes a sublimation of violence that releases a series of detours, unfoldings or relational strategies that deflect or delay the moment of apocalypse into a patient accumulation of everyday, incomplete truths. This attempt at demystifying the apocalyptic imagination and replacing it with a poetics of patient unfolding seems itself to get caught up in a need for the "fulgurance" of "vérités décisives". There is a sense in which, despite the attempt to write back to Fanon and deconstruct his apocalyptic *fulgurance,* Glissant, in his early essays, seems to want to propose the new poetics of accumulation as a decisive truth. It almost makes one wonder if the main thrust of Glissant's writing is a desperate attempt to free himself from the epistemic violence of apocalyptic discourse. This tendency is arguably most apparent in a list of "binarités dépassables ou non" at the end of the notes in *Poétique de la relation,* a list in which a comma between terms signifies a relating function, a dash an oppositional function and a colon a consequential relationship (1990, 236).

Therefore, we are more than a little sceptical when we are told by the usually insightful Cuban literary theorist Antonio Benítez-Rojo some thirty years later that "The notion of apocalypse is not important within the culture of the Caribbean", that these are "ideological propositions articulated in Europe which the Caribbean shares only in declamatory terms" (1992, 10). What Glissant calls *fulgurance* is more deeply ingrained in Caribbean thought than Benítez-Rojo is willing to concede. Benítez-Rojo's very use of an apocalyptic tone in this passage, while declaring apocalypse to be profoundly un-Caribbean, is evidence of how easy it is to become enmeshed in ideological prescriptiveness. This paradox of a triumphantly non-prescriptive discourse is by no means unusual in Caribbean writing today. A quick glance at the profoundly Caribbean manifesto *Eloge de la créolité* is enough to give us the distinct impression that Bernabé, Chamoiseau and Confiant are (at least rhetorically) brandishing "vérités décisives" while repeating their mentor's need to "sortir des cris, des symboles, des communications fracassantes, des prophéties déclamatoires . . . afin d'entrer dans la minutieuse exploration de nous-mêmes, faite de patiences, d'accumulations, de répétitions, de piétinements" (1989, 22). Indeed, this manifesto is so contaminated by the "apocalyptic" vocabulary of alienation versus authenticity, of either/or and inside versus outside, that its perpetrators could well be reminded, today, that a *créoliste* tiger should not persist in proclaiming his *tigrité* or *mangrovité* or *diversalité.* The tiger should cease creating abstract nouns with essentialist suffixes and simply move on – in the spirit of constant, patient, inexorable unfolding.

My own view is that apocalyptic thought in the Caribbean as a whole and in the French Caribbean in particular is indeed very much a part of a Caribbean intellectual tradition, and a discursive practice that may be far more insidious than might be first realized. The succumbing of a Fanon, once wary of the lure of "vérités décisives", to the need to envisage violent closure to the colonial struggle in the Third World is not much different from the case of the Haitian novelist Jacques Stephen Alexis. The latter is as renowned for his contestation of the "vérités décisives" of Negritude in 1956 with his theory of Haitian hybridization, "le réalisme merveilleux", as he is for losing his life at the hands of the Duvalier regime in a failed attempt to bring final, violent closure to Duvalierism. Perhaps symbolically, Alexis's death occurred in 1961 – the very year in which Fanon's fiery manifesto was published. Had Alexis waited, he would have seen the Duvalier dynasty come crashing down in 1986. We should, therefore, be paying more attention to the source of this apocalyptic discourse that drove some to tragic attempts at closure. This is especially the case at this second post-apocalyptic Caribbean *fin de siècle,* which is marked by a growing sense that it is really too late for the eruption of "fulgurances essentielles". After a century of failed "revolutionary truths", the francophone Caribbean, with its unexploded volcanoes, may well have become exemplary of the Caribbean condition as a whole.

Verrition: Vérité

. . . la poésie noire de langue française est, de nos jours, la seule grande poésie révolutionnaire. (Sartre 1948, xii)

Pour avancer, pour améliorer leur progrès social et culturel, les hommes ont inventé la révolution. Depuis deux siècles au moins il a semblé aux êtres humains que pour sortir de l'oppression, pour réduire le champ des injustices, le chemin le plus court passait par la révolution. Je l'ai pensé a mon tour à vingt ans. A l'âge d'homme, en pleine soixantaine, les faits m'en éloignent. . . . Une nouvelle révolution? Chat échaudé, je n'ai pas de schéma révolutionnaire à suggérer. (Depestre 1989, 33)

In the last fifty years, we have come a long way, from seeing black poetry as uniquely revolutionary in 1948 to the confession by a Haitian "chat échaudé", immersed in the cold reality of failed revolutions, who has no "schéma révolutionnaire" to propose. The assertion by the most important cultural broker or intellectual mediator in French Caribbean literature, Jean-Paul Sartre, that black poetry is the only revolutionary poetry in existence is firmly inscribed in oppositional notions of here versus elsewhere. Here, in Europe, according to Sartre, the poetics of an eruptive emancipation have been lost since the white proletariat "opprimé par la technique" conceives of its struggle in exclusively materialist and technological terms (1948, xii). However, in that bastion of vitality and authenticity, the generic Third World, the generic black writer is able to reanimate the ideal of climactic "vérités décisives". In contrast to this apocalyptic schema of exhausted "here" as opposed to vital "elsewhere", an ageing poet from elsewhere residing in the "here" of Lézignan-Corbières cannot share the complacency of Sartre's easy dichotomy and is, therefore, unable and unwilling to launch yet another ideology based on the ideal of final, definitive resolution. Such a position, I would suggest, has little to do with René Depestre's advanced age or his fear of revolutionary politics as a kind of "Man Zabyme" who is capable of swallowing him should he succumb to her allure. Rather, I would suggest that Sartre and Depestre are useful markers who indicate the passage in French Caribbean thought from the grounded centrism of the past to the postcolonial eccentricities of the present.

To trace the emergence of apocalyptic thought in the francophone Caribbean is to consider critically the way in which the modernist dream of fiery closure becomes crystallized in an ideological form in the movement of Légitime Défense. This movement has been largely ignored because of the mythification of the ideology of Negritude as the authentic beginning of a Caribbean poetics. It is Sartre's "Orphée noir" essay, as René Ménil reminds us in his too often overlooked *Tracées*, that asserts the lack of authenticity in the poetry of Légitime Défense: ". . . ses poèmes sont des devoirs d'élève, ils demeurent des strictes imitations: ils ne se dépassent pas, bien au contraire ils se ferment sur eux-mêmes" (Sartre 1948, xxvi).

Ménil, who was as much a part of Légitime Défense as of Césaire's *Tropiques*, is clear on the role of the avant-garde modernist Jean-Paul Sartre in the formulation of the poetics of Negritude. His point is that Negritude was no blacker or more authentic than Légitime Défense, since André Breton was to Légitime Défense as Sartre was to Negritude. At least in the case of Légitime Défense, Etienne Léro singlehandedly composed the manifesto of his short-lived movement in his fiery essay "Misère d'une poésie", which incidentally ends with the apocalyptic image of a rising wind that will sweep away from the French colonies "les fruits avortés d'une culture caduque" (1932, 12). This apocalyptic image returns at the end of Césaire's *Cahier d'un retour au pays natal,* where an all-encompassing wind sweeps all before it:

> dévore vent
> je te livre mes paroles abruptes
> dévore et enroule-toi
> et t'enroulant embrasse-moi d'un plus vaste frisson.

> (1956, 90)

Ménil's analysis is well worth repeating as he sees in Negritude, and in Sartre's formulations of the poetics of the movement, complicity between the naivety of a progressive European intellectual and a local bourgeoisie which used the mask of progressive credentials to further its neo-colonial agenda. In "Orphée noir", the Negro envisaged by Sartre has no concrete reality but is reified outside of national context and class relations. As Ménil rather amusingly puts it in his essay on Negritude in *Tracées,* black Orpheus looks a lot like Sartre in blackface: "Sartre brasse les poèmes des poètes noirs dans le chapeau du prestidigitateur pour en faire sortir le nègre! Mais le nègre en question est un nègre qui ressemble à Sartre, à Sartre dont on aurait foncé et parfois renversé les couleurs. C'est un nègre bien angoissé, bien existentialiste, pittoresque!" (1981, 65). Ménil's point is that Negritude, trapped in this Sartrean exotic-for-itself identity, simply consented to this reification, allowing itself to be defined by an external consciousness, and capitulated to the class interests of a native bourgeoisie.

By historicizing Negritude and seeing it as a particular mentality that was created in particular historical circumstances and responding to certain local exigencies, we can more clearly separate the poetics of the movement from what Depestre, in *Bonjour et adieu à la négritude,* called its "métaphysique soma-tique" (1980, 82). It is my contention that Negritude, no more and no less than Légitime Défense, Haitian Indigenism, *noirisme* and Fanon's revolutionary nationalism, is a product of the temptation to apocalyptic thought in the French Caribbean. As I have argued in *The Other America: Caribbean Literature in a New World Context,* the most important of Césaire's neologisms in his *Cahier d'un retour au pays natal* is not Negritude but *verrition* (Dash 1998, 64). This frequently mistranslated coinage means "to scrape clean or sweep away". It also echoes the word *vérité* and *vert,* suggesting a fresh, green truth that explodes from this fiery conflagration. Césaire's epic poem ends, therefore, not with a return to a literal island homeland but with the apocalyptic fantasy of the tongue or language of fire that spurts from the reanimated volcano and triumphantly announces a new, disalienated future. An equally dramatic res-olution can be found at the end of that other Caribbean master text written in the apocalyptic mode, *Gouverneurs de la rosée.* Here the Caribbean is reduced to a "plaine couchée dans l'embrasement de midi" and the fiery tongue of the Césairean volcano is replaced by "une mince lame d'argent" which makes its way, or rather writes its way, across the burning surface of the plain (Roumain 1944, 219).

Roumain's "lame d'argent" and Césaire's "langue de la nuit" are both tied to the single greatest consequence of this modernist poetics of fiery elsewheres, the concept of language as, to use Fanon's terminology, "une praxis totalisante". There is in this tradition of apocalyptic thought a belief in language as a closed system, a privileging of *langue* as abstract system over *parole* as individual utterance. As Césaire triumphantly cites in his essay "Poésie et Connaissance", "Au commencement était le verbe / Jamais homme ne l'a cru plus fortement que le poète" (Césaire [1944] 1973, 119). His disciple Fanon is not far behind in declaring categorically, "Parler une langue, c'est assumer un monde, une culture" (Fanon 1952, 33). This new sovereignty of the Word, apocalyptic *langue,* can never include the idea of the individual speaking within a given situation. That every utterance refers to something already uttered or exists in terms of a Bakhtinian dialogic relationship of intonation, inflection or particular choice within a system is unthinkable in the language of closure. The shift from apocalyptic *langue* to deconstructive *parole* means the shift from the concept of the originating Word to a formulation such as "In the beginning, words were already there."

It is a non-heroic *parole* of diversion and accommodation that is now being (sometimes too triumphantly) advanced. For instance, we have shifted from "In the beginning was the word" to a formulation that would be closer to "water is the beginning of all things" for a theorist such as Benítez-Rojo. Glissant's theory of a "Forced Poetics" also fits into this new post-apocalyptic approach to language. It should be noted that Glissant's interest in Creole is not in establishing it as the *langue maternelle* of the Caribbean, as the true source of cultural authenticity. This view is closer to the apocalyptic view of Creole, which characterizes the *Créolité* movement. (In a sense, Raphaël Confiant's [1993, 114] insistence that Césaire's *Cahier* could and should have been written in Creole is a non-issue since it would mean retaining the same apocalyptic poetics. The impulse to Oedipal rage should be diverted towards a deconstructive *parole* – maybe in the manner of archly postmodern Daniel Maximin.) The concept of a Forced Poetics, sometimes overly contaminated by the lament that Creole is not yet a national language, relies on the concept of a creative release of the individual *parole* within a situation of anxiety or in a problematic relationship to the *langue* or to a system: "J'appelle poétique forcée, ou contrainte, toute tension collective vers une expression qui, se posant, s'oppose du même coup le manque par quoi elle devient impossible, non en tant que tension, toujours présente, mais en tant qu'expression, jamais accomplie" (Glissant 1981, 236). This is as much a perfect description of Glissant's own poetics as it is a theorizing of a *parole*-based *langage* which never achieves plenitude but remains in a state of banal or everyday opposition to prevailing systems or *langues*. It is not a case of overt linguistic resistance or blind cultural mimesis.

What Glissant offers, somewhat apologetically, in *Le Discours antillais* as the linguistic practice of a yet to be liberated Martinique has, I would like to propose, become precisely the creative indeterminacy of a post-apocalyptic poetics. As Glissant suggests in *Le Discours antillais*, while waiting for the volcano to explode and for a non-alienated, natural poetics to emerge, a poetics of errant trajectories across language becomes "natural" to the Martinican or marginal condition: "Notre perspective est de nous forger, par l'une ou l'autre de ces voies d'ailleurs non contradictoires, et à partir des usages débilités de deux langues dont le contrôle ne nous fut jamais collectivement acquis, un langage par quoi nous poserions volontairement l'ambigu et enracinerions carrément l'incertain de notre parole" (Glissant 1981, 283). In this vision of contestation from within which he seems to savour paradoxes (*usage débilité, poser l'ambigu, enraciner l'incertain*), Glissant is saying something more important than even he realized at the time. Herein lie the seeds of 'la pensée archipélique", with its image of diffracted opacities scattered across a sea of relational possibilities

Mitan-Milan

. . . whenever history makes its move it catches us unawares. And since the general purpose of every society is the safety of all its members, it must first postulate the arbitrariness of history. . . . It would therefore be prudent for society as a whole to develop patterns of motional irregularity (ranging from erratic foreign policy to mobile habitats and shifting residences) to make it difficult for a physical enemy or a metaphysical enemy to take aim. If you don't wish to be a target, you've got to move. "Scatter", said the Almighty to his chosen people, and at least for a while they did. (Brodsky 1995, 123)

I would like to stress that all the cultures of the small Central European countries have, at the beginning of the twentieth century, become important centers for world culture. . . . All these small countries have shown a dynamism typical of young nations, together with the experience of ancient nations, and have supplied a new and surprising vision of the world which often enough, shocks through the lucidity of its relentless skepticism born of defeats and experiences painful to a degree unknown to bigger peoples. (Kundera 1981, 22)

We can debate whether the French Caribbean contains "God's chosen people" or is an "important center for world culture". However, the concepts of "motional irregularity", scattering and a "skepticism born of defeats" are very familiar to the Caribbean and are of acute importance in the present post-apocalyptic phase. It is no coincidence that there are affinities between Joseph Brodsky and Derek Walcott as there are between Milan Kundera and Patrick Chamoiseau. The relationship may help position the Caribbean in general and the French Caribbean in particular as the twenty-first century begins.

The French Overseas Departments and Haiti, once seen as polar opposites – the exploded volcano versus the unexploded volcano; independence and isolation versus dependence and overdevelopment – are now both similar and exemplary in the way they have been thrust onto the global stage. It seems ironic that Haiti, where one-sixth of the population depends on USAID for nutrition, and the French Overseas Departments, which have the highest consumption of Yoplait yogurt in the hemisphere, should share a common fate. Both, however, are thrust into a situation where they must be what they were and what they are with no idea as to what they will be. If, as Glissant continually repeats, "le lieu est incontournable", this "lieu" is not fixed but subject to relational change. The francophone Caribbean no longer has a clear choice (if it ever did) between nation and elsewhere, or Africa and France, or even, as Glissant once posed it, between "humanisme réducteur" and "opacité particulière" (1981, 190–91). The question is rather whether they will be European, regional, hemispheric and yet Franco-Caribbean all at the same time. How will the geographic nation of Haiti relate to the tenth Department – the million or so Haitians now living in North America who represent a new extraterritorial concept of nation? Will French survive in Haiti, or do we have the makings of a situation (not unknown in the Caribbean) where English and Creole will coexist in the future? These are the realities of a francophone Caribbean fully in the grip of post-colonial anxiety (which still contains elements of the neo-colonial and anti-colonial) of which the French Caribbean arguably represents the cutting edge, and even more so those outside of the Caribbean who have an even more acute sense of the oppositional ambivalences and the chaotic cohabitations of the present.

To bring this essay to an inconclusive, post-apocalyptic, non-triumphalist conclusion, I would like to cite a few instances of tactical eccentricity as currently practised to suggest a sense of the shape of things to come in francophone literature. The first instance, not surprisingly, is that of the recent work of Glissant. I say "not surprisingly" since I feel that I personally and, maybe, French Caribbean literature as a whole have "ripened" along with Glissant in his sustained effort to deconstruct the discourses of apocalypse. His most recent work, however, is even more daring in its effort to step away from an old form of Caribbean identity politics. The novel *Tout-monde,* whose title seems to suggest a transcendence of the old binarisms – West and the Rest, here and elsewhere – is not set in Martinique but in a decentred space where "La procession des 'Là-bas' s'est soulevée en une tempête d''Ici'. Le Tout-Monde est rayonnant d''Ici' qui se relaient" (Glissant 1993, 490). This is where Caribbean narrative is now sited, as Glissant puts increasing distance between himself and the adversarial identity politics of inside versus outside that drive the *Créolité* movement.

The main protagonist in this novel, Mathieu, is stung by a jellyfish early in the story. This image of the medusa or *méduse* can be easily seen as an intertextual reference to Walcott's claim in "The Muse of History" that "History" is "that Medusa of the New World" (Walcott 1998, 36) However, Glissant, in the appendix to this novel, draws our attention to Mathieu's exclamation in Italian, "Sono battuto delle meduse", and, I suspect, to the idea of being stung as opposed to being petrified or wounded (1993, 516). The image of the bite is included in two major texts of the Caribbean: at the end of Césaire's *Cahier d'un retour au pays natal* and in Walcott's *Omeros,* where the character Philoctete is "blest" with his wound, which is both a product of the past of slavery and an extension of the sulphur wound of Soufriere on the island itself. The "sceau de douleur" inscribed on Mathieu's chest by one of the three *méduses* is not a symbol of redemptive knowledge – as it is in Césaire, where the bite is administered by a snake - nor is it a symbol of stoic suffering as in *Omeros.* It is non-explosive in its meaning. Mathieu's cry of pain in bad Italian is turned into an in-joke for his group of friends. The transparent, floating creature of the *méduse* is not mythic and has no point of origin. In a sense, we are all *battuti,* inevitably stung by history. We only differ in terms of where we were bitten. But even that "where" is not an easily understood, *incontournable Ici* since the place where Mathieu is stung is "Là-bas". The novel ends with another gratuitous and arbitrary wounding by two human medusas, "vagabonds errants", which causes Mathieu to slip into a coma, away from the "Ici" to a "Là-bas" of dream. The novel ends with the voices of two gendarmes, from Angers and Pézenas, saying to each other, "à tout considérer il l'avait bien cherché" (512). *Tout-monde* represents for Glissant the beginning of a new cycle of novels that will deal with the plural cosmopolitan world of the indefatigably errant *batoutos*.

The deconstructing of the traditional polar oppositions between *Ici* and *Là-bas* has also been practised by Haitian writers since the 1960s. Duvalierism has forced a deconstruction of the idea of a heroic modernism, which has been the most fruitful vein in Haitian literature for the last two decades. This rupture with the triumphalist poetics of the past is as apparent in Franketienne's early *spiraliste* novel *Ultravocal,* where the symbol of the tree turns diabolical in the character Mac Abre, as it is in the early novels of Jean-Claude Charles (*Manhattan Blues*) where *Là-bas* becomes the only *Ici* that is liveable. The precariousness of *Ici* is the main theme of Dany Laferrière's original version of the narrative of return to the native land, *Pays sans chapeau.* In this work, his *Ici* is little more than "une petite table bancale sous un manguier" (1996, 13). The narrator can make no clear distinctions in his narrative between subject and object, outside and inside. He confesses, "Aujourd'hui, je n'arrive point à écrire si je ne sens pas les gens autour de moi, prêts à intervenir à tout moment dans mon travail pour lui donner une autre direction. J'écris à ciel ouvert au milieu des arbres, des gens, des cris, des pleurs" (14).

Unexploded volcanoes, banyan identities, drifting medusas, rhizomatic branchings now abound in francophone Caribbean writing as a new discourse emerges built on the ruins of the language of Apocalypse. In this new era of errancy and eccentricity, of *lieux contournables,* the question of what francophone Caribbean identity is or will be remains unresolved. Perhaps the best provisional answer comes from Milan Kundera, who, when asked about the future of Czech identity, invoked the Pascalian wager: "Il n'y a pas de réponse définitive à ces questions. L'existence tchèque est et restera un pari" (1995, 34).

References

Benítez-Rojo, Antonio. 1992. *The Repeating Island: The Caribbean and the Postmodern Perspective.* Durham, NC: Duke University Press.

Bernabé, Jean, Patrick Chamoiseau and Raphaël Confiant. 1989. *Eloge de la créolité.* Paris: Gallimard.

Brodsky, Joseph. 1995. *On Grief and Reason: Essays.* New York: Farrar, Straus and Giroux.

Césaire, Aimé. [1944] 1973. "Poésie et Connaissance". In *Aimé Césaire, l'homme et l'œuvre,* ed. Lilyan Kesteloot and Barthélemy Kotchy, 112–26. Paris: Présence Africaine.

———. 1956. *Cahier d'un retour au pays natal.* Paris: Présence Africaine.

Confiant, Raphaël. 1993. *Aimé Césaire, une traversée paradoxale du siècle.* Paris: Stock.

Dash, J. Michael. 1998. *The Other America: Caribbean Literature in a New World Context.* Charlottesville: University Press of Virginia.

Depestre, René. 1980. *Bonjour et adieu à la négritude.* Paris: Laffont.

———. 1989. *Entretiens avec René Depestre.* Port-au-Prince, Haiti: Etzer Depestre.

Fanon, Frantz. 1952. *Peau noire, masques blancs.* Paris: Seuil.

———. 1968. *Les Damnés de la terre.* Paris: Maspero.

Glissant, Edouard. 1969. *L'Intention poétique.* Paris: Seuil.

———. 1981. *Le Discours antillais.* Paris: Seuil.

———. 1990. *Poétique de la relation.* Paris: Gallimard.

———. 1993. *Tout-monde: roman.* Paris: Gallimard.

Kundera, Milan. 1981. "The Czech Wager". *New York Review* 27, no. 21–22: 21–22.

———. 1995. "Le Pari tchèque". *Le Nouvel Observateur* (25 October): 34.

Laferrière, Dany. 1996. *Pays sans chapeau: roman.* Outremont, Que: Lanctôt.

Léro, Etienne. 1932. "Misère d'une poésie". Légitime défense: 10–12.

Ménil, René. 1981. *Tracées.* Paris: Laffont.

Roumain, Jacques. 1944. *Gouverneurs de la rosée: Roman.* Paris: Editeurs Français Réunis.

Sartre, Jean-Paul. 1948. "Orphée noir". In *Anthologie de la nouvelle poésie nègre et malgache de langue française,* edited by Léopold Sédar Senghor, viii–xliv. Paris: Presses Universitaires de France.

Walcott, Derek. 1990. *Omeros.* New York: Farrar, Straus and Giroux.

———. 1998. "The Muse of History". In Derek Walcott, *What the Twilight Says: Essays,* 36–64. London: Faber.

4

Re-membering Caribbean Childhoods
Saint-John Perse's "Eloges" and Patrick Chamoiseau's *Antan d'enfance*

Mary Gallagher
University College Dublin

Memory, Recovery and Writing

The literature of traumatized cultures typically abounds in first-person *récits de vie,* that is, in narratives which implicitly claim a certain status of authenticity. French Caribbean writing is no exception to this apparent rule; indeed, it is particularly rich in first-person fictional or autobiographical narratives, belonging to what one could loosely term the Bildungsroman tradition. Chronicles of a coming of age, these texts trace the trajectory of and the influences upon a (possibly fictional) life through childhood towards maturity. As such, they might be expected to function as a literature of recovery in two senses of the term: in organizing an individual life into a narrative (recovery as recording), they could perhaps facilitate a recovery (recovery as rehabilitation) of the collective pysche. Taking the Caribbean Départements d'Outre-Mer alone, one could cite as part of this Bildungsroman tradition such key works as Françoise Ega's *Le Temps des madras* (1965, 1989), Joseph Zobel's *La Rue Cases-Nègres* (1950), Michèle Lacrosil's *Sapotille et le serin d'argile* (1960), Simone Schwarz-Bart's *Pluie et vent sur Télumée Miracle* (1972) and Myriam Warner-Vieyra's *Le Quimboiseur l'avait dit* (1980). However, not all of these texts chart paths of recuperation in the sense of healing. Lacrosil's and Warner-Vieyra's, for example, concentrate rather more on the aetiology of trauma than on its treatment.

In this paper, we shall consider two French Caribbean texts which present themselves as recovering authentic Caribbean childhood experience: Saint-John Perse's "Eloges" and Patrick Chamoiseau's *Antan d'enfance*. Yet although both are concerned with recovery as recording, and although the second may also facilitate a certain cultural therapy, neither fits squarely into the generic tradition mentioned above. Arguably, neither text is primarily about the unfolding of a "real" life, nor even about the shaping of a fictional individual's character and destiny by ambient influences. Instead, both concentrate on foregrounding poetically the texture of memory and nostalgia. They do chart specific memories of a Caribbean childhood, but in a manner which is not just framed but completely overshadowed by their primary preoccupation, which is poetic and reflexive.

In analysing here the poetics of remembering presented by two very different literary works, we shall also look at how the writing of Patrick Chamoiseau, born in Martinique in 1952, recalls the poetry of Saint-John Perse, the poetic alter ego of Alexis Léger, born in Guadeloupe in 1887. Hence, in the case of Chamoiseau, we shall be looking at a double process of remembering, one aspect of which, enacting a certain intertextuality, is specifically literary. Furthermore, as so much of Caribbean literature is based on an implicit problematic of textual (as well as other forms of) remembering, and as many contemporary texts, including works by Raphaël Confiant and Daniel Maximin, look back towards the writing of Saint-John Perse, this analysis may suggest a useful map for the reading of other Caribbean texts in French which are traversed by similar paths of revisitation.[1]

From Saint-John Perse to Patrick Chamoiseau

The more recent of the two works under scrutiny in this paper, Chamoiseau's *Antan d'enfance* (1990), is a relatively short autobiographical narrative in lyrical prose, although the prose is punctuated at regular intervals by brief illuminations of poetry in verse. The other text which we shall consider is Saint-John Perse's "Eloges", a sequence of eighteen poems, dated 1908 but first published in the *Nouvelle revue française* in 1910, almost eighty years before *Antan d'enfance*.[2]

Like Chamoiseau's memoirs, "Eloges" was inspired by the experiences of a Caribbean childhood. It is a significantly more opaque and problematic text than its shorter sister-sequence, "Pour fêter une enfance". But if I have chosen to concentrate here on "Eloges" rather than on the more limpid text of "Pour fêter une enfance" – that relatively transparent and elegiac benediction of a privileged, white, *fin de siècle* Caribbean childhood – this is not simply because it is the more challenging of the two works; it is also because, like Chamoiseau's *Antan d'enfance,* and unlike "Pour fêter une enfance", it is situated in the urban Caribbean.[3] However, the principal reason for my choice is that the difficulties which one encounters in trying to interpret "Eloges" are accounted for precisely by the poet's oblique approach to the process of remembering, a process which is also central to the poetic composition and to the literary complexity of *Antan d'enfance.*

At the outset of this reading, it is important to mention the significance of the intertextual resonances[4] through which *Antan d'enfance* seems less to reply to Saint-John Perse's writing than to appropriate it. These stylistic and referential correspondences are neither fortuitous nor insignificant; indeed, they might be read as a confirmation of a recent sea change in the reaction of Caribbean writers and critics to Saint-John Perse's writing, from alienation, challenge or at best cautious acceptance to less-qualified repossession. However, the change in Saint-John Perse's Caribbean reception reflects, in addition, the more general ideological revisionism currently being promoted by certain prominent French Caribbean intellectuals and indeed by Chamoiseau in particular. This ideological shift is most clearly marked in the cultural programme of *Créolité*. While the new vision of Caribbeanness represented by the *Créolité* project owes much to Aimé Césaire's programme of Negritude and even more to the writings of Edouard Glissant on *Antillanité,* its originality seems to lie essentially in its new emphasis on celebration and benediction at the expense of lament. This sense of "recovery" – or at least this move away from a preoccupation with the pathology of the Caribbean colonial inheritance – is evident in the very title of the movement's "manifesto", *Eloge de la créolité* (Bernabé, Chamoiseau and Confiant 1989), which inevitably calls to mind that of Saint-John Perse's first poetic masterpiece.

Clearly, the sociocultural Caribbean milieu of the Guadeloupe-born *fils de béké* was vastly different from that of the *négrillon* portrayed in *Antan d'enfance.*[5] Furthermore, *Eloges* was written in France rather than Fort-de-France, several years into the poet's definitive exile from the *pays natal.* And yet Chamoiseau, like a significant number of contemporary Caribbean writers, apparently feels drawn to situate his writing on childhood in relation to that of Saint-John Perse. Indeed, *Eloges* seems to be an obligatory, or at least preferred, point of reference not just for francophone Caribbean writers such as Glissant, Chamoiseau or Raphaël, but also for Derek Walcott.[6] Hence, although the greater part of the oeuvre of the poet who was awarded the 1960 Nobel prize for literature retains little of the Caribbean inspiration which marks *Eloges,* this text has remained a touchstone for subsequent Caribbean writing.

Not only do "Eloges" and *Antan d'enfance* evoke many of the same daily sights and experiences of an urban Caribbean childhood, but both texts share, in addition, a predominantly celebratory tone; even the humblest and potentially most sordid of street scenes are the object of lyrical attention. Both texts also have in common an intense, exalted poeticity, and both bear the explicit imprint of the spoken word in their constant use of apostrophe and direct speech, metadiscourse and reported speech. However, there are, of necessity, formal and generic differences between, on the one hand, the numbered sequence of discrete poems in *versets* which forms "Eloges" and, on the other hand, the autobiographical prose narrative of Chamoiseau's text. Superimposed upon, if not actually imposed by these differences, are further disparities, both in coherence and in the meaning or mission ascribed to the programme of remembering which each text has set itself.

Although it is not the text's sole motivation, the autobiographical status of *Antan d'enfance* is articulated in a much more unambiguous fashion than is that of "Eloges". Saint-John Perse's text is presented and structured in a manner which, even in comparison with his own "Pour fêter une enfance", shows a marked tendency towards abstraction, impersonality and discontinuity. In contrast, Chamoiseau's narrative offers a chronological and personal reconstruction. But while it is true that this linearity contrasts very strongly with the disconcerting elliptical transitions between and within the poems of *Eloges,* narrative continuity and transparency is by no means the whole story of Chamoiseau's text.

In fact, both works are self-consciously constructed around an explicit and poetic approach to memory. For Chamoiseau, writing about his childhood offers the healing possibility of reconstructing, conserving and sharing a collective past, even if, in so doing, the writer recovers a certain pre-eminently poetic reality. For the speaker in "Eloges", it presents, above all, an exalting creative opportunity for the subject; an opportunity to re-view and to communicate past perceptions and experiences which are less communal than personal, while simultaneously composing a song, a story, a poem. Although they differ, then, in the emphasis placed on the subject's aesthetic experience and creative act, both texts situate memory within the context of nostalgia and community, and both are organized around a communicated return to the past. In addition, not only is each work formally and structurally determined by its definition of its specific project of remembering and commemoration, but it is also saturated and directed by reflection on this subject.

Remembering in "Eloges"

Nostalgia and the Structure of the Poem Sequence

The structural pivot of "Eloges" is a conventional trope, well aired in the French poetic tradition, namely, a comparison likening the processes of memory or imagination to a departure on a sea voyage. If the internal coherence of the poem sequence seems problematic, it is partly because this pivotal comparison is expressed elliptically and because it is not introduced until poem III. Since the images presented in the first three poems are hallucinatory in quality, and since the discursive context is most mysterious, the reader is, so to speak, at sea right from the beginning of the sequence. Suddenly, however, the third poem presents a transition: the speaker calls, presumably on himself, to return in silence as a man to the things he saw, presumably as a child; he is to return like someone who has made "promises of islands", like someone assuring a younger person, "You will see!":

> Sois un homme aux yeux calmes qui rit,
>   silencieux qui rit sous l'aile calme du sourcil,
> perfection du vol (et du bord immobile du cil il fait retour aux choses
> qu'il a vues, empruntant les chemins de la mer frauduleuse . . . et du bord
> immobile du cil
>   il nous a fait plus d'une promesse d'îles,
>   comme celui qui dit à un plus jeune: «Tu verras!»
>   Et c'est lui qui s'entend avec le maître du navire). (35)

The imagery used in this context implies that the return will be an internal or imagined one, a return of the mind's eye ("du bord immobile du cil"), represented as flying ("perfection du vol") or sailing back across a fraudulent sea ("la mer frauduleuse"). We can thus read into this poem advance clarification of the organization and purpose of the remainder of the sequence. And indeed, after several poems evoking a boat journey, we read a poem (numbered x) about disembarkation and, finally, a further set of poems presenting things said or seen on land.

Clearly, the programme of poem III, as fulfilled by the remainder of the sequence, enacts an etymological definition of nostalgia, involving as it does a return to the islands across a fraudulent sea. The sea is fraudulent in that the return is merely imagined, effected on board an immobile vessel ("et du bord immobile du cil") – the dreamer's eyelashes or the wings of his eyebrows.

Nostalgia (from the Greek *nostos,* meaning "return") consists precisely in the organization of images and memories into a movement of return; and "dans le mot 'nostalgie', le but n'est presque rien, *le mouvement est tout*" (Laurent Dispot, *Manifeste archaïque,* quoted in Taconet 1986, 116). The distress or pain involved in this process derives from the subject's acknowledgement of the illusory nature of the movement. If one considers the etymological definition of nostalgia, then "Pour fêter une enfance" is both more and less nostalgic than "Eloges". It is more so in that the principal theme of the sequence is loss; the island childhood is represented as a paradise praised and mourned. As the following examples illustrate, the tone of "Pour fêter une enfance" is intensely elegiac: "Je parle d'une haute condition, alors"; "Je parle d'une haute condition, jadis"; "Alors, les hommes avaient une bouche plus grave, les femmes avaient des bras plus lents" (23);

> Sinon l'enfance, qu'y avait-il alors qu'il n'y a plus?
> Plaines! Pentes! Il y
> avait plus d'ordre!   (25)

Yet, although "Eloges", less elegiac in tone than its sister sequence, does seem to overlook the pain of loss, it is, nevertheless, entirely constructed around the etymological definition of nostalgia. Similarly, Chamoiseau's reflection on memory as a return to childhood vision and experience is very extensively developed; indeed, his remarks on this subject frame and determine the structure and significance of the entire text.[7] Furthermore, Chamoiseau, like Saint-John Perse, also acknowledges the illusory or perfidious quality of his memories.[8] Of course, for the Martinican writer, the displacement effected by memory is only temporal, whereas Saint-John Perse's lyrical return involves a much more radical lie or illusion, in that a cultural and spatial displacement is superimposed on the return voyage back through time. In that sense, the poet's use of the spatial image (the sea journey) has literal relevance, since he is writing in and from his exile in France, leagues away from the *pays natal.*

Singing the Dream of the Past

From the poem which announces the programme of recovery (poem III) to the poem of disembarkation (poem X), "Eloges" makes constant reference to the sea, to the deck of the boat and particularly to the sail. The sail as the means of the illusory return can be read as an image of memory and imagination; it is associated in the text primarily with the internal domain of the mind and soul: "la grand'voile irritable, couleur de cerveau" and "la présence de la voile, grande âme malaisée" (41). The sail is also, however, compared to a cheek puffed out with breath: "la voile étrange, là et chaleureuse révélée, comme la présence d'une joue ... O / bouffées! ... Vraiment j'habite la gorge d'un dieu" (41). Several further allusions to breath ("une aisance du souffle" [38]) and to song ("le chant qui étire les yeux" [38]); "ces poissons qui s'en vont comme le thème au long du chant" [39]) underline the fact that these poems are concerned not just with the process of memory as imagined or illusory return, but with remembering as a source of poetic inspiration and lyrical expression.

At another level, however, the imaginary return to the islands, presented as sea voyage or flight, becomes superimposed on specific childhood memories of real boat outings. Appropriately, the first seven sections which follow the crucial third poem evoke things seen and said on board a boat;[9] however, the dreamlike haze surrounding their evocation is a constant reminder of the purely imaginary nature of recollection.

As though to underline the illusory quality of the recovery of the past in "Eloges", the poems treating of the (imaginary) return sea voyage abound in references to the strangeness of the visions communicated: "qu'il est étrange d'être là" (37); "la voile étrange" (41). Moreover, these references are reinforced by frequent allusions to dreaming: "Je m'éveille, songeant au fruit noir de l'Anibe" (36); "Le pont lavé, avant le jour, d'une eau pareille en songe au mélange de l'aube" (37); "Tout l'intime de l'eau se resonge en silence aux contrées de la toile" (41). This sense of the unreality of the return of the mind's eye thus echoes (and explains) the other-worldly, hallucinatory visions of the first three poems of the sequence in which the *Songeur* is a key figure.

Memory and Communication

"Eloges" does not simply evoke the mechanism of memory in terms of a programme which the remainder of the sequence will then execute. Rather, the programme is presented in terms of an intention to communicate images and visions to another person; after all, the avowed function of the speaker's return to things he has seen is, as we have seen, to share them with another. In this way, memory is presented as serving a declared function of revelation or initiation. Indeed, the mission of communication is dramatized several times subsequently in the sequence; in poem xi, for example, we read, "Pour voir, se mettre à l'ombre. Sinon, rien" (43). Then in poem xiv, "ô mes amis où êtes-vous que je ne connais pas? Ne verrez-vous cela aussi?" (46).

Remembering in *Antan d'enfance*

Following the Trajectory of Childhood

Antan d'enfance is divided in the first instance into two sections: the first is entitled "Sentir", meaning "to smell" or "to sense", the second "Sortir", or "to go out". In a way, a similar division is marked in "Eloges", but only towards the end of the sequence. There, the poet/child (or at least the first-person speaker) indicates that he is leaving the house as he truculently submits to having his hair combed on the threshold and finally crosses the same threshold, dismissing all around him (including the reader) and demanding to be left alone to conduct his business with nature.[10] Both texts thus defer to the almost inevitable progression of childhood from home-centredness to self-assertion in a realm beyond the limits of the house. However, in "Eloges", the wider realm is not a social one; it is, rather, the realm of nature. The final poems of the sequence express the speaker's peremptory intention to withdraw from the original programme of reviewing and communicating the things he has returned to see and his determination to retreat into a private world, where communion with his own body or with nature will be paramount. In this sense, the trajectory of *Antan d'enfance* is the opposite of that of "Eloges": at the beginning of *Antan d'enfance,* the child is absorbed in solitary games at home with fire, insects, rats and the elements, and only gradually turns towards the wider human community and its doings, which then become the new centre of his preoccupations. The entire second section of *Antan d'enfance* presents, indeed, not just the child's increased curiosity towards the outside world, but also, even more forcefully, his desire for increased contact with the wider community and the town.

It is also interesting to note that towards the end of "Pour fêter une enfance", having detailed at length what goes on in the house and in the *habitation* more generally, the poet/child concentrates on comings and goings across the sea.[11] "Eloges", as we have seen, concentrates throughout on the presence of the sea. In *Antan d'enfance,* on the other hand, the centrifugal movement of the child's development does not include any wider awareness of the Caribbean environment as insular; in fact, the sea hardly features at all in the childhood memories detailed by Chamoiseau.

Reliving the Child's Reality: Between Prose and Poetry

The narrator of *Antan d'enfance* enunciates at some length a philosophy of childhood according to which childhood is a period or state of grace in which human beings perceive the true nature of reality. But it is also the time when one gradually learns to secrete around oneself a shell which will later make that reality imperceptible to one's adult self; hence it is only by not growing up that one can avoid this gradual corruption of one's capacity to see things as they truly are. Chamoiseau's narrator distinguishes, therefore, between what the adult regards as "la réalité" in all its comfortable and reassuring stability and squareness, and on the other hand, true reality, or "le réel",[12] to which the child has immediate perceptual access and which is uncomfortable, complex and shifting, full of possibilities and impossibilities. Growing up means no longer having the courage or the strength to face true reality, that is, squarely to countenance this fragmentation, disturbance and complexity. It is thus a matter of establishing "entre cette perception et soi le bouclier d'une enveloppe mentale. Le poète – c'est pourquoi – ne grandit jamais, ou si peu" (Chamoiseau 1990, 79). Maturity is thus a process of loss in that, paradoxically, as the child proceeds in his or her inventory of the world, reducing the strangeness and singularity of the experience of things by classifying them, this very process strips off the magical capacity of childhood to perceive unmediated reality, and so the world is denuded not just of its mysterious aura but also of its immediacy and truth.

Above all, Chamoiseau wants to reconstruct this poetic or childlike way of looking at a particular world. Thus he attempts to pace out childhood instead of describing it: his project is "retrouver son arcane; non la décrire mais l'arpenter dans ses états magiques" (1990, 11). Recovering childhood will mean recovering the chaos in which fact is mixed up with illusion; it will mean reconstituting the discontinuity, the missing beginnings and the ambiguity which are associated with that state or vision apart. In attempting to recover the past, to wander through it and to communicate his findings, the author is obliged, however, to resort more and more often to snatches of poetry. The poetic puncturing of the prose and the disruption of the chronological flow of the narrative are thus among the ways in which he attempts to restore the discontinuity and ambiguity germane to the child's vision of the world. He had pointed out explicitly, after all, that the child's gaze is similar in quality to that of the poet.[13]

Chamoiseau's concern with reconstruction, or what we have termed "re-membering", emerges clearly from the manner in which his narrative respects chronological order, from his explicitly articulated concern with the location of the beginning[14] and from his frequent invocation of witnesses as guarantors of the accuracy of his memories.[15] Nonetheless, authenticated, accessible and linear as the resulting narrative may be, flashes of more opaque poetic allusion intervene ever more often, and the entire narrative is framed by extensive lyrical passages of reflection on the problematic nature of memory (1990, 11–12, 164–65). Hence, while attempting to recover the past, this text underlines and almost undermines its own effort by emphasizing at regular intervals that certain qualities of the past are almost irretrievable and that the gaze of the child survives only in the discontinuities, detours and ellipses germane to poetic insight. Chamoiseau indeed expresses a certain anxiety (or at least a constant preoccupation) concerning memory as recovery of that which may prove to be irrevocably irrecoverable: "O mes frères, vous savez cette maison que je ne pourrais décrire . . . ô mes frères, vous savez, elle meurt dans ses poussières. Elle s'étouffe de souvenirs" (164).

Communication and Community

Much of the striking intertextuality between *Antan d'enfance* and "Eloges" centres on the congruent patterns of orality which mark each text. These patterns involve extensive use of direct address and prevalent self-referential discourse, for example, "Je parle d'un Noël sinon amer, du moins très sobre" (Chamoiseau 1990, 58). In their use of direct address, both texts address memory in the first place and, in the second, a certain audience or readership. In "Eloges", memory is indirectly addressed as the "maître du navire", whereas in *Antan d'enfance,* it is directly identified: "Mémoire ho, cette quête est pour toi!" (11). Chamoiseau's narrator tries to reassure and to cajole memory, urging it to lower its guard, announcing that he comes not to pillage or to conquer but rather in intoxication and in docile joy.[16]

It is important to note in this connection that in "Eloges", those who are to share the poet's memories are referred to as "O mes amis . . . que je ne connais pas", whereas in *Antan d'enfance,* they are "Oh mes frères". Thus, Saint-John Perse's readers are not identified in time or in space, whereas the identity of the projected readers of *Antan d'enfance* is quite clear, since they are assumed to share the same past as the narrator. A dedication at the beginning of the text is addressed to these readers who will be able to identify with the narrator's childhood: "Partageurs ô / vous savez cette enfance!" (7). *Antan d'enfance* thus presents itself as written for and addressed primarily to a specific community of Caribbean readers.

Furthermore, for its community of projected readers, the remembered world will be familiar. This sense of solidarity resonates with the attempt on Chamoiseau's part to reconstruct, to re-collect or to re-member the experience of an entire generation and way of life:

> Oh mes frères, je voudrais vous dire: la maison a fermé une à une ses fenêtres, se détachant ainsi, sans cirque ni saut, du monde, se refermant à mesure sur sa garde d'une époque – notaire fragile de nos antans d'enfance.
>
> Mes frères O, je voudrais vous dire. (Chamoiseau 1990, 165)

Although throughout Chamoiseau's text the narrator claims that as a child he was identified as and identified himself as a loner, this solitude is never privileged at the expense of solidarity with a certain named community. In this sense, the universalizing connotations of the rather abstract and remote figures of the *Songeur,* the *Conteur* and the *Enfant* of "Eloges" ("L'enfant veut qu'on le peigne sur le pas de la porte" [51]) contrast very clearly with Chamoiseau's reference to himself as the *négrillon.* This latter term is not simply an affectionate diminutive – it is also a social and racial marker identifying the narrator's ethnic allegiance.

It is true that the child speaker of "Eloges" demonstrates an isolation and a marginality which go far beyond the necessary solitude of childhood and its marginalization from the active adult world. Indeed, he betrays an isolation beyond even the extra eccentricity which one would expect of a bookish child with a poet's eye and a special sensitivity to nature. In his wilful withdrawal from communication ("A présent laissez-moi, je vais seul / . . . et vous me laissez également, / assis, dans l'amitié de mes genoux" [52]) and in his (apparently) involuntary exclusion from communication ("Et moi, plein de santé, je vois cela, je vais / près du malade et lui conte cela: / et voici qu'il me hait" [39]), the child speaker of "Eloges" is in no sense as socially integrated as the narrator or the *négrillon* of *Antan d'enfance*. Indeed, even when the fraternal voice of the narrator of *Antan d'enfance* is finally broken off, channelled into the silence of desire, ("Mes frères O, je voudrais vous dire" are the final words of the text), the desire expressed remains a desire to communicate community. In "Eloges", on the other hand, the speaker seems to have a dysfunctional relation to others – so much so, in fact, that the final poem corresponds to a dismissal, as the first-person declares his desire to be left alone.

De l'enfant au négrillon: Convergence and Divergence

It could be argued that the less marked autobiographical status, the more remote – or at least the less socially explicit – affiliation and the significantly greater opaqueness and discontinuity of Saint-John Perse's text are mostly accounted for by the vastly different positions, milieux and readerships of the two writers. And yet, unlike "Pour fêter une enfance", "Eloges" does not directly confirm the prevalence of the considerable social and historical differences between the childhood experiences evoked by each text. The world of the Caribbean town, as presented in "Eloges", is a significantly less hierarchical milieu than the Caribbean plantation or *habitation* evoked in "Pour fêter une enfance". Consequently, the passages which gradually and economically outline in *Antan d'enfance* what Chamoiseau terms the "ruine intérieure" of racism resonate less in relation to "Eloges" than in relation to the casual privilege of the childhood celebrated in "Pour fêter une enfance". Yet even in its manner of treating the same preoccupation as the one which directs *Antan d'enfance* – that is, the poetics of literary memory – "Eloges" reflects a very different ideological position from that of Chamoiseau. Thus, while the two authors converge to a certain extent in the picture which they present of the Caribbean environment, in their evocation of its cultural and racial diversity, for example, or of the quality of the urban environment, this evocation is located in Chamoiseau's case in relation to an explicitly stated collective affiliation and cultural agenda. "Eloges", on the other hand, although it is also an exploration of the process of memory as imagination and dream, has as its agent the figure of an *Enfant* and/or *Songeur* who eschews all social labels and who serves, instead, a universalizing and idealizing function.

Between the writing of the self-styled *Français des Iles* – a Frenchman and poet first and foremost – and that of the *Créole* who identifies himself as the *négrillon* turned *Marqueur de paroles* this disparity is predictable. However, a closer reading of the convergences between the two works (in tone, genre, and self-reflexive or metadiscursive discourse) can provide more than confirmation of a crudely determinist thesis. Apart from obliging us to dwell on the texture of memory instead of reading through it, these two texts, and *a fortiori* a comparative reading of both, encourage us to review the complex relation (in the Caribbean context) between self and community, past and present, memory and poetry, imagination and reality, personal expression and collective *engagement*.

Notes

1. I have concentrated elsewhere on the implications of the specifically intertextual dimension of Chamoiseau's relation to Perse. See, for example, Gallagher 1994, 1999, 2001.
2. All references to Saint-John Perse's writings are taken from the *Oeuvres complètes* (1978); page numbers are given in parentheses after the citations. Somewhat confusingly, when "Eloges" appeared again in 1911, one year after its first publication, it was accompanied by another poetic sequence ("Pour fêter une enfance", dated 1907), in a volume which was also entitled "Eloges". These two sequences are included in the definitive 1925 edition called *Eloges,* but this time along with a poem entitled "Ecrit sur la porte" and a third sequence, "Images à Crusoe", both of which evoke the Caribbean, although not a Caribbean childhood specifically. In the remainder of this paper, references to the title of the poem sequence "Eloges" will be in inverted commas, to that of the 1925 volume in italics.
3. "Pour fêter une enfance" evokes the world of the Caribbean plantation (or *habitation*) rather than the Caribbean town.
4. The precise intertextual references between Chamoiseau's writing and that of Perse are particularly striking when one considers "Pour fêter une enfance": "O! j'ai lieu de louer" (28) or "je me souviens du sel, je me souviens du sel" (24) echoed in Chamoiseau's text by "Je me souviens de l'icaque / oh je me souviens de l'icaque" (1990, 161). This poem sequence opens with the unforgettable image of

the child's bath: "Palmes . . .! / Alors on te baignait dans l'eau-de-feuilles-vertes" (23). Chamoiseau evokes a very similar scene in *Antan d'enfance*: "le négrillon bénéficiait d'un bain de feuilles gardiennes – géranium, coquelicot, patchouli, fromager – qui lui adoucissait la peau" (1990, 93).

5. See Rosello's study (1992). Writing about the ongoing polarization which undermines the unity of Caribbean society, Rosello notes that "A quelques exceptions près, les Antillais sont tous des descendants d'esclaves, ou des descendants de maîtres" (7).

6. Not only does Glissant's poetry reply to that of Saint-John Perse, but this key Martinican author has written several highly lucid essays on the importance of Saint-John Perse's writing in the Caribbean context; each of the three collections of Glissant's essays (1969, 1981, 1990) contains a chapter on Saint-John Perse. Like *Antan d'enfance,* Confiant's memoir of his childhood, *Ravines du devant-jour* (1993), alludes to and quotes from *Eloges,* while the text of Walcott's Nobel speech (1993) refers extensively to the poetics of Saint-John Perse.

7. Not only does *Antan d'enfance* open and close with invocations of memory, but such invocations are prevalent right throughout the text, for example: "O mémoire sélective. Tu ne te souviens plus de sa disparition. . . . Mémoire, c'est là ma décision" (Chamoiseau 1990, 49); "Mémoire, je vois ton jeu: tu prends racine et te structures dans l'imagination, et cette dernière ne fleurit qu'avec toi" (58).

8. "Enfance, c'est richesse dont jamais tu n'accordes géographie très claire" (Chamoiseau 1990, 11); "mémoire, pourquoi accordes-tu cette richesse sans pour autant l'offrir? Et quand s'écoule d'un au-delà des yeux, sans annonce ni appel, un lot de souvenirs, quand s'élève en bouffée la mensongère estime d'un temps heureux . . ." (12).

9. "Et d'autres montent, à leur tour, sur le pont / et moi je prie, encore, qu'on ne tende la toile" (38); "– Cependant le bateau fait une ombre vert-bleue; paisible, clairvoyante, envahie de glucoses où paissent / en bandes souples qui sinuent / ces poissons qui s'en vont comme le thème au long du chant" (39); "– Ce navire est à nous et mon enfance n'a sa fin. J'ai vu bien des poissons qu'on m'enseigne à nommer. . . . / ce poisson buissonneux hissé par-dessus bord pour amuser ma mère qui est jeune et qui bâille" (40).

10. "Et la Maison! la Maison? . . . on en sort!" (48); in poem XVII, "L'enfant veut qu'on le peigne sur le pas de la porte" (51); and further on, "A présent, laissez-moi, je vais seul. / Je sortirai, car j'ai affaire: un insecte m'attend pour traiter. Je me fais joie du gros œil à facettes . . . / Ou bien j'ai une alliance avec les pierres veinées-bleu: et vous me laissez également, / assis, dans l'amitié de mes genoux" (52).

11. "Alors / une mer plus crédule et hantée d'invisibles départs, / étagée comme un ciel au-dessus des vergers, / se gorgeait de fruits d'or, de poissons violets et d'oiseaux" (28); "La barque de mon père, studieuse, amenait de grandes figures blanches . . ." (29).

12. "On ne quitte pas l'enfance, on se met à croire à la réalité, ce que l'on dit être le réel" (Chamoiseau 1990, 78).

13. "Commença une longue attente, ô frères, la plus terrible je crois de nos communes enfances" (Chamoiseau 1990, 57).

14. "Où débute l'enfance?" (Chamoiseau 1990, 13).

15. The narrator's mother, for example, usually referred to as "La haute confidente" (Chamoiseau 1990, 13), is frequently invoked as a guarantor of the narrator's memories.

16. "Mémoire, passons un pacte le temps d'un crayonné, baisse palissades et apaise les farouches, suggère le secret des traces invoquées au bord de tes raziés. Moi, je n'emporte ni sac de rapt ni coutelas de conquête, rien qu'une ivresse et que joie bien docile au gré (coulée de temps) de ta coulée" (Chamoiseau 1990, 12).

References

Bernabé, Jean, Patrick Chamoiseau and Raphaël Confiant. 1989. *Eloge de la créolité*. Paris: Gallimard.

Chamoiseau, Patrick. 1990. *Antan d'enfance*. Paris: Hatier.

Confiant, Raphaël. 1993. *Ravines du devant-jour: récit*. Paris: Gallimard.

Ega, Françoise. [1965] 1989. *Le Temps des madras: récit de la Martinique*. Paris: L'Harmattan.

Gallagher, Mary. 1994. "Saint-John Perse et la nouvelle créolité". *Souffle de Perse* 4 (January): 75–91.

———. 1999. "Seminal Praise: The Poetry of Saint-John Perse". In *An Introduction to Caribbean Francophone Writing*, edited by Sam Haigh, 17–34. London: Berg.

———. 2001. "Saint-John Perse: créole, donc moderne?" In *Modernité de Saint-John Perse? actes du colloque de Besançon, des 14, 15 et 16 mai 1998*, edited by Catherine Mayaux, 363–75. Besançon, France: Presses universitaires franc-comtoises.

Glissant, Edouard. 1969. *L'Intention poétique*. Paris: Seuil.

———. 1981. *Le Discours antillais*. Paris: Seuil.

———. 1990. *Poétique de la relation*. Paris: Gallimard.

Lacrosil, Michèle. 1960. *Sapotille et le serin d'argile*. Paris: Gallimard.

Perse, Saint-John. 1978. *Œuvres complètes*. Bibliothèque de la Pléiade. Paris: Gallimard.

Rosello, Mireille. 1992. *Littérature et identité créole aux Antilles*. Paris: Karthala.

Schwarz-Bart, Simone. 1972. *Pluie et vent sur Télumée Miracle: roman*. Paris: Seuil.

Taconet, Noël. 1986. *"Eloges" de Saint-John Perse: la nostalgie*. Paris: Belin.

Walcott, Derek. 1993. *The Antilles: Fragments of Epic Memory*. London: Faber and Faber.

Warner-Vieyra, Myriam. 1980. *Le Quimboiseur l'avait dit*. Paris: Présence Africaine.

Zobel, Joseph. 1950. *La Rue Cases-Nègres: roman*. Paris: Présence Africaine.

5

From Exile to *Errance*
Dany Laferrière's *Cette grenade dans la main du jeune Nègre est-elle une arme ou un fruit?*

Sam Haigh
University of Warwick

Haitian literature is, almost by definition, a literature of "exile": from the founding, Caribbean exile from Africa, to what Yanick Lahens has called the "internal exile" entailed when writing either in an oral culture with severe problems of illiteracy, or under occupation and dictatorship (1992, 742), to the literal exile of the growing Haitian diaspora in France, Cuba, the United States, Canada and elsewhere. It has become almost obligatory to begin discussions of this latter type of "literature of exile" by addressing the issue of how to define it: is it "migrant", "emigrant", "immigrant", "diaspora" or, as Maximilien Laroche has termed it, "haïtienne", but "du dehors" as opposed to "du dedans" (1987, 26)? (See also Jonassaint 1996.) Is it the subject matter of the work or the nationality of the author which determines the definition? And how might the nationality of these authors be defined in any case?

In the case of those resident in Quebec, answers from writers themselves are varied. Emile Ollivier has famously described himself as "Haïtien la nuit, Québécois le jour" (interview in Jonassaint 1986, 88); Nadine Magloire has called herself "néo-québécoise" (interview with Nicole Ass-Rouxparis in Rinne and Vitiello 1997, 68); while Liliane Dévieux sees herself as simply "haïtienne" (Jonassaint 1986, 50). Anthony Phelps calls himself "canadien" (Jonassaint 1986,

108),[1] Gérard Etienne, "un écrivain du monde, point final" (Jonassaint 1986, 64). Dany Laferrière, meanwhile, whose work will be the focus here, has stated that he feels neither Haitian nor Québécois, but "Plutôt Américain" (Bordeleau 1994, 10).

These types of questions are also, inevitably, bound up with writers' own attitudes towards the experience of "exile", about which they are frequently asked in interviews. Once again, their answers are varied. Many, such as Ollivier, admit to experiencing an acute sense of exile which, even after he has lived outside Haiti for over thirty years, marks his writing profoundly. Others, especially among the younger generations to which Laferrière belongs, do not readily define themselves as "exiles", and their work may not always explore issues of immigration, figure Haitian characters or refer to Haiti at all. However, conscious as almost all of these writers are of the practical benefits that exile has brought them – in terms of enabling them to write at all – an increasing preoccupation in their work is a desire to imagine exile differently, and in particular to see it as potentially productive rather than paralysing. Again Ollivier, in an interview with Jean Jonassaint, is a case in point:

> La littérature d'exil a été une littérature fondamentalement nostalgique dans les premiers temps, mais de plus en plus, *l'exil travaille* les œuvres des écrivains haïtiens de la diaspora. . . . Irrémédiablement, l'exil est un acquis à «positiver». Il faut s'éloigner des brumes de la nostalgie, du larmoiement. . . Oui, l'exil, blessure, n'est pas fatalement un lieu de malédiction, il peut ouvrir la voie à une grande fertilité. (1986, 85–86)

This sentiment is shared by others among the writers interviewed by Jonassaint, notably Phelps and Etienne, as well as by Joël des Rosiers, poet and critic, whose essay *Théories caraïbes: poétique du déracinement* calls throughout for a positive re-evaluation of "l'effet de l'ex-île" (1996, 3). Laroche, too, in his 1987 study *L'Avènement de la littérature haïtienne*, describes the way in which, especially among those writing in the 1980s, like Laferrière, "l'exil devient non plus une condamnation mais une chance" (5). Often, however, such attempts are accompanied both by an acute sense of the importance of remembering the very real alienation entailed by the experience of emigration and by an awareness that the notion of exile itself, "one of the most dominant tropes in the ideologies of high modernism" (Gikandi 1992, 19) and the condition of every (post)modern – especially writing – subject, is in danger of becoming overworked.

Realizations such as these have provoked a desire not simply to "revalue" the term "exile", but instead to use different terms to express the positive potential of the experience of forced emigration. Ollivier, in the interview with Jonassaint quoted above, seems to slip almost imperceptibly from using terms such as "l'exil", "le déracinement" and "l'excision" to the term "errance" as he begins to voice his desire to imagine its positive potential. This, too, is the case in an essay by Lahens, *"Manhattan blues* de Jean-Claude Charles ou quand l'exil devient errance"*, in which she argues that "alors que l'exilé est taraudé par la hantise du retour, l'errant est avant tout celui qui, à force de bouger, finit par emporter ses racines avec lui" (1986, 9). "L'errance" would seem, for these writers, to be almost automatically a more enabling means of conceiving of the idea of emigration.

This is also the case in the work of René Depestre, who, writing from his own experience as part of the Haitian diaspora, feels, like Ollivier and Lahens, that exile has traditionally been defined in terms of tragedy. The exile, for him, has been imagined as "cet être humain qui, arraché à son sol natal, coupé de son enfance et sa langue maternelle, vivait en terre étrangère une douloureuse épreuve de deuil et de nostalgie" (1998, 11). For him, such a definition is part of a fundamentally Western – and therefore, of course, colonial – fixation with rootedness, with what Edouard Glissant calls "l'identité-racine", in which "la racine est unique, c'est une souche qui prend tout sur elle et tue alentour" (1990, 23). This is the same fixation out of which nationalism grows, Western or otherwise, as well as nationalist literature written either from within the *pays natal* or from a position of exile in which the *pays natal,* idealized or reviled, remains the exclusive focus and sole means of self-definition. For Haitian writers like Depestre, who know more than many "les misères atroces du nationalisme" (Depestre 1998, 140), such a model of diaspora writing seems to be particularly inappropriate and limiting.

Instead, both personally and in literary terms, Depestre also prefers the idea of *errance* to that of *exil.* For him this is a more accurate description of the migrant Haitian's frequent experience of wandering between several host countries rather than settling only in one. Famously, he refers to himself as "ce nomade enraciné", and he has often described the way in which, instead of seeking out diaspora communities when living abroad, he has preferred to allow himself to be "Français à Paris, Brésilien à Sao Paulo, Tchèque à Prague, Italien à Milan, Cubain à La Havane" (1998, 13). In the work of Depestre, *errance,* or *nomadisme,* is a means of imagining identity differently, and he names this reimagined identity "l'identité-banian", after the banyan tree, "dont les racines ont la faculté, après un premier développement en tronc unique, de redescendre à la terre nourricière pour s'assurer d'autres remontées à la lumière" (14). Depestre's description of his own *identité-banian,* which he also sometimes refers to as "l'ensemble des rhizomes de mon parcours existentiel" (137), is extremely similar to Glissant's description of the reimagined identity, which for him, too, comes from valorizing *errance* over *exil.* By means of an engagement with the work of Gilles Deleuze and Félix Guattari on "la pensée rhizomatique" and "le nomadisme", he names this identity "l'identité-rhizome". As he explains, if "la racine est unique", then the *rhizome* is

> [u]ne racine démultipliée, étendue en réseaux dans la terre ou dans l'air, sans qu'aucune souche y intervienne en prédateur irrémédiable. La notion de rhizome maintiendrait donc le fait de l'enracinement, mais récuse l'idée d'une racine totalitaire. (Glissant 1990, 23)

In the work of both theorists, what emerges is a notion of identity in relation, rather than in opposition, to the other. The *errant* remains linked to what Depestre calls the *chez soi* of the native land, but unlike the *exilé,* it is also open to the many cultural influences of the *chez autrui.* In his own case, "ces différentes racines, ajoutées à mon héritage haïtien, ont fait les *moi* . . . [d'une] identité multiple" (Depestre 1998, 13). Glissant's notion of *errance* is one of "une recherche de l'Autre" (1990, 30). If "l'identité comme racine condamne l'émigré . . . à un écartèlement laminant" (157), *les errants* are those who, like Depestre, take their roots with them, who do not abandon or renounce their origins but who add to them as they move from place to place. This, as Glissant comments, entails a more positive sense of identity: "si l'exil peut effriter le sens de l'identité, la pensée de l'errance . . . (qui est la pensée du relatif) le renforce le plus souvent" (32).

Glissant's notion of *errance* finds its concretization in Patrick Chamoiseau's figure of "le driveur". A Creole wanderer, the *driveur* – from the *marron* to the *affranchi* to the post-abolition town-dweller – has continued to move "sans cesse (driver)" (Chamoiseau 1992, 33) and has therefore resisted, if not necessarily consciously, the sedentary lifestyle imposed by the French from the time of the *habitation* on. "La Drive", for Chamoiseau, is both "la forme élémentaire de résistance" and "un projet de réalisation de soi" (31). Though not restricted to the Creole *En-ville,* today's *driveur* is nonetheless largely an urban figure and, for Chamoiseau, the Haitian and Dominican immigrants who live in the most dispossessed areas of the towns of Martinique and Guadeloupe are, along with musicians, artists and writers, *the* contemporary examples of "la Drive".

This modern-day *driveur* seems especially resonant of those Haitian writers of the diaspora, the vast majority of whom have gravitated towards cities such as Paris, New York and Montreal. This is certainly true of Dany Laferrière, a Haitian-born writer living between Montreal and Miami, whose first novel, when it appeared in 1985, won its author notoriety, acclaim and criticism alike – not only because of its provocative title, *Comment faire l'amour avec un Nègre sans se fatiguer,* but also because of its subject matter: the sexual relationship between "la Blanche" and "le Nègre". This novel paved the way for a prolific writing career, which has seen a continued preoccupation with *la question raciale*, as well as with *la réalité américaine*, in particular in the four novels which are often referred to as "le roman américain" (Bordeleau 1994, 10): *Comment faire l'amour, Eroshima* (1987), *Cette grenade dans la main du jeune Nègre est-elle une arme ou un fruit?* (1993) and *Chronique de la dérive douce* (1994). In his other novels, however, which are sometimes referred to as "le volet haïtien" (Pelletier 1994, 11), Laferrière explores memories and memoirs of Haiti: of a childhood and ado-lescence there, in *L'Odeur du café* (1991), *Le Goût des jeunes filles* (1992), *La Chair du maître* (1997) and *Le Charme des après-midi sans fin* (1997), and of a more recent return to the native land, in *Pays sans chapeau* (1996). If in the other Haitian novels childhood is seen somewhat as "un paradis perdu", in this latter novel Haiti is by no means simply idealized or reviled; rather, it is a place which is still real, which is revisited and re-evaluated, not imagined only from afar.

It is immediately obvious that Laferrière's entire oeuvre lends itself to an auto-biographical reading, not only because the novels explore experiences which are evidently very close to those of the author himself, but also because the narra-tor is frequently a writer struggling to write a novel similar to the one that we are reading. Of the "Haitian" novels, this is especially marked in *Pays sans chapeau,* in which the narrator has returned to Haiti after twenty years' absence and is trying to write about the experience while struggling with the difficult role of the writer in Haitian culture. And even in the most recent novel at the time of writing, *Le Charme des après-midi sans fin,* the narrator refers in the final chapter to the publication of *L'Odeur du café* in 1991. It is especially true of the "American" novels, however, and in particular of *Comment faire l'amour* and *Cette grenade,* the two novels on which I shall focus here.

In the first novel, the narrator is a poor black immigrant living in Montreal and trying to write a first novel, *Paradis du Dragueur nègre,* which he hopes will bring him the success, fame and money to enable him to escape from poverty. In *Cette grenade,* the narrator begins by reflecting on the success of his first novel, entitled *Comment faire l'amour avec un Nègre sans se fatiguer,* and on the fame and financial benefits that it has brought him. This, together with the conversations between the narrator and readers of his first novel which make up much of *Cette grenade,* inevitably leads the reader, at the very least, to consider this novel as the sequel to *Comment faire l'amour.*[2] It has equally inevitably led to the conflation of the author and narrator of these novels: as Michel Terrien points out, even Laferrière himself, in an interview, "passait directement du narrateur à sa personne" (1998, 173). Despite this, there are several indications within *Cette grenade* itself that such easy conflations should be guarded against. The very first reader with whom the narrator of *Cette grenade* speaks about *Comment faire l'amour* asks him, "Est-ce que c'est votre histoire? . . . Je vous ai vu à la télé, l'autre jour, et je me demande si tout ça vous est vraiment arrivé" (Laferrière 1993, 31). As he sets out for her the familiar argument about the impossibility of faithful autobiography, it is clear that his question – "pourquoi est-ce si important de savoir que l'histoire s'est réellement passée?" (Laferrière 1993, 32), which she is unable to answer – must also be directed at us as readers. However, it is difficult – if not impossible – to read these two novels without taking at least the narrator to be the same, with *Cette grenade* acting as a supplement to and constant commentary on *Comment faire l'amour.* Nonetheless, Terrien's own approach is instructive, and it must be remembered that the two novels remain part of "une œuvre littéraire où le 'je' est fictif" (Terrien 1998, 173).

Given the continued autobiographical resonances in Laferrière's work, it is perhaps initially surprising that neither *Comment faire l'amour* nor *Cette grenade* focuses upon the issues of exile or immigration – a sustained examination of these is left to *Chronique de la dérive douce* later. In *Comment faire l'amour,* we never know the narrator's origins for sure, while in *Cette grenade,* it is at least made clear that the narrator is from the Caribbean. Apart from referring once in *Cette grenade* to "chez moi" (Laferrière 1993, 37), however, his "native land" is not identified in more precise terms, and never does he refer to himself as an "exile". Instead, he chooses to refer to his time in North America as "mes années d'*errance* à travers les chambres crasseuses . . . de cette ville [Montreal]" (Laferrière 1993, 110, emphasis added). Describing scenes familiar from *Comment faire l'amour,* he also refers to the time spent, during the writing of his first novel, "[à] arpenter la rue Saint-Denis", watching people in restaurants and cafés that he can only dream of being able to enter and wishing that he could cross over to this "other side" of life in North America (110).

As the narrator of *Cette grenade* describes it, then, and echoing Ollivier, Lahens and Depestre, the time spent writing *Comment faire l'amour* was not a time of "exile-as-nostalgia". Rather, like them, he makes a deliberate effort to avoid nostalgia, and entitles one of his chapters "Comment revivre le bon vieux temps sans nostalgie" (1993, 113). It is a future in the host country and not a return to the native land which is envisaged, both in *Comment faire l'amour* and throughout *Cette grenade.* Indeed, when the narrator goes to see the editor of the magazine for which he ends up writing what we read as *Cette grenade,* it has already been assumed that he will write something on the Caribbean for their "numéro spécial sur l'Amérique" (Laferrière 1993, 12). He is outraged at the assumption that he is naturally fixated on his native land: "toujours la même connerie! Les gens doivent écrire sur leur coin d'origine!" (15). Indeed, the editor's assumption is part of a much wider phenomenon in which people that he meets insist on seeing him as deeply unhappy (see, for example, pages 76 and 90) – that is, a tragic, exiled figure as described by Depestre. Just as the narrator repeatedly finds such an attitude bemusing, so he informs the magazine editor that he is interested in writing about North America, where he achieved his "indépendance": "j'écris sur ce qui se passe aujourd'hui, là où je vis" (15). As we learn a little later, before coming to America the narrator had always seen it as "la terre promise", one which *owed* him success, and it is this success which, from his arrival, he has been determined to achieve (38). As he explains, "Je voulais tout. . . . Tout ce que l'Amérique m'avait promis. Je sais que l'Amérique a fait beaucoup de promesses à un nombre incalculable de gens, mais moi, j'entendais lui faire tenir ses promesses" (36).

The narrator of *Cette grenade* is by no means idealistic about America as "terre promise": not only has it failed to keep its promise of success to so many of those immigrants, like himself, from the "Third World", but, as he acknowledges, "le Tiers-Monde existe aussi en Amérique du Nord. Ce sont les ghettos où pullule une fourmilière noire, pauvre, analphabète" (Laferrière 1993, 26). He is well aware of the difficulties entailed in making a life in North America and in attempting not to be consigned to the America of the ghettos. Like Chamoiseau's *driveur,* who is most often "ce personnage affecté par une déveine", Laferrière's narrator, especially as he struggles to write his first novel, "déambule sans arrêt" (Chamoiseau 1992, 29). As Chamoiseau makes clear, the *driveur,* like the *nomade* whom Glissant refuses to follow Deleuze and Guattari in celebrating (see Glissant 1990, 23–24), wanders primarily to survive, not as a consciously con-testatory strategy. He is *unable* to settle, in the urbanized, increasingly assimi-lated and gallicized environment of the French Caribbean. However – and crucially, although the *driveur* himself may not be aware of it – while "c'est un malheur [d'être le jouet de la Drive] . . ., *c'est un défi*" (Chamoiseau 1992, 33). In the case of Laferrière's narrator, who also wanders, at first in order to survive, this is a challenge which he was, and still is, determined to take up. It is the chal-lenge of the *errant,* of finding a way in which to remain focused on a future in the country or countries in which he finds himself, and not, like the *exilé,* to be haunted by the impossible dream of a return to an idealized past.

Of course, since this narrator is also the author of a novel called *Comment faire l'amour* whose subject matter, it would seem, is broadly the same as that of Laferrière's novel of the same name, it is sexual success, promised "par les revues, les posters, le cinéma, la télé", which he feels is primarily owed by America to him and to "tous les jeunes gens du Tiers-Monde" (Laferrière 1993, 38). It is this, in his usual provocative way, that he feels is the principal lure for all those immigrants – all those nomads, in fact, as he imagines Bedouins in the desert watching American television – who have been tempted to the "Terre Promise" (39). Thus the sexual preoccupations of *Comment faire l'amour* are, in part, con-tinued in *Cette grenade.* In each novel, but especially in *Comment faire l'amour,* the narrator could be described not only as an "un errant", but as "un sexe itinérant" (76) whose wandering is highly sexualized and always masculine, virile, effected at least in part through sexual relationships with (white) women.

The most obvious reading of this continued preoccupation, particularly with the relationship between "le Nègre et la Blanche" is, of course, via Frantz Fanon's *Peau noire, masques blancs* – that is, as a classic example of the "lactification com-plex" so famously described by Fanon, in which the neurotic black man seeks inte-gration into the white world through sexual relationships with white women: "je ne veux pas être reconnu comme noir, mais comme Blanc. . . . [Q]ui peut le faire, sinon la Blanche? . . . Dans ces seins blancs que mes mains ubiquitaires caressent, c'est la civilisation et la dignité blanches que je fais miennes" (Fanon 1952, 51). Certainly, the narrator of *Comment faire l'amour* sees his own preoccupation with white women in similar terms: "Je prends fermement ses seins blancs. Le léger duvet de son ventre blanc (marbre). JE VEUX BAISER SON IDENTITÉ. Pousser le débat racial jusque dans ses entrailles" (Laferrière 1985, 74). And, again like the *névrosés* described by Fanon, this narrator, throughout *Comment faire l'amour,* conceives of his relationships with white women – the union of "l'inférieur avec la femme du supérieur", as he describes it in *Cette grenade* (83) – as a form of revenge on white men.[3]

As Anne Vassal has pointed out, however, by the end of *Comment faire l'amour* the narrator's writing has begun to take over from "la drague" as a primary means of gaining entrance into and acceptance from his "host" culture (Vassal 1998, 186). Success as a writer – "voler la science des Blancs" – is even seen as yet another form of revenge on white men: "être musicien ou athlète, ça on connaît, mais les mots nous résistent encore, et voilà ce jeune rusé qui s'est frayé un chemin jusqu'au cœur de l'alphabet" (Laferrière 1993, 48). And throughout *Cette grenade,* it is writing, not sex, which is seen as having been the means of obliging America to keep its promises, as having given the narrator access to the financial success and celebrity that he so desires. Here, sex with white women becomes simply part of the narrator's aspirations, something that he hopes to attain once he has gained some sort of place in the host country, and not itself a means of gaining such a place. As he explains in *Cette grenade,*

> A l'époque de mon premier roman, c'est simple, je manquais de tout. Je manquais de vin, de nourriture, du rire des jeunes filles insouciantes, je manquais d'argent pour payer le loyer, de conversations libres et interminables dans les bars sans penser de l'addition. C'est pour cette raison qu'il y a tant de vin (mauvais quand même), de jeunes filles insouciantes et de rires dans ce foutu premier roman. On n'a qu'à regarder la peinture haïtienne pour comprendre cela. Les paysages sont toujours comme un jardin d'éden. Les fruits, toujours trop beaux. Les poissons, trop gros. Les sourires des enfants, trop larges. C'est le pays rêvé contre le pays réel. (108–9)[4]

And, indeed, now that he has achieved a modest level of acceptance into his host country, gone from *Cette grenade* are the claustrophobic sex scenes of *Comment faire l'amour.* White women are still omnipresent, largely as people with whom he discusses his first novel, but actual, personal relationships with them are rarely mentioned. Instead, we are left to assume that these have now become more securely a part of "le pays réel".

Of course, that relationships with white women should be a desired outcome rather than a means of finding a place in the host society is no less bound up with the complex described by Fanon. Jean Veneuse, the protagonist of René Maran's *Un Homme pareil aux autres,* who is examined by Fanon in *Peau noire masques blancs,* is read even by Fanon as having educated – "civilized" – himself to such a point that he deserves the love of a white woman, and that a relationship with a black woman would seem impossible. However, even in *Comment faire l'amour,* the level of self-awareness on the part of the narrator is such that it becomes difficult to believe that he is simply another black man suffering from the neurosis described by Fanon. In *Comment faire l'amour,* the narrator, describing his relationship with Miz Sophisticated Lady, asks,

> Existe-t-il une psychanalyse possible de l'âme nègre? N'est-ce pas, véritablement, le «Continent noir»? Je vous pose la question, Dr Freud. Qui pourrait comprendre le déchirement du Nègre qui veut à tout prix devenir Blanc? . . . Moi, je voudrais être Blanc. Bon, disons que je ne suis pas totalement désintéressé. Je voudrais être un Blanc amélioré. Un Blanc sans le complexe d'Œdipe. (72–73)

This is a moment of self-reflexivity and playfulness typical of Laferrière's work: Fanon's Freudian probings of the black unconscious and his analysis of the particular form that the Oedipus complex may take in the Caribbean are clearly referred to here, and the narrator's "bon, disons que je ne suis pas totalement désintéressé" goes little way to convincing us that he is seriously in search of a white identity through his relationships with white Canadian women.

Throughout this novel, as well as in *Cette grenade,* it is clear that the role adopted by the narrator with regard to white women is precisely that: a role. He, along with a number of other black men described by him, deliberately adopts the role of "le Nègre" in order to attract as many women as possible:

> Hier soir, j'étais dans un bar du centre-ville. Il y avait, à côté de moi, un Noir et une Blanche. Je connaissais le type. C'est tout juste s'il ne disait à la fille qu'il était un amateur de la chair humaine, qu'il venait de la brousse, que son père était le grand sorcier de son village. Et moi, je voyais la fille hocher la tête, en extase devant un vrai de vrai, l'homme

primitif, le Nègre selon *National Geographic,* Rousseau et Cie. . . . Je
connais très bien ce type et je sais . . . [que] c'est un urbain et un
Occidental . . . mais devant la Blanche, l'Afrique doit lui servir, en quelque
sorte, de SEXE SURNUMERAIRE. (Laferrière 1993, 146–47)

Like Fanon, this man is quite aware of the stereotypes, primarily sexual, which
exist in the white imagination; and, as for Fanon, they are stereotypes which
depend upon an equally stereotyped view of the white women as simultaneously
terrified of, and fascinated by, the idea of having sex with "un Nègre". As Fanon
asserts, such is the famed sexual prowess of the black man that "une Blanche qui
a couché avec un Nègre accepte difficilement un amant blanc" (Fanon 1952, 148).
Unlike Fanon, who frequently presents the stereotypes about white female sexuality as true, for Laferrière's narrator, both "le Nègre" and "la Blanche" – especially "la blonde . . ., la-plus-que-blanche" (Laferrière 1993, 83) – are stereotypical
roles which certainly contain an element of truth but which were invented by
the white man. And they are roles of which Laferrière makes use in his work
simultaneously to shock and delight a North American readership.

Indeed the same desire to shock can be seen to be at work in the decision
to use the word *Nègre* rather than *Noir* in the title of *Comment faire l'amour* and
then throughout these novels. As the narrator of *Cette grenade* explains, this decision led to the censorship of the title in the US press; he was even asked to change
it for the US market (Laferrière 1993, 23–24).[5] In an attempt to set out his reasons
for insisting upon the continued use of the word *nègre,* the narrator of *Cette
grenade* explains that he was motivated by a desire to empty it, as a Western invention, of its negative connotations: "dire le mot nègre si souvent qu'il devienne
familier et perde tout son soufre" (198). It must, however, be remembered that
the narrator of these two novels is not Laferrière, and that even within the fictional world in which the narrator of *Cette grenade* is the writer of a novel entitled *Comment faire l'amour,* motivations and intentions cannot necessarily be
taken at face value. Once again, we are reminded of this within the text of *Cette
grenade* itself, for the narrator changes his stated motivations for writing according to the requirements of a given situation. As he admits, although a desire for
wealth and success – even vengeance on the landlord who tried to prevent him
writing – were his personal motivations for writing, "naturellement, je réserve
un autre langage à la presse. Je leur dis que j'écris pour exprimer certaines vérités
restées tapies dans quelque recoin de mon âme" (114). His constant use of the

term *nègre,* far from being motivated by a grandiose desire to challenge received perceptions, may in fact be motivated more simply by a desire to exploit the unacknowledged expectations of the white liberal readers with whom *Comment faire l'amour* was so popular. Like the white women seduced by the role playing of the "dragueur nègre", a white American readership is given exactly what it wants and expects from "un écrivain nègre": a novel preoccupied with sex and white women. In return, that "écrivain nègre" – and this is a role which he consciously adopts, as opposed to that of "un écrivain noir" or, simply, "un écrivain" – gains publication, wealth and notoriety – that is, the success owed to him by "America".

It thus seems less easy to read the early focus on white women as simply another example of the Caribbean neurosis described by Fanon. Indeed, when the sexual preoccupations of *Comment faire l'amour* and *Cette grenade* are read alongside those of Laferrière's other works, a different reading becomes possible, for his other narrators are certainly also preoccupied by sexual relationships with women, but these women are by no means necessarily white. In *L'Odeur du café* and *Le Goût des jeunes filles,* the first two novels of "le volet haïtien", it is the narrator's sexual *apprentissage* among the young *Haïtiennes* of his childhood and adolescence which is recounted. And in Laferrière's second novel, *Eroshima,* which takes place, like *Cette grenade,* largely in the United States, the white women of *Comment faire l'amour* are replaced by "les Jaunes". When the treatment of sexuality across Laferrière's wider oeuvre is thus examined, it begins to look very similar to what J. Michael Dash calls the "global libertinage" of Depestre (1997, 154; see also Jones 1981).

For Depestre, *errance* in particular is very much a sexual, and masculine, phenomenon, in which a Caribbean *érotisme solaire* informs an attitude towards sexual relationships and women which renders the emigrant's wandering from country to country an even more enriching experience. According to Depestre, love and sex, like exile, have in the Western tradition typically been associated with the tragic, an association which has led to a Western preoccupation with sex as sin and with pornography rather than eroticism. Running counter to this, he believes, is a Creole culture of (strictly heterosexual) eroticism which is "superbement libre" (Depestre 1998, 127) and in which "la femme s'épanouit en jardin du paradis dans les bras du fermier enchanté qui pioche et bêche passionnément ses adorables profondeurs" (125; see also Depestre 1981). This is something which seems to have informed Depestre's attitude towards sexual relationships throughout his own *errance érotique* as a Haitian emigrant.

Certainly his concepts of "la femme jardin" (Depestre 1998, 28–30) and of free, reciprocal love without sin or consequences – "l'érotisme solaire" (130) – are ones which are repeated throughout his oeuvre. It displays an attitude towards women which has much in common with that found in the poetry of Negritude and the work of the Martinican *créolistes:* women are rarely assigned an active role of any sort, and when they are not a hindrance to the male hero's quest for or assertion of cultural identity, they figure primarily as the means of his attainment of it and, like the banished Chinese woman in Depestre's *Eros dans un train chinois* (1990), are frequently sacrificed for it.

There are certainly similarities between the *errance érotique* of Depestre and that of Laferrière's narrators, from the adolescent sexual experiences in Haiti to those of *Comment faire l'amour* and *Eroshima*. However, the playfulness and self-reflexivity of Laferrière's work belie the seriousness of Depestre as much as they resist a straightforward Fanonian reading. As we have seen, in *Cette grenade* the obsessive focus on personal sexual relationships disappears. Instead, the narrator's insistence on continuing to examine the relationship between "le Nègre et la Blanche" is constantly undermined – by the narrator himself, by his friend ("c'est un peu dépassé, ton histoire de blonde . . ." [93]), by the readers of his first novel and, most important, by the presence of Erzulie. This dream-like, almost magic realist incarnation of the voodoo goddess appears from time to time in order to berate the narrator for including only white women in his novels and to make a plea for her own inclusion in his work. If this were a less playful book, she could be taken for the outward manifestation of his conscience. At the very least, she is emblematic of the novel's, and the narrator's, self-awareness and self-reflexivity. Their lengthy discussions of the missing black woman in literature, his objections that she would be better represented by a white man ("ça fera drôlement colonialiste" [99]), his brief flirtation with the idea that he may write his next book on black women, and her unremitting criticism of him ("tu crois vraiment à ces sornettes?" [100]) all work to remind us that he, unlike Depestre, does not take his own clichés very seriously. Once again, Laferrière's narrator constantly teases and provokes the reader, seeking a reaction to his self-aware political incorrectness and, consequently, seeking to make the money which will assure his future in his adopted country.

It is thus writing about sex and not sex itself which allows this narrator to take up the challenge of *la Drive* and enables him to orientate himself towards the future and not the past – to become *un errant* and not *un exilé*. And now that he has achieved the success that he wanted, and is freed from the constraints of finding a way simply to survive, he finds himself in the somewhat unfamiliar (and luxurious) position of being paid to wander – and much farther than around the streets of Montreal. As his friend points out at the beginning, "tu te balades un peu, à leurs frais, et tu écris tes impressions, et, vieux, crois-moi, ça paie rudement bien. . . . C'est ça, l'Amérique" (Laferrière 1993, 13). "L'Amérique", it would seem, is a land of opportunity both in financial terms and in terms of travel. As the narrator himself comments before embarking upon his journey, it is a nomadic space: "En Amérique, on bouge. L'espace américain est une invitation à la vitesse" (12).

Thus the narrator spends his time "à parcourir l'Amérique et à noter, en toute liberté, ce que je vois" (Laferrière 1993, 94). *Cette grenade* becomes a sort of road novel – although, as the narrator himself comments in relation to his project, it is actually "plus proche du cinéma que du roman, du montage rapide que de longs enchaînements, de scènes se téléscopant que d'un ordre régulier" (27). After the opening three sections devoted largely to the discussions with readers of his first novel, the narrator then travels from one American city to another, avoiding the small, identical towns of the South that he so detests because of the racism in which they are steeped. In the course of his journey, he meets countless Americans, both ordinary readers of his first novel and famous figures, giving us "vidéoclips" (27) of "la boîte à surprises de la vie américaine" (187). In "Chroniques d'Amérique", he meets Spike Lee and argues over the filming of *Malcolm X*; in "Hall of Fame", he imagines meetings with "dix héros américains contemporains" (149), including figures as diverse as Ice Cube, Toni Morrison, Derek Walcott, Magic Johnson and Naomi Campbell; in "L'Amérique est un énorme téléviseur avec plein d'images dedans", he examines the American obsession with baseball and finds it indicative of the homosociality of American culture. In the final section, entitled simply "Retour", he returns not to Haiti, but to Montreal, the place of his "birth" as a writer.

As the narrator travels, he is certainly aware that he is only able to do so because his success as a writer has freed him from the daily struggle for survival. However, he by no means feels compelled to use this new-found freedom in order to embark on an examination of his own subjectivity, as may perhaps have been expected. Just as the wandering of Chamoiseau's *driveur* is never an overt "projet de réalisation de soi" (1992, 31), so this narrator's journey never becomes a traditional quest for identity. On the rare occasions that he even alludes to the question of identity, he does not do so directly in relation to himself, and his references to "les Antillais sans identité" (Laferrière 1993, 36) or to African Americans who "cherche[nt leur] identité dans les mots" (13) are subjected to his usual ironic tone. Nonetheless, throughout his journey he is interested, as we have seen, in defining himself in at least one sense: as "un écrivain nègre" (35), with the potential to become "le plus grande écrivain nègre vivant" (35), and he is certainly unclear about what makes "un grand écrivain nègre" (35).

Although this is clearly a role that the narrator of *Cette grenade* has consciously chosen, and although, as we have seen, it is a role which has allowed him to attain a certain level of personal success in America, he is never clear whether there is another side to such a role, and he is certainly unclear about what makes "un grand écrivain nègre" or "un bon écrivain nègre". However, as his travels continue and as he encounters examples of black writers and artists, it becomes clearer what "un (grand) écrivain nègre" is not. It is not someone – and here we are inevitably reminded of the long Haitian tradition of "commited" writing – who writes "littérature engagée", for he sees this as being "du passé", while he is a writer "du présent" (Laferrière 1993, 66–67). Nor, like the Nigerian taxi driver he meets, is it someone who writes thousand-page volumes rehabilitating the history of "le dernier royaume africain" (191). Nor, most crucially, is it a writer of politically correct, black nationalist novels. As we see when he meets Spike Lee and Ice Cube, he abhors such over-investment in black identity politics because it fixes "black America" in a motionless opposition to "white America" (154) which simply plays into the latter's hands. It ensures that *la question raciale* continues to be one of irreconcilable difference and, more crucially in capitalist America, it ensures that vast amounts of money are made by the film and music industries out of the highly marketable subject of racism: "s'il n'y avait pas le racisme, tout le showbiz américain s'écroulerait du jour au lendemain!" (147). For him, the issue of racism is simply "une bonne mine à exploiter" (147), a means of appealing both to the guilty white liberal and to the black militant.

Despite these views, and despite the narrator's usual apparent unwillingness to examine such matters seriously, "la question raciale", as he explains to the magazine editor, "reste très importante pour moi" – and not solely "du point de vue sexuel" (Laferrière 1993, 14). His wider interest in issues of race and racism is most marked in the final chapter of the section entitled "Hall of Fame", in which James Baldwin, "le seul écrivain en qui j'ai pleinement confiance" (165), crosses over from the land of the dead in order to speak with him. It is here that we meet the writer who serves as his model of "un grand écrivain nègre", as he traces a line of filiation from Richard Wright to Baldwin and then, implicitly, to himself. As he describes Baldwin's life after his arrival in Paris, it is impossible not to see the parallel with his own life as a new immigrant in Montreal:

> Baldwin à Paris. Maigre, sans le sou, enragé, écrivant la nuit, flânant le jour. Le Nègre est plus libre à Paris mais il crève de faim. . . . Baldwin prenant enfin son repas tout seul dans sa chambre de bonne. Il n'y avait place que pour le lit et la machine à écrire. . . . C'est dans ce réduit qu'il se prépare à bombarder l'Amérique blanche. (166)

Like Baldwin, Laferrière's narrator "a voulu comprendre l'Amérique"; like Baldwin, he received shocked media attention after his work was published; and, like Baldwin, he was "cet homme que les Noirs et les Blancs ont détesté à tour de rôle" (167).

Yet such comparisons may at first seem misplaced, self-inflating or even offensive. The apparently frivolous subject matter of *Comment faire l'amour* and the narrator's insistent heterosexuality (though not, like Fanon, an equally insistent homophobia) do not sit easily with Baldwin's representations of homosexuality – at first tentative, then explicit – and his commitment to the struggle against racism and the promotion of black civil rights. However, the narrator's continued esteem for Baldwin, which culminates in the conversation they have here, may signal a seriousness about racial issues to which he has until now seemed almost afraid to admit and has therefore constantly underplayed or undermined. What is more, in this conversation the narrator's repeated use of the word *nègre* suddenly loses its pejorative undertones and ceases to shock, contextualized as it is by the fact that Baldwin, in the 1950s and 1960s, would have been described with pride as "un écrivain nègre". Indeed, it is difficult not to wonder at this point if the narrator's use of the term is not in some measure an effort to reconnect with an era in which the role of the black writer was more clear: to examine racism and to struggle against it. It is therefore unsurprising that it is to Baldwin, such an icon of his time, that he turns in order to ask the crucial question: "Comment devenir un bon écrivain des années quatre-vingt-dix?" (171). And, in reply to Baldwin's "Qu'est-ce que ça veut dire?" answers "un écrivain de son temps" (171). Baldwin fades away before he is able to answer, but he has already advised him, nonetheless, to leave the subject of racism alone:

Ce n'est pas ton affaire. . . . Tu ne peux pas être à la fois la maladie et le remède. . . . C'était notre problème à l'époque. . . . Aujourd'hui, je crois qu'il faudrait laisser un peu de place aux autres. . . . Il faut absolument que le Blanc puisse s'occuper du racisme lui aussi. (168–69)

The narrator – and the reader – therefore continues to be left with no clear idea of the precise role of the "écrivain nègre" beyond that of personal gain – except, that is, for a quite vague notion that it entails some form of contestation. Not that simplified contestation of "black" against "white", but a more complex and sustained attempt to trouble the fixed, racialized oppositions in which American culture has become entrenched, oppositions which in many ways make all sides, black and white, comfortable because the rules of the game are clear. Thus the narrator's constant attempts to shock may be seen as the manifestation of his desire to question what is acceptable when talking about "race" in America. However imprecisely articulated, his is a refusal to see only "ce qu'on me recommande de voir" (Laferrière 1993, 94), and to write only what America wishes to hear on the subject of "race".

By the end of his journey, however, he is unsure even of this role. Where more traditional journey-as-identity-quest narratives may reveal in the final pages the protagonist's renewed sense of identity, *Cette grenade* allows its narrator only a sense of what he is not. Or, rather, what he no longer is: "je ne suis plus un écrivain nègre" (199). It is, of course, never clear which element of this self-definition he rejects, and indeed there is never any implication that he himself knows who or what he is either. And this, it would seem, is the point. Michael Jackson, an apparently unlikely icon, becomes for him someone who has succeeded, and here "success" is not defined solely in material terms: "il a réussi le pari difficile de n'avoir ni sexe, ni couleur, ni race . . . ni identité. . . . Je ne parle pas ici d'identité raciale, nationale, ou autre connerie de ce genre. Je parle d'identité profonde" (146). By the end of the novel, all that can be deduced is that any form of fixed, singular identity, even initially contestatory like those of Spike Lee and Ice Cube, is to be resisted as potentially limiting. Like the title of the novel, on which the last "chapter" dwells, the only certainty at all, is that nothing is certain or singular.

The title of this last chapter – really only a paragraph – is "Feu sur l'Amérique", which refers to the narrator's meeting with Baldwin and to the news headline "L'Amérique est en feu" which, presumably alluding to the Little Rock school segregation riots of 1957, sent Baldwin back to the United States and began his commitment to the civil rights movement. Thus it is signalled that, at least for the narrator, issues of race and racism are still as relevant in the 1990s as they were when Baldwin wrote the collection of essays *The Fire Next Time,* for which he received so much media attention in 1963. Although it is never made clear who, in this last chapter, is running along the street ("le voilà qui arrive . . . gracieux mouvement sautillant du ghetto" [201]) it is clear that whoever it is – Bouba, the narrator's friend from his early days in Montreal, or simply one of the many poor black inhabitants of America's *tiers monde* – he is ready, as was Baldwin and his generation, and as is the narrator now, to take up the challenge of life in contemporary America. He is "ce jeune animal qui s'apprête à bondir ou à lancer quelque chose". And the final question, "Ce truc vert qu'il tient dans sa main, est-elle une arme ou un fruit?" (201) – although never answered or resolved – once again recalls, among many things, the question of the role of the narrator and his writing. Is his writing "une arme" – is he, as he flippantly suggests earlier, "le griot de cette Amérique minable" (38)? Or is it simply the means to personal success – "un fruit", picked from "les arbres de cette terre promise [qui] ploient sous les fruits sauvages, lourds et succulents" (41–42)? It is, perhaps, both or neither. For the only thing which is at all clear by the end of *Cette grenade* is, as Dash points out, that "what predominates is the relative, mobile meaning of things, always open to the vagaries of new readings. Identity here is not fixed but always subject to contact and conjecture" (1997, 159).

Upon arriving in Canada , and while embarking on his first novel, the narrator of *Cette grenade* saw North America as "ce monde à conquérir" (109). "L'errant", however, according to Glissant, "n'est plus . . . le conquérant"; instead, "[il] cherche à connaître la totalité du monde et sait déjà qu'il ne l'accomplira jamais. . . . [Il] renonce volontiers à la prétention de la sommer ou de la posséder" (1990, 33). And indeed, by the end of *Cette grenade* the narrator, by now more sure of his position in America on a practical level, no longer feels the need to "conquer" his host country, to oblige it to pay him his due. Like Baldwin, he was "l'homme qui a voulu comprendre l'Amérique" (Laferrière 1993, 167), but with the benefit of Baldwin's hindsight, he now knows that such a task is impossible and is able, instead, to wander his new world and observe its diversity. There is no sense that he wishes to achieve real or complete integration into this world – despite the initial similarities with Fanon's *névrosés* – or that he feels such an integration to be possible. Neither is there a sense that he wishes to reject his native land in favour of his host country. As Glissant again points out, "l'errance ne procède pas d'un renoncement, ni d'une frustration par rapport à une situation d'origine qui se serait détériorée (déterritorialisée) – ce n'est pas un acte déterminé de refus, ni une pulsion incontrôlée d'abandon. On se retrouve parfois, abordant aux problèmes de l'Autre" (1990, 31). Like Depestre, Laferrière's narrator, always uncertain of his precise role or identity, is nonetheless free to add to his sense of himself as he travels through his world.

It is thus perhaps unsurprising that if the narrator can be seen to have gained a sense of himself as anything by the end of the novel, then, at least by implication, it is as "American". Before his journey begins, he informs us that the cinematic, "videoclip" quality of American life makes it difficult for American writers to write novels: "le roman contemporain américain est, généralement, une collection de textes brefs reliés entre eux par un fil souple et solide (le sentiment d'être américain). . . . Ce livre n'échappe pas à cette règle" (Laferrière 1993, 27). And while the narrator of *Cette grenade* persists in the use of *Amérique* to describe a journey across the United States and back to Quebec, the term *américan* is, of course, potentially very open in meaning. As the magazine editor points out at the beginning of the narrator's project, "nous travaillons sur toute l'Amérique, vous savez. . . . L'Amérique centrale, l'Amérique du Nord, du Sud, et aussi la Caraïbe" (15). Such a vague and multiple "host country" is, of course, entirely appropriate for someone whose identity, as an emigrant, is also resolutely vague, multiple and mobile. However, the magazine editor very obviously omits Canada from his list – or, rather, subsumes it within "l'Amérique du Nord" – and in the Québécois context within which Laferrière's work is published, this would certainly not go unnoticed. Indeed in this context, in particular, the use of the word *américan* is never unproblematic, as a Haitian living in Quebec would be well aware.

In Quebec literature, invested as so much of it is in asserting a specifically Québécois "national" identity, "America", at its origin, is often Nouvelle France, and the "first Americans" are those explorers who, before their achievements were written over by anglocentric versions of American colonization, discovered the first territories of the continent. Jacques Poulin's *Volkswagen blues* (1988), for example, a Québécois road novel which bears many similarities to *Cette grenade*, explores in particular the nomadic lifestyle of those early colonizers who, as legend has it, resisted France's call to *sédentarité* and chose instead to "go native", or to hybridize themselves and adapt to a different life in the *Terre Promise*. *Néo-québécois* writers such as Laferrière could perhaps be usefully seen as a new generation of nomads, exploring *l'Amérique* in ways which not only intersect with the concerns of Québécois writers, but which may also begin to revitalize Quebec literature. As Québécois critics and writers have suggested, Quebec literature has a tendency towards introspection, preoccupied as much of it is either by overtly nationalist concerns or by the "humiliation" of being Québécois and the need to counter anglo-Canadian and US dominance. Such concerns are obviously understandable and justifiable, given Quebec's history of marginalization and exclusion. However, they are also, some feel, too nostalgically focused on an idealized past and run the risk of entailing marginalizations and exclusions of their own – of the concerns of Native peoples, for example, as well as of those of the *néo-québécois*, immigrants and their descendants.

Within this context, writers such as Laferrière may find themselves at the forefront of contemporary efforts to reimagine Quebec and Québécois culture, for they occupy a position which is at once inside and outside of it. Haitians, like the Québécois, are both "American" and francophone, and perhaps understand the threat of US dominance – as well as the potential pitfalls of nationalism – better than many. At the same time, however, they come from a country whose present situation has its roots in an experience of French colonialism that the Québécois nostalgia for Nouvelle France frequently fails to take into consideration. This, of course, as La Grande Sauterelle tirelessly reminds Jack in *Volkswagen blues,* is the colonial experience in which the French were not colonized and humiliated but were themselves the agents of violent colonization. While plenty of Québécois writers are interested in exploring this side of Quebec's past, the arrival of writers such as Laferrière can only accelerate a reexamination, and perhaps even redefinition, of Quebec's collective identity, national as well as literary. Novels such as *Cette grenade* which are future-orientated, characterized by the openness, mobility and inclusiveness of meaning and identity, certainly represent an exciting development for Haitian literature, diaspora and otherwise. At the same time, they may have the potential to infuse Quebec literature with a new vitality which will help to assure its place within the increasingly diverse field of "American" literature.

Notes

1. While Magloire, as she explains in her interview with Aas-Rouxparis, rejects the term *néo-canadien* because she would like to see Quebec become independent, and therefore *québécois* become a separate nationality, Phelps feels uncomfortable with the term *québécois* precisely because he feels that it is too politically charged.

2. This, indeed, is how Dash (1997) reads *Cette grenade*.

3. This aspect of the narrator's relationship with white women, within the Québécois context of Laferrière's novel, also goes beyond a strictly Fanonian reading. As Lamontagne points out, that the women chosen by the narrator of *Comment faire l'amour* are primarily anglophone Canadians is something which was immediately popular with francophone readers of the novel:

    > comme les "nègres blancs de l'Amérique" se sont fait historiquement, soci-
    > ologiquement et économiquement exploiter par les anglophones depuis la
    > Conquête de 1760, ils trouveraient une énorme compensation à voir d'autres
    > minoritaires profiter des femmes anglophones. . . . Le Québécois francophone
    > se reconnaît donc dans cette volonté de "baiser l'inconscient d'une fille de
    > Westmount". (1997, 34)

4. The interaction between "le pays rêvé" and "le pays réel", for both the artist-as-writer and the ordinary Haitian, is something which is explored in detail by Laferrière in his later, "Haitian" novel, *Pays sans chapeau*.

5. Laferrière encountered similar difficulties when promoting the English translation of this novel in New York: he was taken to task by the African American public for the use of the word "Negro" in the English title (Lamontagne 1997, 41).

References

Bordeleau, Francine. 1994. "Dany Laferrière sans arme et dangereux." *Lettres québécoises* 73: 9–10.

Chamoiseau, Patrick. 1992. "Les Nègres marrons de l'en-ville". *Antilla* 473: 29–33.

Dash, J. Michael. 1997. *Haiti and the United States: National Stereotypes and the Literary Imagination*. 2nd edition. Basingstoke, UK: Macmillan.

Depestre, René 1981. *Alléluia pour une femme-jardin: récits d'amour solaire*. Paris: Gallimard.

———. 1990. *Eros dans un train chinois*. Paris: Gallimard.

———. 1998. *Le Métier à métisser*. Paris: Stock.

des Rosiers, Joël. 1996. *Théories caraïbes: poétiques du déracinement*. Montreal, Canada: Editions Tryptique.

Fanon, Frantz. 1952. *Peau noire, masques blancs*. Paris: Seuil.

Gikandi, Simon. 1992. *Writing in Limbo: Modernism and Caribbean Literature*. Ithaca, NY: Cornell University Press.

Glissant, Edouard. 1990. *Poétique de la relation*. Paris: Seuil.

Jonassaint, Jean. 1986. *Le Pouvoir des mots, les maux du pouvoir*. Paris/Montreal: Arcantère/PUM.

———. 1996. "Migration et études littéraires: essais de théorisation d'un problème ancien avec contours nouveaux". *Journal of Canadian Studies* 31, no. 3: 9–20.

Jones, Bridget. 1981. "Comrade Eros: The Erotic Vein in the Writing of René Depestre". *Caribbean Quarterly* 27, no. 4: 21–30.

Laferrière, Dany. 1985. *Comment faire l'amour avec un Nègre sans se fatiguer*. Montreal: VLB.

———. 1987. *Eroshima*. Montreal: VLB.

———. 1991. *L'Odeur du café*. Montreal: VLB.

———. 1992. *Le Goût des jeunes filles*. Montreal: VLB.

———. 1993. *Cette grenade dans la main du jeune Nègre est-elle une arme ou un fruit?* Montreal: VLB.

———. 1994. *Chronique de la dérive douce*. Montreal: VLB.

———. 1996. *Pays sans chapeau*. Outremont, Que: Lanctôt.

———. 1997a. *La Chair du maître*. Outremont, Que: Lanctôt.

———. 1997b. *La Charme des après-midi sans fin*. Outremont, Que: Lanctôt.

Lahens, Yanick. 1986. "*Manhattan blues* de Jean-Claude Charles ou quand l'exil devient errance". *Conjonction* 169: 9–12.

———. 1992. "Exile: Between Writing and Place". *Callaloo* 15, no. 3: 735–46.

Lamontagne, A. 1997. "'On ne naît pas Nègre, on le devient': la représentation de l'autre dans *Comment faire l'amour avec un Nègre sans se fatiguer* de Dany Laferrière". *Quebec Studies* 23: 29–42.

Laroche, Maximilien. 1987. *L'Avènement de la littérature haïtienne*. Quebec: Grelca.

Pelletier, Jacques. 1994. "Toutes couleurs réunies". *Lettres québécoises* 73: 11–12.

Poulin, Jacques. 1988. *Volkswagen blues: roman*. Quebec: Babel/Leméac.

Rinne, Suzanne, and Joëlle Vitiello, eds. 1997. *Elles écrivent des Antilles: Haïti, Guadeloupe, Martinique*. Paris: L'Harmattan.

Terrien, Michel. 1998. "Conjonctions et disjonctions dans *Chronique de la dérive douce* de Dany Laferrière ou poésie de la condition immigrante". In *Cultural Identities in Canadian Literature / Identités culturelles dans la littérature canadienne*, edited by Benedicte N. Maugière, 173–82. New York: Peter Lang.

Vassal, Anne. 1998. "Lecture savante ou populaire: *Comment faire l'amour avec un Nègre sans se fatiguer* de Dany Laferrière". *Discours social / Social Discourse* 2, no. 4: 185–202.

6

Creole in the French Caribbean Novel of the 1990s
From Reality to Myth?

Marie-Christine Hazaël-Massieux
Université de Provence
Translated by Gertrud Aub-Buscher

In trying to draw a panorama of the place of Creole in the contemporary novel of the Lesser Antilles, it is interesting to discover that though there is much talk of Creole and though it is perhaps given a greater place than thirty years or so ago in daily communication, including in more formal contexts, its place in the novel and even in shorter works of fiction remains very restricted. There is no doubt that after the publication of a number of novels and short stories in Creole between 1975 (the year of *Dezafi*) and 1990, there has been a considerable reduction in output (except perhaps in Haiti)[1] and that the novel remains the poor relation of writing in Creole.

What is more, one cannot fail to notice that since 1987 novels have been produced, often encouraged by literary prizes, written in a French which is very different from the written norm: should we speak of "regional French", "Caribbean French" or "creolized French"? All these terms as well as others have been proposed at one time or another. In this francophone literature, only a small place is reserved for Creole, a Creole somehow "moulded" into the fractured structure of the French sentence but no longer present as such, apart from occasional sentences or quotations, which are then translated in a footnote or between parentheses. I should like to stop for a moment here to look precisely at these Creole passages in novels mainly written in French in order to find out what leads an author to turn to Creole when writing a novel in French.

I have often had occasion to point out (see especially Hazaël-Massieux 1993, 228 ff.) that most writing in Creole, in the context of an instrumentalization which is far from complete, is writing which closely approximates oral language:[2] transcribed, or even "written", stories appeared well before the phonetic scruples of linguists incited them above all to be faithful to the reproduction of speech, publishing stories collected at wakes, such as the stories of Ina Césaire and Joëlle Laurent (1976) for example. From the outset,[3] there were of course a great number of poems written in Creole. Though these are no doubt of unequal quality, many authors have ventured into the realm of poetry, and the twentieth century saw the publication of a large number of collections as well as of single poems appearing in newspapers; it would be impossible to draw up an exhaustive inventory. As for plays in Creole, they have delighted audiences for decades, and they are still just as popular when they are performed in one of the countries concerned. There are examples in Haiti (for example Numa, but also Felix Morisseau-Leroi, with his famous *Antigone,* and Franketienne, whose *Pèlen-tèt* did very well until it was forbidden by the censors) and in French Guiana (particularly the works of Elie Stephenson), and of course in Guadeloupe and Martinique (we would mention, beside Maurice Jallier's famous *Famille Marsabé,* the plays of Gilbert de Chambertrand as well as Georges Mauvois, several of whose very significant works have been published by Editions Ibis Rouge in French Guiana).

The relative rarity of Creole novels in a literary landscape which includes much of interest can be explained both by the difficulties arising quite simply from the length expected for a novel (you have to "keep going" for a long time) and by the fact that the novel is the literary genre furthest removed from oral speech (Hazaël-Massieux 1993). While poetry is based on rhythmic, melodic and more generally prosodic features which presuppose production as speech, the novel is the written genre par excellence, in which everything must be explicit so that it can be understood by the reader, who stands outside the novel's world. The writer cannot really rely on intonation, for punctuation marks are very limited, and therefore ambiguous, in their capacity to render the richness of oral language, in which not only expressive but also grammatical functions are constantly indicated by intonation. The use of those punctuation marks is in any case modelled mainly on writing in a language which has a long written tradition (such as French), and the Creole-speaking writer, who always speaks French as well, is not going to take it into his or her head to develop a specific use of punctuation for Creole.[4] While Creole is still deeply a language of allusion to a situation, in which deictics are an important element, in which the silences themselves, carrying all that is left unsaid, can play a part in oral communication, the writing of a novel implies the reduction of the implicit (for fear of not being understood) and hence the development of what I have called elsewhere a "language of distance" (Hazaël-Massieux 1993, 233), in which everything that cannot be said by the discourse situation alone – the facial expressions and gestures of the speaker, the attitudes of the partners in the interaction, and so on – has to be made explicit by linguistic processes. Whereas in the spoken language complicity plays an important part in the comprehension of utterances, in writing, especially when an audience outside the situation or even foreign to a particular universe is being addressed, it is necessary to say, to describe, to make explicit. This is necessary to ensure minimal comprehension, even if, following the current concept, one wants to keep a certain opacity.

At the grammatical level, which must also be mentioned, one could stress that the sentence, which is the fundamental unit of the written language, implying certain rules of construction, certain elaborations and explicit syntactic relations, corresponds only partially to the period, the unit of speech in which information is most often accumulated in a non-linear way (Hazaël-Massieux 1995). When going into written mode, Creole speakers, who normally use periods in their everyday expression, have to create a model for the Creole sentence – an operation which can be carried out only progressively and which may even take centuries. If they merely turn to the French model (the model available to them through their schooling) even when using Creole vocabulary, they risk creating an artificial written Creole. The difficulty of developing a specifically Creole written sentence, with its own rules, means that writers often make do with short sentences, thus avoiding questions of syntax, to limit as much as possible linguistic complexity (the use of long sentences leading almost inevitably, for example, to the production of subordinate clauses which resemble French subordinate clauses, or interrogative sentences which resemble French interrogatives, and so on). Hence they end up, more or less consciously, with a reduced syntax which is neither French (as is their aim) nor specifically Creole but in fact common to many oral languages (the term often used in that case is *parataxis*), devoid of all syntactic complexity. It is possible to write poetry using limited structures, with few variations (parallelisms, such as the accumulation of nominal phrases, can be a poetic device), whereas it is quite difficult to compose a novel (a work which by definition is long) with sentences created according to a limited number of models – unless one plays precisely on the effect of repetition, as Franketienne did in *Dézafi,* a work which is perhaps incorrectly called a novel, written as it is using many techniques which might easily be designated as "poetic" (such as typographic effects and significant rhythm).

It is for all these reasons, and others, that the novel is such a difficult genre, even if we are far from putting forward Balzac as the only model of a novelist. The authors who – in exploring the *nouveau roman,* for example – set out to be less descriptive and to convey content through dialogues, snippets and more or less fractured sentences, sometimes even systematically refusing the argumentative use of language or a logical coherence deemed a little too laboured or heavy, cultivating short and very concise sentences (such as Marguerite Duras, though one might also mention Michel Butor or Nathalie Sarraute as authors more deeply committed to the *nouveau roman*), have not always been able to achieve what they set out to do (that is, find readers or retain attention to the point where the reader is ready to get involved in a communication which is after all far from easy), unless they were very talented and at the same time ready to undertake the sometimes rather contrived and always quite visible task of writing and formal construction. In any case, for them it was a matter of deliberately impoverishing a very rich language with a long tradition of the novel, not of "getting by" in a language which is not yet ready to fulfil all functions, to be used in all situations, to allow all the play and linguistic inventiveness expected of a literary language, while (as is the case with Creole) it is only one of the codes of a system of communication which until now has preferred to turn to French for "elaborated" communication and writing.

In the Americano-Caribbean zone which interests us here, and not altogether irrelevant to the novel, there are, however, a number of novellas which, being shorter than real novels, no doubt favour the use of Creole. Although there are not very many of them either, their authors seem to feel more comfortable with this shorter genre, in which it is easier to get away with a complete unity of tone and where, moreover, the marks of oral literature are important (for example, characters chosen to recall oral traditions, motifs taken from folk tales and events sequenced as in the framework of the folk tale). In addition, the novellas published in the Lesser Antilles in recent years are accompanied by a translation into French, which allows for a book of about 150 pages to be put together more easily, with two, three or four relatively short Creole texts accompanied by a French version. This shows that authors writing in Creole are increasingly aware of the sociolinguistic characteristics of the use of Creole: all the debates about writing Creole have shown that readers consistently complain that they cannot read Creole. In order to have readers, it is therefore necessary to offer an occasional short text in Creole, translated and preferably surrounded by a number of texts in French. This is the gamble Ralph Ludwig took with his *Ecrire la "parole de nuit": la nouvelle littérature antillaise* (1994). In that collection, Sylviane Telchid is the only author to have contributed in Creole, a version of her short story *Mondésir (Mondézi)*.

About the same time, Georges-Henri Léotin gave us in *Mémwè latè* (1993) a novella in Creole (a mere fifty-two pages) accompanied by its French version (sixty pages). It must be said that the inspiration for the story is profoundly marked by Creole folk tales and oral traditions. Folk tales generally remain an important resource for anyone wishing to write in Creole: being a characteristic genre of oral literature, a folk tale can perfectly well be expressed in the oral language that is Creole even when it is put down on paper. In 1990, Hector Poullet hence gave us *Tibouchina*, following Alain Rutil's *Les Belles paroles d'Albert Gaspard*, published in 1987; Telchid herself, who gave her *Ti-Chika . . . et d'autres contes antillais* in a bilingual version to the Editions Caribéennes in 1985, has published a (short) novel, *Throvia de La Dominique*, entirely in French.

Faced with these phenomena, one may feel that authors who want to write in Creole but who also want readers (the two propositions being more or less irreconcilable) think that Creole probably has a slightly better chance of being accepted or even read if it is administered in homeopathic doses. This is of course a gamble, and one may wonder if readers who possess *Mondésir* in French have often been curious enough to go and read *Mondézi*, which, as they themselves confess, is difficult to read for those who, while no doubt speaking Creole, are not accustomed to reading it. This is true even when the text in question is a short story very similar to a folk tale and hence marked by the characteristics of oral language, whose "Creole" version is certainly less difficult to read than certain more elaborated texts. More systematic work on the reception of Caribbean writing needs to be done in order to gain a better understanding of the readers, what they expect and what they accept, independent of the sales figures put out by publishers (especially in the case of books which have won prizes), figures which tell us nothing about actual reading habits – we may know that 100,000 persons have bought a certain book, but we do not know if they have read it. I myself have seen enough examples of people buying a book that has been hyped in the press, often with every intention of reading it, but giving up after ten pages, put off by the language (French or Creole), to refuse to consider that sales figures give even an approximate idea of the number of real readers.

This disaffection of readers for written Creole, of which authors are increasingly aware, explains in part why those who had begun to write in Creole no longer do so: the enormous amount of work required to write in a language which is still little or not at all codified is not made worthwhile by literary success, for there is none at the end of a path strewn with pitfalls. The case of Raphaël Confiant, who now translates (or has translated) – and is at last selling – his novels originally written in Creole, published at the author's expense and bought by nobody, is extremely significant.

Should one therefore think that after "the age of Creole" we have now moved into the "age of translation"? That might turn out to be a somewhat hasty judgement, especially as when there is a translation, it is no ordinary translation: it is translation into the language whose "inventor" is currently thought to be Patrick Chamoiseau and whose main characteristics I described as early as 1988 (Hazaël-Massieux 1988).

Until the last few years (until Edouard Glissant?),[5] the French of Caribbean authors was a very "well-behaved" French, merely containing more or less numerous insertions of regional terms (such as are found in Joseph Zobel, Simone Schwarz-Bart or Maryse Condé), a vocabulary which has moreover become classic in its exoticism (*ravet, annoli, gaule, man Untel* and all the names of plants, animals and fruits which give a certain local colour to what is for the most part Standard French). But now a particular French is gradually developing, in which creations have their place, and not only the vocabulary but also the grammar of Creole are partially reproduced, recast and represented.[6]

Has Creole, which is part of everyday reality in the West Indies (albeit sometimes a "difficult" one – difficult to accept, difficult to handle, difficult to write), become a myth for writers? They no longer write in Creole but in French "as if it were Creole": they are writing in a French which seeks to create an illusion. And when they – accidentally – resort to Creole, in a quotation or a brief insertion, in order to underline stylistically the characteristics of a person or situation, they do it in an emblematic way, using a sentence belonging to a specific type (see below the importance of exclamations), frequently repeated (for example, Félix Soleil's "Yin ki fanm, fanm ki an tÿou mwen" in Table 6.1 below). They are again short sentences, which sometimes look like proverbs. A systematic study of Creole insertions which go beyond the "word" (and hence forms other than lexical, which would also be worth considering for their role in the construction of a mythical Creole[7]) is certainly interesting, and leads us to draw up a list by structure (sentence types – often exclamatory, always "expressive", strongly marked by intonation and so on) as well as by situation (in exchanges marked by emotion or confusion, when the character represented loses control of his language and so on, but even more often when there is aggression or violence). It goes without saying that there is some variation in the use of these Creole sentences according to the social context depicted – there are more in Confiant, fewer in Chamoiseau, almost none in certain works. These preliminary observations, which lie behind the more systematic study presented here, have far-reaching consequences and raise questions about the image of Creole which is thus created for the reader.

The non-West Indian reader, who often does not understand but is always ready to appreciate the picturesque, the exotic and the disorientating, certainly reacts to this image, without being very sure what is being said. But the image is also ambiguous, with probably more serious consequences, for the Creole-speaking West Indian, who already has difficulties reading Creole, who comes with strong prejudices ("Creole isn't a real language, you can't write it") and who quickly risks having his opinions confirmed by the image the authors are ready to show him of a completely marginal usage, of a Creole which is vulgar or designed mainly for insults.

Creole is thus not totally absent from the novel. In this connection it is interesting to note that the work of linguists and anthropologists and its dissemination to a wider public, which of course includes writers, has certainly heightened the latter's awareness of the relationship between Creole and French in the Creole world. The now well-known facts concerning diglossic situations have reached the educated public, and what before was merely intuitive (the fact that Creole is reserved for certain situations while French is used in others, which is perfectly reflected in the distribution of languages to be found in the plays of Chambertrand in Guadeloupe, Mauvois in Martinique or Elie Stephenson in French Guiana) is now entirely conscious; its implementation in the novel is often an application of what the writer has learned at university. For example, in *Chronique des sept misères,* one can see Chamoiseau playing very skilfully with styles: Césaire's language is not the same as Pipi's, nor is Afoukal's that of Félix Soleil, and in this stylistic usage, Creole of course has its place. Here I should like to point out precisely the place of Creole in the meeting between Césaire and Pipi. Whereas throughout the book, Chamoiseau has not given any particular features to Pipi's language (he talks "as the author", that is, usually in a French which is quite literary though coloured by Creole; see Hazaël-Massieux 1988), at the point of that meeting with Césaire, in order to mark Pipi's emotion and to underline the tension of the passage, Pipi's language allows Chamoiseau to indulge in play: in reply to the mayor of Fort-de-France, who has addressed him in spontaneous, very abstract French – "Cher ami, je défendrai personnellement toute entreprise à grande échelle employant vos méthodes" – Pipi replies in a stumbling, mainly expressive Creole: "Ebyen, misié limè, séti manmay la té fin, dann!" (Chamoiseau 1988, 201).

Pipi's reply is, incidentally, also the occasion for the author to mimic another group, namely journalists, who, in order to be what today would be called "politically correct", translate Pipi's sentence "le soir au journal télévisé, après un dossier sur le Loir-et-Cher . . ." as *"Monsieur le Maire, les enfants avaient telle-ment faim!"* Chamoiseau adds, "C'est pourquoi au marché, durant une charge de temps, tout le monde crut Pipi docteur en langage de France" (1988, 201).

This passage is a real anthology piece, which should be studied by young West Indians in school while the debate about the place of Creole is still so lively: the discovery of Caribbean literature can also lead to the discovery of languages. But one might also mention all that pertains to the discovery of French by "le négrillon" in *Chemin d'école:* "Le maître parlait français comme les gens de la radio ou les matelots de la Transat" (Chamoiseau 1994, 68).

In fact, examples of the use of Creole can be found in certain novels – in dialogue, whether direct or reported, or occasionally in quotations of proverbs, sayings or songs (categorized as "quotations" in the table below). When Creole is used in these novels, it is normally translated at the foot of the page or in parentheses, in an attempt to emphasize, for reasons of "realism", the social affiliation or the involvement of the character, his emotion and so on. It must be stressed, however, that the introduction of Creole for stylistic reasons remains marginal, and that it occurs only in particularly "marked" cases, such as Pipi, who expresses himself in French throughout the *Chronique* even though the character he embodies is basically a Creole speaker. Man Ninotte, in *Chemin d'école,* about whom Chamoiseau tells us that "elle utilisait de temps à autre des chiquetailles de français" (1994, 67), does not really speak Creole but a form of French which at most suggests or is supposed to represent Creole.

Most of the novels currently being published in the French West Indies have examples of these insertions in Creole, which remain marginal even though the existence of a "recommended" writing system such as that of the Groupe d'Etudes et de Recherches en Espace Créolophone (GEREC) to which authors can refer might facilitate the graphic representation of Creole and its differentiation from French; the strictly gallicizing orthographies favoured by authors in the 1930s and 1940s did not highlight as clearly the passage from Creole to French.

By way of example, before calling for a more systematic study which would be of great interest, I have analysed Chamoiseau's *Chronique des sept misères* (Table 6.1) and *Chemin d'école* (Table 6.2), and Confiant's *L'Allée des soupirs* (Table 6.3). It is noticeable right away that Creole sentences in these novels are infrequent and at the same time relatively short. We need, however, to look in more detail, to show possible differences between Chamoiseau and Confiant in this matter, and in particular to examine the contexts in which the Creole sentences appear.

The analysis of Chamoiseau's *Chronique des sept misères* presented in Table 6.1 includes only Creole sentences, even if they consist of only one word, but ignores words borrowed from Creole in the middle of a French sentence. There are 31 Creole sentences in a work of 240 pages (without the appendices), making an average of about 1 sentence in Creole for every 8 pages. Of the 31 sentences, 19 are exclamations, and 12 appear explicitly in a context of anger or insult. The average sentence length is 4.8 words.

Table 6.2 shows that there are 10 Creole sentences in Chamoiseau's *Chemin d'école,* a novel of 202 pages, or one for every 20 pages (with the school context explaining perhaps this significant reduction compared with *Chronique*). The sentences are interrogatives or exclamations, and they almost all appear in the context of a fight or some other agitation. The average length here is 4 words per sentence.

In analysing Confiant's *L'Allée des soupirs* (Table 6.3), I stopped noting examples after 200 pages, corresponding to the average length of a work by Chamoiseau (while Confiant's novel runs to 404 very compact pages).[8] This time there are 72 Creole sentences on 200 pages, making a little more than 1 every 3 pages.

The average length of Confiant's Creole sentences is greater than Chamoiseau's, at 6.75 words per sentence. In addition, it is noteworthy that whereas there is no Creole sentence of more than 9 words in Chamoiseau, in Confiant there are occasionally sentences of 17, 20 or even 23 (the longest, a declarative, which in itself is significant). Is this a sign of greater mastery of written Creole by this author (who, let us not forget, has published three novels in Creole)?

The speakers of Confiant's Creole sentences always come from a very working class background, the slums of Fort-de-France. They are gangsters, prostitutes or "mères maquerelles", or else occasionally the *Béké* Salin du Bercy, as an indication that he is "going to the dogs" and that he can resort to Creole in his dealings with the common people. The sentences are still mainly exclamations and have for the most part been taken from direct or indirect, mainly antagonistic dialogues, together with some quotations (such as of proverbs and songs). It must be pointed out, of course, that most of the time these characters also speak French in the text (which includes far more dialogue in French than in Creole): the use of Creole is always motivated by the context of a fight, act of aggression, insult or sexual exchange, all often abusive or at least very violent. There are occasional cases of complicity: the use of Creole may, for instance, underline proximity to or membership in the same group.

It must nevertheless be noted that although there is a relatively large number of Creole sentences in Confiant's *L'Allée des soupirs,* there are practically none in his *La Savane des pétrifications* or *Bassin des ouragans.* In these two works, Anna-Maria de La Huerta sets the tone of the principal protagonists with her ridiculously refined language; the narrator says of her that "Sa gouvernante lui lisait du Crébillon le soir à la veillée afin qu'elle affûtât ses imparfaits du subjonctif" (1994b, 27–28). It would seem that *L'allée des soupirs* represents a somewhat special case in Confiant's work: one has the impression that he is letting off steam by introducing a large amount of Creole – perhaps as a consequence of the appearance of characters from the lowest strata of society – whereas there is less Creole in his *Eau de café* (1991), except the occasional very coarse remark (there is about 1 Creole sentence every 10 or 15 pages), and very little in *Chimères d'en-ville* (1997). In *La Vierge du grand retour* (1996), there is a little more Creole, still in the same contexts of fights or the appearance of people from very lower class backgrounds: about 14 sentences in the 100 pages analysed, or 1 sentence every 7 pages.

Table 6.1: Patrick Chamoiseau, *Chronique des sept misères*

Sentence[a]	Dialogue or Narrative	Character	Situation	Sentence Type	Number of Words
Yin ki fanm, fanm ki an tÿou mwen! (19)	dialogue	Félix Soleil	anger	exclamation	8
Fanm fanm yin ki fanm ki an tÿou mwen![b] (20)	quotation	Félix Soleil	anger	exclamation	9
Fanotte véyé sé ich ou-a! (20)	dialogue	Félix Soleil	anger	exclamation	6
Man ni bel yanmes vini ouè mwen (21)	dialogue	Ginette	market	exclamation	4 + 3
Sé fanm-la mi mwen! (22)	dialogue	Félix Soleil	anger	exclamation	5
Tonnan di sò! (23)	dialogue	Félix Soleil	insult	exclamation	3
Fouté likan bôbô et saletès! (24)	dialogue	Félix Soleil	insult	exclamation	5
Aaah, koutala aké an ti bolomm! (25)	dialogue	Félix Soleil	emotion	exclamation	5
Ese cé an tigasson? (25)	dialogue	Félix Soleil	emotion	interrogative	4
Apa kouyonnad (60)	narrative	narrator	epic character	interpolated phrase	2
Vié chabin, épi mwen Obè pé jan tué'w! (62)	dialogue	Clarine	emotion	exclamation	9
Sa anké fè bô maché? (67)	dialogue	Clarine	not clear from context	interrogative	5
Sé . . . sépa ich mwen kilà non . . . Sé ich an adanm (72)	dialogue	Clarine	agitation, emotion	declarative	(1+) 5 + 4
Sa anté pé fè? (95)	dialogue	Man Joge	emotion ("gémissait Man Joge")	interrogative	4
Anlé sav là ti-manmay la pasé, Pipi . . . (95)	dialogue	Man Joge	emotion	declarative	7
Ich tig paka fèt san zong (101)	quotation	narrator	proverb	declarative	6
jou malè pani pwan gad (102)	quotation	narrator	saying	declarative	5
Anpaka goumen épi i-anmay (104)	dialogue	Zouti (laghia fighter)	anger	declarative, exclamation	5
Hè Mérilo hè Mérilo / Saki vayan lévé lanmin / Saki vayan tombé si mwen (104)	quotation	Kouli (laghia fighter)	song	exclamation	4 + 4 + 5

Sentence	Dialogue, Narrative or Quotation	Character	Situation	Sentence type	Number of words
Saki disa (141)	dialogue	Pipi	market	interrogative	2
Pa koké la, pa koké la, pa koké la! (191)	quotation	crowd	insult	exclamation	3 + 3 + 3
Ebyen misié limé, séti manmay la té fin, dannè! (201)	dialogue	Pipi	emotion	exclamation	9
Anpa save (203)	dialogue	Pipi	emotion	declarative	2
An landièt manman zot! (210)	dialogue	Madame Carmélite (market woman)	insult	exclamation	4
Yo andidan, an tann yo hélé! (225)	dialogue	Pin-Pon	irritation	exclamation	6

a French translation is given in the text of *Chronique des sept misères* on the page indicated.
b This sentence recurs several times in the first part of the *Chronique* (five in total).

Table 6.2: Patrick Chamoiseau, *Chemin d'école*

Sentence	Dialogue, Narrative or Quotation	Character	Situation	Sentence type	Number of words
Eti? (22)	dialogue	Man Ninotte	with her son	interrogative	1
Ou pa ni an ti tablo?! (27)	dialogue	Man Ninotte	with her son (irritated)	interrogative, exclamation	6
Eti? (46)	dialogue	Man Ninotte	with her son	interrogative	1
I pa konnèt non'y! (I pa konnèt non'y!) (62)	dialogue	children in the playground	fight	exclamation	5
I fè an kawô (88)	dialogue	children	fight	declarative, exclamation	4
iii salé iii salé iii salé iii sicré (121)	quotation	children	fight	exclamation	10
Iii salééé, les Biwoua, les Wacha, les Wouap wouap wouap . . . les Mi ta'w mi ta mwen (130)	quotation	children	fight	exclamation	2 + 6?a
Andièt sa! (136)	dialogue	children	fight and insult	exclamation	2
Mèt-la pala! (177)	dialogue	children	magic	exclamation	4

a The question mark indicates my uncertainty about the status of the onomatopaeias in this sentence.

Table 6.3: Raphaël Confiant, *L'Allée des soupirs*[a]

Sentence	Dialogue or Quotation	Character	Situation	Sentence Type	Number of Words
Nou kay fan fwa zòt! (15)	dialogue	"un jeune mâle nègre surexcité"	fight	exclamation	5
Sé mésyé blan-an, ranjé kòzòt fout! (15)	dialogue	"un jeune mâle nègre surexcité"	fight	exclamation	7
Hé, tì manzèl, viré ba mwen, souplé! (16)	dialogue	chaperones, working-class matrons	to their protégées, about to misbehave	exclamation	7
Kon sa, i ké montré yich mwen an pli byen! (18)	dialogue	mother of Ancinelle to those around her	anger, resentment	exclamation	10
An nou fè'y, non! (30)	dialogue	Ancinelle	coarse sexual talk	exclamation	5
Gran-Zonng, isalòp ki ou yé, Bondyé ki nan syèl ka atann ou pou sa menyen tjou'w ba'w! (31–32)	quotation	"Quelques bougres courageux"	insulting Grand Z'Ongles, a hooligan	exclamation	2 + 4 + 14
Wouvè! Wouvè la ba mwen, souplé! (32)	dialogue	Grand Z'Ongles	fight	exclamation	1 + 5
Doubout la épi anchouké anlè kò "w, sakré popilè ki ou yé! (35)	dialogue	Grand Z'Ongles	fight	exclamation	7 + 5
Ramirèz, fidji'w blan, pyé'w nwè / Sa ou fè Bondyé kon sa, monchè? (40)	quotation	crowd	song	declarative + interrogative	7 + 7
Way! Mi i tjwé mwen kouman! Sa mwen fè'y, non? (53)	dialogue	Eugène Lamour	fear	exclamation	1 + 5 + 5
Annou brilé komisarya Lakwa-Misyon! (55)	dialogue	"un bougre hurlait"	riot	exclamation	4
Woy-woy-woy! Mi fwansé déwò mi! (55)	dialogue	crowd	before someone making a speech in French	exclamation	5
Konmen ou lé? (67)	dialogue	Salin du Bercy, béké	attack	interrogative	3
Mi Boriga! (70)	dialogue	workers	fear	exclamation	2
Si zòt wè i pa déviré avan dé zè di matin, nou ka bay désann, lézòm (70–71)	dialogue	Salin du Bercy's overseer	fear	declarative	16
Boriga, sòti la ou yé a si ou ni dé grenn, fout! (72)	dialogue	Salin du Bercy	insult	exclamation	12
Boug! Sòti la, nou ni palé pou nou palé, fout! (73)	dialogue	Salin du Bercy	to the fleeing Maroon	exclamation	10

Lannuit-tala sé an lannuit ba soukiyan, sa ou di? (73)	dialogue	Salin du Bercy	complicity	interrogative	10
Ou pé di sa! (74)	dialogue	Beauregard	complicity	exclamation	4
Man sé an bètjé kréyòl manmay! (77)	dialogue	Salin du Bercy	aggression + complicity	exclamation	6
Sa ki'w? (77)	dialogue	aggressor	attack	interrogative	3
Sé mwen ki mèt lizin Larenti a. (77)	dialogue	Salin du Bercy	aggression + complicity	declarative	7
Eskizé, patwon, nou pa té wè sé'w ki té la. Annou, ba'y pasé! (77)	dialogue	(black) aggressor	complicity	command	2 + 9 + 4
Wou taa, ou pé di ou fini bat!	dialogue	(black) aggressor	attack	exclamation	9
Malaba, pa di mwen sé'w ka palé kon sa jòdijou, èbé-bondyé? (77)	dialogue	Salin du Bercy	attempt at complicity	interrogative or exclamation	11 + 2
Chapé . . . chapé kò'w! (77)	dialogue	(black) aggressor	complicity	exclamation	3
Sa ki fèt? (93)	dialogue	(lower working-class) woman	attempt at conciliation	interrogative	3
Konpè, fèmen djèl ou, non ! Ou konpwann ou pé fè djendjen épi an bagay kon sa? (93)	dialogue	(lower working-class) woman	anger	exclamation + interrogative	5 + 11
Fè sa ou ni pou fè! (97)	dialogue	(working-class) father to son	emotion	exclamation	6
Ou sé an makoumè oben ki sa? (102)	dialogue	Eugène Lamour	irritation	interrogative	7
Ejèn, ou toujou té an frè ba mwen. . . . (104)	dialogue	Jean	emotion	declarative	8
Hon! . . . palé palé'w non! (104)	dialogue	Eugène Lamour	annoyance	command	5
Mennen an vè wonm vini ba mwen, souplé (119)	dialogue	Salin du Bercy	anger + drunkenness	command	8
Ou pa sav bètjé pa ka bwè Kouvil, ou pa sav sé Néson nou ka bwè, fout! (119)	dialogue	Salin du Bercy	anger + drunkenness	exclamation	8 + 9
Man là an fanm! Ba mwen an fanm, fout! An madigwàn! (120)	dialogue	Salin du Bercy	anger + drunkenness	command	4 + 5 + 2
Ba mwen wè'y! (120)	dialogue	Salin du Bercy	coarse sexual talk	exclamation	4
Pyés pa! (121)	dialogue	Salin du Bercy	sexual talk	exclamation	2
Mi an tjou'w! (121)	dialogue	Salin du Bercy	coarse sexual talk	exclamation	4
Sa ki taa? (128)	dialogue	working-class women	jealousy, verbal aggression	interrogative	3
Ga fidji tikté kon an fig mû'ya! (128-129)	dialogue	working-class women	jealousy, verbal aggression	interrogative	8

Table 6.3: Raphaël Confiant, *L'Allée des soupirs* a (continued)

Sentence	Dialogue or Quotation	Character	Situation	Sentence Type	Number of Words
Fout fès fanm Fdfwans fann fon! (130)	dialogue	hooligan	insult	exclamation	6
Pli ta, pli tris! (138)	dialogue	daughter of madame	situation not clear	exclamation	4
Ki tan Bondyé ki nan syèl ké fè fimèl tjo-tala pèd chimen istya, tonnan di sò? Nou pa za asé an banbanm kon sa? (157)	dialogue	working-class woman	insult	exclamation	17 + 8
Sa ou fè a? Ou pa wè ou tjwé siléma san pèyé nou an, sakré chenfè ki ou yé! (159)	dialogue	Eugene Lamour	insult	interrogative + exclamation	4 + 15
Sa ki ni? (161)	dialogue	Ziguinote (Indian)	situation not clear	interrogative	3
Nou paré kon sa yé a (169)	dialogue	working-class man	fight	exclamation	6
Man pa sav poutji nou ka goumen men sèl bagay man konnèt sé ki man fouté bon wòch nan tjou sé vyéblan-an. (173)	dialogue	working-class woman	fight	declarative	23
Tjenbwazè-a sòti pwan tjèk fanm (184)	dialogue	working-class man	sexual attack	declarative	6
A laj mwen, zòt konpwann man pé tjenbé an bann san ladjé'y déwò, sakré isalòp ki sòt yé! (185)	dialogue	Grand Z'Ongles, sorcerer	insult + sexuality	exclamation	18
Ga sa tibolonm, man sé pé papa'w alò pa djè fè lestonmak anlè mwen ou tann mwen di'w! (185)	dialogue	Grand Z'Ongles	insult	exclamation	20
Zòt ka séré men li, Gran-Zònng, i pa-a séré, fout! (186)	dialogue	Grand Z'Ongles	insult	exclamation	11
Man pa ni konpè blan! (187)	dialogue	Chartier	insult, fight	exclamation	5
Péla, chenfè ki ou yé! konpè CRS ou ka tiré anlè jenn manmay (187)	dialogue	rascal	Insult, fight	exclamation+ declarative	5 + 8
Pa pè! (199)	dialogue	Malaba	attack	exclamation	2

a First 200 pages only.

What remains typical in both Chamoiseau and Confiant is the context in which Creole is used: it appears only to express insults or very coarse emotions, or else to speak in very crude terms of facts relating to sexuality. This tendency, which is already very clear in Chamoiseau, is reinforced in Confiant: Creole is found only in people from very lower class backgrounds, people who live on the very fringes of society or who have at least broken with the practices of a society which may be poor but dignified; they are nearly always prostitutes, quarrelsome men or something similar, and Creole occurs when they are hurling insults at each other or speaking about sex.

Given all this, questions arise about the representation of Creole conveyed by these novels written primarily in French. While the authors have frequently been keen to stress that Creole is a language worthy of being esteemed, learned and developed like any other,[9] the image which they, consciously or unconsciously, give through their novels is very different: Creole clearly appears as the language of loose women and criminals from the places of ill repute in Fort-de-France; it is the language of fights and violent sexuality, the language of the margins of society and illicit practices.

Is there still a place for Creole writers in the Caribbean? The future will tell us, for it may be risky to make a definitive choice between the hypotheses available to explain the ways in which literature is evolving in the French West Indies. The production of the last few years does seem to suggest, however, that a profound discouragement has overcome those who certainly have things to say and who could say them in Creole – with a great deal of work on the language no doubt, and with the occasional great setback[10] – but who could despite all that be the initiators of a literature in Creole. The attempts to write novels wholly in Creole and the insertion of Creole in French novels serve only to reinforce very traditional ideas of the distribution of the languages, of their use and status. Curiously, the essay by Chamoiseau and Confiant, *Lettres créoles: tracées antillaises et continentales de la littérature, 1635–1975*, written in 1991, stops at 1975. Why? It has not occurred to anyone yet to translate *Eloge de la créolité* into Creole. Why?

Appendix

Principal Works of Fiction Published Wholly in Creole in the Caribbean

Date	Work (with publication information where avaiable)	Country
1885	Parépou, Alfred. *Atipa: premier roman en créole: 1885.* Paris: Editions Caribéennes, 1980.	Guyane
1905	Tonton Dumoco. *Les mémoires d'un vonvon.* Fort-de-France: Impr. de la Martinique, 179 pp. [written in French, but with enough insertions in Creole to be worthy of mention]	Martinique
1906	Lhérisson, Justin. *Zoune chez sa ninnaine.*	Haiti
*c.*1918	Chambertrand, Gilbert de. *Dix bel conte avant cyclone.* Basse-Terre: Editions Jeunes Antilles, 1976, 62 pp.	Guadeloupe
1929	Lhérisson, Justin. *La famille des Pitite-Caille.* [These two novels by Llérisson are written mainly in French but with a large number of dialogues in Creole. Published in Haiti in the early twentieth century and republished by Fardin in 1975, these works have been made accessible to a wider public by Editions Caribéennes, Paris, who published an edition in 1978, 149 pp.]	Haiti
1975	Franketienne. *Dézafi.* Port-au-Prince: Fardin, 312 pp.	Haiti
1975	Célestin-Mégie, Emile. *Lanmou pa gin baryè (woman).* 3 Vols. Port-au-Prince: Fardin, 1975–81, 215 pp. + 179 pp. + 181 pp.	Haiti
1976	Paultre, Carrie. *Amarant,* 48 pp.	Haiti
1977	Paillère, Marie-Madeleine [Madlèn Payè]. *Insèlbadjo: Kont chanté,* 109 pp.	Haiti
1979	Jean-Baptiste, Pauris. *Peyi Zoulout (pawoli).* Port-au-Prince: Fardin, 140 pp.	Haiti
1979	Jean-Baptiste, Pauris. *Sogo nan kouazman granchimin.* Port-au-Prince: Edisyon Bon Nouvèl, 119 pp.	Haiti
1979	Confiant, Raphaël. *Jik dèyè do bondyé: istwé kout.* Fort-de-France: Grif An Tè.	Martinique
1980	Vali, Wojé. *Jédi: nouvelles.*	Guadeloupe
1981	Vali, Wojé. *Lèt-la: nouvelles.*	Guadeloupe
1982	Vali, Wojé. *Chofé taksi-la: nouvelles.* Paris: Présence Africaine.	Guadeloupe
1982	Morisseau-Leroy, Félix. *Ravinodyab.* Paris: L'Harmattan, 108 pp.	Haiti
1982	Paultre, Carrié. *Tonton Libin.* Port-au-Prince: Boukan, 114 pp.	Haiti
1983	Vali, Wojé. *Louké: nouvelles.*	Guadeloupe
1985	Jean-Baptiste, Pauris. *Nan lonbray Inosans.* Port-au-Prince: Henri Deschamps, 128 pp. [Prix Deschamps, 1985]	Haiti
1985	Jean-Baptiste, Pauris. *Lavi an miyèt.* Port-au-Prince: Impression Magiqe, 20 pp.	Haiti
1985	Confiant, Raphaël. *Bitako-a.* Fort-de-France: GEREC, 77 pp.	Martinique
1986	Confiant, Raphaël. *Kòd yanm.* Fort-de-France: KDP/Désormeaux, 131 pp.	Martinique
1987	Confiant, Raphaël. *Marisosé.* Schoelcher, Martinique: Presses Universitaires créoles, 141 pp.	Martinique
1987	Franketienne. *Adjanoumelezo (Espiral),* 522 pp.	Haiti
1989	Deyita. *Esperans dézire.* Port-au-Prince: Deschamps, 191 pp.	Haiti
1990	Leotin, Térèz. *Lèspri lanmè.* Paris: L'Harmattan/Presses Universitaires Créoles, 103 pp. [Bilingual edition, Creole/French]	Martinique
1991	Deyita. *Kont nan jaden peyi Titoma.* Port-au-Prince: L'Imprimeur II, 174 pp.	Haiti
1993	Leotin, Georges-Henri. *Mémwè latè.* [Martinique] Editions Bannzil Kréyol [The Creole text is followed by a very free French "translation".]	Martinique
1994	Heurtelou, Maude. *Lafami Bonplezi.* Coconut Creek, Fla.: Educa Vision, 273 pp.	Haiti
1995	Heurtelou, Maude. *Sezisman! Pou lafanmi Bonplezi.* Coconut Creek, Fla.: Educa Vision, 207 pp.	Haiti
n.d.	Legagneur, M. Denise. *Ti Rozali,* 41 pp.	Haiti
n.d.	Jeanty, Edner. *Man Lé,* 24 pp.	Haiti

Notes

1. The list of novels given in the Appendix makes it clear that no real novel in Creole has appeared in the French West Indies since 1987 (the year of *Marisosé*).

2. If the situation is a little different in Haiti, where the production of fiction written in Creole has not ceased since 1990 (see Appendix), it is certain that it still occupies a limited place in the whole of written production in Creole.

3. One of the first works in Creole, which is always quoted by linguists, is the famous poem "Lisette quitté la Plaine" of Divivier de La Mahautière, which dates from 1757. One might also mention, in no particular order, the work of François Achille Marbot, Gilbert Gratiant, Gilbert de Chambertrand and Georges Mauvois, but also Monchoachi, Joby Bernabé, Hector Poullet and others, as well as less well known authors who have been trying their hand at writing in Creole away from the limelight, notably in the context of Floral Games, such as R. Bogat, Ancelot Bellaire, Germain William, and many others. In this connection, the DEA (Diplôme d'études approfondies) dissertation of Gilberte Coranson (1997), which gives a nearly exhaustive panorama of publications in and on Creole in Guadeloupe between 1935 and 1970, opens very interesting perspectives for a better understanding of writing in Creole.

4. Bernabé (1976, 55) noted, "Standard punctuation: full-stop, semicolon, question mark, exclamation mark, etc. In this system, it functions as in French, since nothing would justify a different treatment."

5. It is interesting to point out that as early as 1987, the Glissant of *Mahagony* wrote in a French which was profoundly marked by Creole, if with rather different aims and characteristics from those of the French of Chamoiseau. The relationship is undeniable, and Glissant can therefore claim to be the father of *Antillanité*, even if his sons must, more or less consciously, kill him in order to take his place and so propose something else, another language; even if, while distancing themselves from Glissant in order to affirm their originality, like Chamoiseau, the apologists of *Créolité* acknowledge the debt they owe him. In *Ecrire en pays dominé*, Chamoiseau situates himself expressly under the patronage of Glissant and acknowledges the debt he owes to the author of *Malemort*:

> J'y avais découvert cette circulation intense entre la langue créole et la langue française, et la liberté créatrice danse une langue dominée, Toutes deux livrées à une libre autorité. Mais il y avait mieux. De lectures en lectures, d'insatisfaction en insatisfaction, d'irritation en désarroi, j'avais pressenti que l'écriture de *Malemort* signifiait une *disponibilité* salutaire qu'il m'était encore impossible de nommer. Cette circulation chaotique, hors recette, sans système, étrangère à toute mécanique, ouvrait à une gourmandise qui dépassait le seul espace des langues dans laquelle elle se jouait. (1997, 92)

6. In an attempt to bring out the complexity of the problem, we like to say that now authors "write Creole directly into French". The logical conclusion of such a formula is given by Fournier, commenting on a passage from the *Lettres créoles* of Chamoiseau and Confiant (1991), who admire Clément Richer for his use of "themes and rhythms which are deeply Creole without ever resorting . . . to Creole lexical or metaphoric elements". Pointing out the paradoxical nature of such a formula, Fournier adds: *"Créolité* without Creole? The concept, as we already suspected, transcends the linguistic material" (1995, 160). It is true that *Créolité,* like *oralité,* often appears as a myth for writers who claim to be part of it but who write in French. It is all the easier to set oneself up as a defender of Creole if one does not use it and does not have to face the difficulties of writing in an essentially oral language.

7. I am currently supervising a thesis by Wandrille Micaux on vocabulary in the novels of Chamoiseau.

8. I have nevertheless checked that there was no significant difference in characteristics of the Creole passages in the rest of the novel: there was the same proportion of sentences per page, the same type (with an enormous preponderance of exclamations and occasional interrogatives) uttered essentially in contexts of aggression or complicity.

9. Even if they concede the difficulty of writing in Creole, in well-known texts or interviews.

10. See the "confessions" about the difficulties of writing in Creole given by Confiant in *Le Monde* (1992).

References

Bernabé, Jean. 1976. "Propositions pour un code orthographique intégré des créoles à base lexicale française". *Espace Créole* no. 1: 25–57.

Bernabé, Jean, Patrick Chamoiseau and Raphaël Confiant. 1989. *Eloge de la créolité.* Paris: Gallimard.

Césaire, Ina, and Joëlle Laurent. 1976. *Contes de mort et de vie aux Antilles.* Paris: Nubia.

Chamoiseau, Patrick. [1986] 1988. *Chronique des sept misères.* Paris: Folio.

———. 1994. *Chemin d'école.* Paris: Folio.

———. 1997. *Ecrire en pays dominé.* Paris: Gallimard.

Chamoiseau, Patrick, and Raphaël Confiant. 1991. *Lettres créoles: tracées antillaises et continentales de la littérature: Martinique, Guadeloupe, Guyane, Haïti, 1935–1975.* Paris: Hatier.

Confiant, Raphaël. 1992. "La bicyclette créole ou la voiture française". *Le Monde,* 6 November.

———. 1994a. *L'Allée des soupirs.* Paris: Grasset.

————. 1994b. *Bassin des ouragans, istwè*. Paris: Mille et une nuits.

Coranson, Gilberte. 1997. "La Langue créole dans les textes publiés en Guadeloupe entre 1940 et 1970". Unpublished DEA dissertation, Université de Provence, Aix-en-Provence.

Fournier, Robert. 1995. "Questions de créolité, de créolisation et de diglossie". In *Poétiques et imaginaires: francopolyphonie littéraire des Amériques*, edited by Pierre Laurette and Hans-George Ruprecht, 149–71. Paris: L'Harmattan.

Hazaël-Massieux, Marie-Christine. 1988. "A propos de *Chronique des sept misères*: une littérature en français régional pour les Antilles". *Etudes Créoles* 11, no. 1: 118–31.

————. 1993. *Ecrire en créole*. Paris: L'Harmattan.

————. 1995. "De quelques avatars de la période en français et en créole: de l'oral à l'écrit". *Travaux du CLAIX* 13: 13–42.

Léotin, Georges-Henri. 1993. *Mémwè latè*. [Martinique]: Éditions Bannzil Kréyol.

Ludwig, Ralph. 1994. *Ecrire la "parole de nuit": la nouvelle littérature antillaise*. Paris: Gallimard.

Telchid, Sylviane. 1996. *Throvia de la Dominique*. Paris: L'Harmattan.

7

La Rue Cases-Nègres (Black Shack Alley)
From Novel to Film[1]

Bridget Jones[†]

In several ways, Joseph Zobel's novel *La Rue Cases-Nègres* and Euzhan Palcy's film of the same title constitute convenient markers, points of reference for surveying the evolution of Martinican culture and society. An interval of about 30 years (1950 to 1983) separates the two creations, while both seek to recreate retrospectively the Martinique of the early 1930s. A largely autobiographical novel by a black man, which was dedicated in the original edition "To my Mother, a domestic for the Whites. To my Grandmother, a plantation worker who can't read" (Corzani 1978, 121n), has been brought to the screen by a young black woman. His tentative and individualistic attempt to bear witness to deeply felt racial injustice has been made accessible by a confident collective act which mobilized community goodwill and performance talent.

There is evidently much to be said about the concentrating and restructuring process inseparable from adapting any novel for the screen, and I do not wish to neglect this formal perspective. In particular, film supplies spatial relationships peculiarly appropriate to that process of cultural "re-positioning" (see Hall 1992) crucial for the construction of post-colonial identity. For example, we can study the metaphors of exclusion by which the black child learns "how far to go" (only the back verandah, wait at the gate . . .) without transgressing, or analyse the patterns of inward- and outward-directed gazing as José tries to follow

M. Médouze into an unknown mental space, "Africa". This process of critical reassessment is much intensified by the concentration in time also possible through the medium of film and by the heightened polemical effect of visual contrasts.

However, in the context of reflecting on Caribbean societies, there are also more general issues to explore: questions about how Martinique has developed socially and economically over these three decades, about education and the Creole language, and about Palcy's intriguing construct of a "tragic mulatto" boy to shadow the narrator-hero in her film. Both works deal in individual, partial truths but also seek to address social injustice and alienation within their society.

Many, probably most "books of the film" distress readers of the original text by the liberties taken or by the deadening literalness with which events and characters are rendered. But we are dealing here with two works which are happily both successful in their own terms, and very closely linked. Palcy was an enthusiastic teenage reader of the book, claiming to have written the first version of the screenplay at 17,[2] before she had any professional training. She was confident enough of her rapport with the author to give him a small role (as the parish priest), and she has undoubtedly pushed up his sales enormously (Présence Africaine very rapidly adopted a still as the cover photograph for their paperback edition). Zobel, from his rural retreat in France, is said to be very happy with the film.

Before looking at some of the key shifts in focus and sensibility from novel to film, it might be useful to recall the broadly shared thematic content. *Black Shack Alley* (*Sugar Cane Alley* was the translation for US release) is the story of a black boy raised by his grandmother on a sugar plantation in Martinique between the wars, a model pupil who climbs the ladder of achievement in the French educational system yet remains loyal to his roots in the African-based oral culture of the village. It is a plantation novel, dominated by the hierarchies of slavery and sugar; it is also a classic Bildungsroman, charting young José's initiation into the adult world.[3] As the portrait of an individual gradually becoming conscious of himself, the novel ends with an explicit pledge to write up the experience. Both versions share a strongly didactic, almost ethnographic flavour, demonstrating the activities of the plantation at work and play, and building up a panorama of town and country between the wars – postcards from the past, as the film's sepia title sequence insists.

Although the film necessarily condenses the balanced three-part structure Zobel organized, the broad lines remain. There were initially three equal sections, ending with two framing deaths – of Médouze the father figure (Part 1) and M'man Tine (Part 3) – and between them the definitive farewell to the self who might have been (working in the cane fields) represented by the scholarship to high school (Part 2). Each section is focused on a layer of the pyramid of colour and class which founds colonial Caribbean society.

First of all, José is deeply embedded in Black Shack Alley itself: a community of agricultural labourers occupying a row of former slave huts on the estate, still economically and psychologically dependent on the white Master or manager in his Great House on the hill (Zobel 1980, 11). Through the naive vision of his pre-school child narrator, Zobel immerses the reader in the experience of harsh labour in the cane fields – long hours, low pay and scarce material resources but relieved by a spirit of community and mutual support with a strong African cultural residue. The first of several father-substitutes, M. Médouze, is used to stress the transmission of an oral tradition, the persistence of that *griot* role, which is an analogue for the work of the filmmaker as she keeps alive the past in the collective memory. He is shown passing on his family history of slavery and failed rebellion, his repertoire of Creole tales and riddles, an animist faith in the values of life. Médouze's wake sets the seal on the boy's initiation into African origins and his socialization into the rural proletariat of Petit-Morne. The film version gives most extension to this phase, reducing the coverage of life in town.

Part 2 shifts the emphasis to Petit-Bourg, where the all-age school provides basic education in French. Now the author deals with a wider world, where interracial relations favour social mobility and *métissage* becomes a crucial issue. Here in fictional guise are similar case histories to those explored by Frantz Fanon (himself one of those better-off "high brown" boys at the Lycée Schœlcher, 1939–43, and writing at about this time the thesis that would become *Black Skin, White Masks*). Zobel's Roc family supply a classic demonstration: outside children of a *béké* (1980, 88), holding positions of privilege on the estate, Justin has a child with his black mistress before marrying "up",[4] his brother is the schoolmaster with "tanned" complexion, while ill-treated children like Jojo suffer deep insecurity from the ambivalent attitudes of the adults close to them. At this intermediate "petit-bourgeois" level, where status is negotiated, with colour as a main but not exclusive factor, comes the portrait of Mme Léonce, the disagreeable black *parvenue,* jealously enforcing her social privilege. The world of school offers Zobel an easy way to diversify the physical portraits. It is also the apprenticeship into schooling in French, both secular syllabus and parish catechism class, which instil by rote the twin discourses of the colonizer. Docile and gifted, José admires his teacher, aspires to pass his *Certificat d'Etudes,* and acquires fluency in French.

Finally, his success – note the role of dictation, in which a pupil can only excel by reproducing exactly the magisterial discourse – brings a quarter-scholarship to the Lycée Schœlcher in Fort-de-France. The focus shifts to the urban population and a more developed portrayal of the white elite: wealthy families "uptown" on the Route Didier (seen from the perspective of their domestic servants), their sons at the lycée, teachers from France. Now the key skills being acquired are in reading French literature and writing in French. However, by now the educational process has equipped José with critical awareness. He has become conscious of the conflict between his two cultures (dramatized, for example, by his inability to name his guardian's profession, since he knows only the Creole term for *amarreuse; 1974,* 181; *1980,* 136). He has indeed "cheated" the system, though not in the way the teacher alleges, when he translates into a French composition the profoundly anti-French significance of the death of Médouze. He introduces black authors such as René Maran and Claude McKay to his friends, and they debate together representations of the Negro in the (mainly Hollywood) films they see.

At the close of the novel, the narrator, grieving over his grandmother's death, comforts himself by rediscovering the ritual activities of the wake: he will tell a story, the life story which is the book we have just read.

In trying to suggest how closely the writer's project is interwoven into the portrait of a society, many elements have had to be omitted. I want now to explore just a few of the indications of social change when we compare novel and film, highlighting areas where Palcy has operated a creative reworking of the original text.

First and most obviously, Zobel writes of a period when Martinique was still a sugar-producing colony, and his own experience was conditioned by the importance of the plantations. He comes from the commune of Rivière-Salée, which included Petit-Bourg (real place names are used in the novel), a well-watered fertile plain southeast of the bay sheltering Fort-de-France, once covered with sugar plantations. In 1935 just 11 per cent of those farming owned 80 per cent of the cultivable land area, and most was under cane. However, by the time Palcy was filming, sugar production had shown a dramatic decline (from 68,000 tons in 1940 to 14,000 in 1974, and from 11 active sugar factories in 1950 to 2, Lareinty and Le Galion, by 1970; Crusol 1980). The amount of rum produced has remained relatively constant, but bananas have often replaced cane. (Palcy's father worked as a mechanic in a pineapple factory, and one of her early short films was set on a banana plantation.) Thus images of labour in the heavily subsidized cane fields, though still iconic for slavery, risk being appropriated into the heritage industry: a few acres grown and harvested in traditional style offer photo opportunities for tourists visiting distilleries for promotional samples of blended rums such as Mauny. Palcy has cunningly composed a representation of a plantation from a collection of surviving cane fields and carefully preserved machinery. It arouses recognition, bitter or nostalgic, but this physical environment is now that of only a small minority, and the harvest is mainly mechanized, with some seasonal labour, including that of St Lucians. In their study of *Lettres créoles*, Patrick Chamoiseau and Raphaël Confiant see Zobel's novel as commemorating the end of an era, M'man Tine's death and José's emancipation as "le chant funèbre de la société d'habitation traditionnelle" (1991, 144).

Nevertheless, one obvious survivor is the Creole language, cherished by Chamoiseau in his Prix Goncourt novel as the "seul fond encore utile si loin des bitations" (1992, 340) for town-dwellers. At the same time, several political analysts, such as Fred Constant, point to a persistence of the residential groupings and loyalties created by the plantation, which "still has the role of a magnet around which memories circulate and the feeling of belonging to a micro-collectivity is rooted" (1988, 69).[5] Fort-de-France has expanded greatly within the last generation, and many of the networks so crucial to voting patterns, to survival in time of need, in a small-scale society are rooted in the rural *commune,* even the *quartier,* felt to identify origins.

If there has been a dramatic decline in the role of the sugar plantation, there has been an equally spectacular improvement in education. A handful of brilliant exceptions, headed by Aimé Césaire, tend to obscure the fact that only very few blacks, and still fewer grandsons of workers in the cane fields (Hauch 1960, 133 ff.), obtained secondary education until the 1946 *départementalisation* took a step forward towards implementing French ideals of access for all. The scenes in the village school recreate for French viewers the ideals of the nineteenth-century educational reformer Jules Ferry: a disciplined classroom confidently creating French citizens for the Republic (reducing regional ties, punishing local languages), free, secular and universal. But in the colonies, a severe de facto selection persisted. Charles Hauch quotes elementary school enrolment ratios as rising from approximately 60 per cent in 1938 to 99.7 per cent in 1958–59. As late as 1942, a governor in French Africa could articulate an officially elitist policy: "Let us consider education as a precious thing which is only dispensed advisedly and limit its effects to qualified beneficiaries" (he has sons of chiefs and local notabilities in mind) (Little 1993, 14). When nowadays surprise is expressed that such a stalwart proponent of black liberation as Aimé Césaire should have campaigned for closer union with France in 1945, it is important to see that the Revolutionary and Republican tradition promised an equality of opportunity which the continued dominance of the *béké* elite (some of whom had sided with Vichy) still withheld. Though success rates remain disappointing, especially in the prestigious Bac C (maths and physics), and every new school year brings some contention, the DOM now score very highly in terms of education provision – in regional terms at least, but then Martinicans compare with France. . . . Moreover, in contrast to the scene introduced by Palcy showing a daughter denied opportunities to proceed to the bac, there is now quite an imbalance favouring girls in secondary school results.

School attendance is still the major instrument of assimilation. It means following a largely French curriculum, untouched by the radical syllabus changes the Caribbean Examinations Council (CXC) has brought to the anglophone Caribbean, and for obvious reasons. French centralization has conditioned parents to expect certificates negotiable in the metropole, where population totals now rival those of the islands, so that there is a great deal of circulation, driven by opportunities for jobs and further study, by tourism and family regroupings. Zobel's text reflects the fierce motivation of an earlier, less mobile population. The prime condition of success was and is to acquire mastery of the French language and its canon of texts, especially those of the seventeenth and nineteenth centuries. Speaking Creole, even in the schoolyard, was punished. There is a dense intertextuality of French sources in Zobel's work – the famous litany recited for the hands of M'man Tine owes much to Flaubert, for example. He seldom gives more than an isolated word or exclamation in Creole. Clearly he seeks acceptability to the French public (see the footnotes he provides to regional and Creole terms in the text), and he only very rarely makes explicit any sense of malaise in using the colonizer's language to express the experience of the colonized.

By the time Palcy made her film, there were, paradoxically, few monolingual speakers of Creole remaining but the acceptability of Creole in literature and the arts had improved radically, due in a great measure to the activities of the Groupe d'Etudes et de Recherches en Espace Créolophone (GEREC), spearheaded by the polemical energies of linguist Jean Bernabé and illustrated by novelists such as Chamoiseau and Confiant. By the 1980s, theatre in Creole was commonplace, a good deal of poetry and media production used "nation language" and most writers felt an imperative to explore the creative interfaces between French and Creole. Thus Palcy works within a new linguistic framework that includes a demand for authenticity in showing a rural community as largely Creole-speaking, and tries to suggest a creolized French without sacrificing intelligibility (for example, the scenes with the children and the recurrent use of voices off-camera).

Probably the most controversial and interesting aspect of Palcy's adaptation concerns her treatment of resistance to the colonial order. Throughout the film, her image of *l'école française* is largely bland and conciliatory. It is true that the curriculum is mocked for its grotesque inappropriateness – the subdivisions of the departments of France, the glaciers of the Alps, the first lesson more like drill, all peremptory commands – but she tempers the harsh discipline of Monsieur Roc and softens the portrait of the lycée teacher to the point of a ludicrously implausible home visit in the slums.[6] José is also a much more successful pupil, his exam failures edited out. The portrait of school as the approved path to upward social mobility is thus reinforced by Palcy, who in interviews has indicated links with her own family history of ambitious parents ready to make sacrifices to educate several children to university level.[7]

However, in what may be a compensatory shift of emphasis, Palcy gives clearer focus to the images of white domination (rejected cane in the factory, overseers bullying in the fields) and constructs an elaborated version of the bad *béké* in the shape of pallid, pith-helmeted Monsieur de Thorail. Drawing on the rhetorical oppositions of Negritude, Palcy associates him with the factory and the machine (his motor car), and implicates him in the largely derisory efforts at catechizing of the Roman Catholic church, an anatomy of repression. In contrast, an Edenic image of men and horses bathing at the pool suggests a harmonious natural order before the incursion of the whites. The horse becomes a "natural" instrument to expel the intruder. De Thorail dies subscribing unrepentantly to the racial superiority of his caste (a scene drawn, in fact, from one of Carmen's tales; Zobel 1980, 162). The reshaping of material in the scene at the ford suggests Césaire's influence on Palcy's filmic discourse,[8] but the imagery also has a noticeably depoliticizing effect.

If the film's portraits of whites tend towards simplified silhouettes, the scenes of black resistance are often developed to create more impact. For example, the screenplay rewrites with much more militant and explicit material the testimony of Médouze's father concerning the Middle Passage, and uses recent research to view emancipation as precipitated by a black uprising and attacks on plantations round St Pierre (for example, additions such as "for the first time the blacks saw the whites trembling, shutting themselves up in their fine houses and dying. . . . That's how slavery ended!"; see Zobel 1980, 32, for contrast). Visual associations are also used to reinforce the cluster of positive connotations for *marronage:* the memory of the Maroons coming down in 1848 brandishing torches, machetes and so on is reiterated when the search for Médouze is shown as a dynamic group activity, reclaiming the upland space of the *morne* with the conch shell signalling and torchlight empowering in the darkness. When Jojo/Léopold runs away from the injustice of home and school, the word *marronner* echoes around the school. Palcy is linking images of vigorous action by blacks, with Médouze as a totem or mask (prolonged in miniature by the carved figure he gives José) who centres that dynamic on a link with Africa (the actor is Senegalese).

By reinforcing hints of a revolutionary potential in the black dispossessed and stressing Médouze as mentor, Palcy leads her audience to expect some critical political insight in her hero as he matures, even a leadership role. Instead she operates a substitution which arouses uneasiness. José is withheld from any overt position of rebellion – astutely, for success with all shades of audience, he figures as an endearingly good boy, at most reproaching racism (as manifested by Mademoiselle Flora) with earnest puzzlement or flinging a well-justified rockstone at Madame Léonce. The risks are taken by the much more radical "Léopold" figure. The mulatto boy, rejected by his father, turns to his mother's people, and we are told of his challenge to the crooked bookkeeper, resulting in violence, imprisonment and "social death" (Zobel 1980, 166). José feels that his own life has been insignificant in comparison. Palcy has created in Léopold a much more substantial character to shadow José, and she uses him as conduit for the protest vein. José docilely retains his aura of simple trust in the system, his gaze progressively more focused on the evidence – at the close, M'man Tine's martyred flesh – whereas Léopold takes on the role of sacrificial victim (visually very strong in the leading rope and bloodied face). The crowd of cane workers provide a frieze of that Caribbean protest icon, a crowd raising machetes and agricultural tools. But they do not liberate Léopold: they express solidarity by singing a protesting lament (still current at meetings of *indépendantiste* parties), "Martinique malade-oh", behind the confining rope. Is this another of these ambiguous shifts which continue to allow Martinicans to enjoy gestures of protest without actually threatening the status quo? The black majority transposes in its chant human agency to an impersonal ill: disease. A marginalized child, belonging to neither group, is led off like a lamb to the slaughter. In emotional terms, this sacrifice to a repressive and unjust colonial order seems to compensate for José's complicity with it.

Palcy is black herself, like Césaire, who has only just at eighty stepped down from active politics. The vast majority of other politicians are of mixed race, often quite fair, notably the most successful leader of the parties campaigning for independence: Albert Marie-Jeanne of MIM (Mouvement Indépendantiste Martiniquais), "notre chabin". There is plenty of evidence that the old prejudices about "good hair", the connotations of *échapper* and so on persist, if more covertly, in the Caribbean, while the rise of racist aggression in Europe hardly needs stressing and certainly has repercussions for Antilleans in the metropole. The cultural ideology currently prevailing is *Créolité*, which makes a virtue of diversity, heterogeneity, locating identity in the Creole language as model of the processes of creolization, a dynamic recombination of elements from many origins. The concept is arguably too all-embracing, though highly successful in literary terms. Palcy's choices in *Rue Cases-Nègres* may be revealing: mulatto leadership failing, a black majority trapped and immobilized by the contradictions of dependency. A critical view of black survival is reinforced when we are shown the men dancing the *laghia*, a reduced version of warriors' mock-fighting, but here interminably repetitive, stuck in a groove, like the freed slaves who ran round Martinique and returned frustrated to the same huts and the same cane fields.

Lastly, I would like to focus briefly on that dimension of film (or theatre) which draws on the recognition value of an actor as a composite of a real individual and a succession of previous roles. The point is worth making because some comments, even by Palcy herself, propagate a myth of the film as the work of a mainly amateur cast; with the overtones of artlessness, of absence of a creative transformation of reality that this implies – ethnography not fiction. First-world audiences may want to believe in the authenticity of the portrait, but there is a dangerously patronizing myth at work here.

Among the performers are these:

- ◆ *M'man Tine:* Darling Légitimus, a highly respected and experienced performer on the Parisian stage.

- ◆ *M. Médouze:* Douta Seck, enveloped in the prestige of his roles as Césaire's Henry Christophe (in *La Tragédie du Roi Christophe*, 1964) and Joueur de Sanza (in *Une Saison au Congo*, 1967) in the original productions by Jean-Marie Serreau; accentuating the sense of a noble African dignity, perhaps also the tragic dimension in these victims "crucified by colonialism" (cf. Médouze as black Christ in Zobel's imagery).

- ◆ *Saint-Louis:* Joby Bernabé, involved in collective protest theatre in 1970s Paris, especially *Kimafoutiesa,* now a well-known performer of his own poetry in Creole in recital, with music, also available on cassette.

- ◆ *Douze-Orteils:* Eugène Mona, celebrated musician, singer and flute player, with a serious interest in the authenticity of musical traditions. His premature death occasioned a protracted wake.

- ◆ *Stephen Roc:* Henri Melon, past director of the Théâtre Populaire Martiniquais, which was founded in 1968 and presented plays and "montages poétiques" in French and/or Creole over a ten-year period.[9]

An audience unaware of this depth of professional performance experience would miss the element of recognition of the familiar face which operates for a Martinican public, just as the strange sense of lost time refound which emerges from some reconstitutions of places – the *yak* chugging down river, the school – has a powerful local appeal.

The film was immensely popular in Martinique, seen over and over by people who seldom went to the cinema. Its success must be attributed to its positive merits – the high quality of acting, the coherence and sensitivity of the screenplay. Many identified very strongly with the image of an indomitable matriarch struggling to give a better future to her grandchild, but the film implies that his future will lead him further from his roots, and its nostalgia may be a comforting substitute for harsher thinking about a society trapped in some very cosy contradictions.

Notes

1. This paper should be dedicated to students, both in the United Kingdom and in the Caribbean, with whom I have worked on *La Rue Cases-Nègres,* especially those in Jamaica who improvised scenes from the novel during "French weekends" in the Blue Mountains, and to Stella Allen and Hugh MacDermott for film analysis.
2. Interview with June Givanni (Cham 1992, 228).
3. References to Zobel's novel are to the French edition by Présence Africaine ([1950] 1974) and to the (sometimes rather shaky) English translation published by Heinemann (1980), with an introduction by Keith Q. Warner.
4. Cf. telling lines in Ina Césaire's *Mémoires d'Isles*: ". . . je n'étais pas assez bonne pour qu'on me reconnaisse et ma maman pas assez demoiselle, pas assez mûla-tresse pour qu'on l'emmène à l'église" (1985, 38).
5. Note also references to the evolution of the sugar estates shown in the *Atlas de la Martinique* (CNRS), 1977.
6. There is no surrogate father for José in Part 3 (though Carmen initiates José into sexual mores corrupted by the racial hierarchy), but crucially the visit is a recognition of José's space by a figure of power.
7. Interview in *Le Monde* (Cournot 1989).
8. Intertextual references abound to Césaire (the mongoose-snake contest recalling the opening of the *Tragédie du Roi Christophe,* the "nègre vieux et laid", etc.), as also to Léon-Gontran Damas (table manners).
9. These plays are listed in *CARE 6* (1980), 69.

References

Atlas de la Martinique. 1977. CEGET-CNRS.

CARÉ (Centre Antillais de Recherches et d'Études). 1980. *Regards sur le théâtre.* CARÉ 6

Césaire, Ina. 1985. *Mémoires d'Isles.* Paris: Editions Caribéennes.

Cham, Mbaye. 1992. *Ex-Iles: Essays on Caribbean Cinema.* Trenton, NJ: Africa World Press.

Chamoiseau, Patrick. 1992. *Texaco.* Paris: Gallimard.

Chamoiseau, Patrick, and Raphaël Confiant. 1991. *Lettres créoles.* Paris: Hatier.

Constant, Fred. 1988. *La Retraite aux flambeaux: société et politique en Martinique.* Paris: Editions Caribéennes.

Corzani, Jacques. 1978. *La Littérature des Antilles-Guyane françaises.* Vol. 8. Fort-de-France, Martinique: Désormeaux.

Cournot, Michel. 1989. "Un entretien avec la réalisatrice, 'Derrière les façades bouchées au ciment'". *Le Monde,* 9 November.

Crusol, Jean. 1980. *Economies insulaires de la Caraïbe.* Paris: Editions Caribéennes.

Hall, Stuart. 1992. "Cultural Identity and Cinematic Representation". In *Ex-Iles:*

Essays on Caribbean Cinema, edited by Mbye Cham, 220–36. Trenton, NJ: Africa World Press.

Hauch, Charles. 1960. *Educational Trends in the Caribbean.* Washington, DC: US Department of Health, Education and Welfare.

Little, J.P. 1993. "The Context of *L'Aventure ambiguë:* Aspects of the School System in L'Afrique Occidentale Française". *ASCALF Bulletin* 6 (Spring/Summer): 10–27.

Rue Cases-Nègres (Sugar Cane Alley). 1983. Directed by Euzhan Palcy. Written by Euzhan Palcy. Produced by Michel Loulergue, Jean-Luc Ormières and Alix Régis. NEF Diffusion/Orca Productions/SU.MA.FA.

Zobel, Joseph. [1950] 1974. *La Rue Cases-Nègres.* Paris: Présence Africaine.

———. 1980. *Black Shack Alley.* Translated with an introduction by Keith Q. Warner. (Original title: *La Rue Cases-Nègres.*) London: Heinemann.

8

The Caribbeanness of Haiti
Simone Schwarz-Bart's
Ton beau capitaine

Anthea Morrison
University of the West Indies, Cave Hill, Barbados

One would assume that Haiti's place in the collective consciousness of Caribbean people would be that position of honour conferred on it several decades ago by Aimé Césaire, who acknowledged, in the non-conformist cartography which gave shape to the *Cahier*'s psychic journeys, "Haiti, où la négritude se mit debout pour la première fois et dit qu'elle croyait à son humanité" (Césaire [1939] 1983, 24). Césaire's sense of affiliation with Haiti would be reinforced after a lengthy visit in 1945, and the biography *Toussaint Louverture* (1962) followed by *La Tragédie du roi Christophe* (1963) further attest to a sense of the centrality of Haiti to the Caribbean experience and more generally to anti-colonial discourse.

Césaire is certainly not alone in his fascination with and respect for Haiti: Caribbean writers of the stature of Edouard Glissant, Maryse Condé and Simone Schwarz-Bart have followed in his footsteps, and the list could be substantially extended if one included non-francophone writers. It would be comforting to conclude that other Caribbean observers are exempt from the excesses highlighted by J. Michael Dash in his penetrating analysis of relations between Haiti and the United States: "Haiti seems to have always had the lure of the extreme case, whether it was virgin terrain, a garden of earthly delights where the black race could begin again or the closest and most histrionic examples of Africa's continental darkness" (Dash 1997, 2–3). While "Honneur et respect", the traditional Haitian greeting of friend to friend, is chosen by Condé as the epigraph to *La Migration des cœurs* (1995), the Guadeloupean novelist has highlighted in an interview the sometimes troubling relationship between Haiti and its Caribbean sister/cousin islands: "When I settled in Guadeloupe, I found that a lot of Haitian children felt marginalized in schools there" (Pfaff 1996, 80). Such marginalization is more marked, and perhaps predictable, in the case of the Haitian diaspora in North America, where the black Caribbean migrant from a country known of late more for its political turmoil than for its glorious past is dramatically Other. Edwidge Danticat has written movingly of this based on her own experience as a migrant child in Brooklyn in 1981 who felt keenly the labels which "were like lashes from a whip, a constant reminder of who we were, and how the children in the school thought of us" (1995, 4).

Yet the injustices and misconceptions to which Haitians are subjected are not all inflicted by the Other, and they cannot all be easily dismissed as examples of racism. Indeed, for many Caribbean people with sluggish memories, Haiti's acknowledged historical role of pioneer is sometimes obscured by the much-publicized saga of the Duvalier and the post-Duvalier years, by the terrible odysseys of the Haitian people braving the Caribbean waters on fragile vessels and, not least of all, by their status as a migrant underclass even within their own region. On the latter point, the emergence of the expression "travailler comme un Haïtien" as a contemporary version of the traditional racist formulation "travailler comme un nègre" is a reminder that linguistic choices translate and perpetuate political realities, and also that those who have themselves been historically victims of social stratification are not above doing the same to "their own". In some configurations of Caribbean identity, Haiti has come then to have a place apart, so that when we in the anglophone territories refer to the "French Caribbean", there is an inferred – and of course historically justified – demarcation of Martinique and Guadeloupe on the one hand and Haiti on the other, a distinction concretized by the 1946 *loi de départementalisation,* which transformed the remaining "American" colonies into departments of France. The concomitant marginalization of Haiti is at the heart of the haunting refrain of David Rudder's tribute to a misunderstood people (1993):

Haiti I'm sorry
We misunderstood you
One day we'll turn our heads
And look inside you
Haiti I'm sorry
We misunderstood you
One day we'll turn our heads
Restore your glory

David Rudder (born in Trinidad in 1953), internationally celebrated soca musician, is well known for his thoughtful lyrics and for his ability to give voice, as a sort of New World *griot,* to the joys and sorrows of Caribbean people (among the cultural influences which shaped his childhood was *Shango,* the African-based religious form).

That Rudder's view of Haiti is predicated on an Afrocentric conception of Caribbean identity is illustrated by the interesting parallel between one of the lines of "Haiti" – "where there is anguish in Port-au-Prince / it's still Africa crying" – and the semi-exasperated comment of Césaire's Christophe: "Pauvre Afrique. Je veux dire pauvre Haïti! C'est la même chose d'ailleurs . . ." (Césaire [1963] 1970, 49). But so many other West Indians are detached from the Haitian epic, preferring to make Haiti the stranger, alone (if it were not for Cuba)[1] in a Caribbean sea of *relative* tranquillity. In this connexion, Edouard Glissant's comments in *Le Discours antillais* on the misunderstandings inherent in some Caribbean approaches to Haiti are instructive:

Les arguments préférés des tenants du système dans les Antilles de langue française tiennent en l'examen complaisant des misères d'Haïti: «Voilà où mène l'indépendance!» L'analyse historique de l'effort de ce peuple, soulignant les inimaginables conditions d'apparition de la nation haïtienne, permet d'approcher les données réelles du problème. . . . L'extraordinaire est que le peuple haïtien ait pu résister à tant d'avanics. Il a résisté, il résiste encore. (1981, 267)

But whether a tale of victims or of heroes, whether neglected or celebrated, the Haitian experience remains quintessentially Caribbean, although in some ways as if seen through a magnifying glass – a story of struggle, of reluctant voyagers and also of survival. In her short play *Ton beau capitaine* (1987), Simone

Schwarz-Bart is perhaps writing back, in a less grandiose, less messianic way to *the* literary forefather of her generation, and like him subverting the assimila-tionist discourse of French colonialism and neo-colonialism by asserting kinship with Haiti. This play may come as somewhat of a surprise for readers of a nov-elist seen by some as the optimist among Caribbean women writers, particularly in comparison to her celebrated novel *Pluie et vent sur Télumée Miracle* (1972): the tale it tells is an unsettling, even tragic one, without the redeeming certainty of the latter text, in which the narrator is at the end of her life, looking back at now distant challenges. In *Ton beau capitaine,* the challenges are immediate, dra-matic and far from resolved. Guadeloupe is, for the male protagonist, the land of exile, a hostile, alien place where Haitians are the subject of disparagement; it is the locus of Wilnor's flirtation with a sort of madness – a madness not unknown of course in *Pluie et vent,* but with the crucial difference that in the novel, the beleaguered female characters are always surrounded by caring family and community.

Ton beau capitaine opens with the disturbing scene of the protagonist talking to himself, disclaiming any connection with Guadeloupe, the same country so lovingly named and embraced as home at the start of *Pluie et vent:*

> Wilnor, mon cher, je t'apprends que rien ne t'appartient ici, pas même l'herbe des chemins, pas même le vent. *(Petit rire)* Et si tu veux savoir, la seule chose qui soye vraiment à toi *(il amène la cassette à hauteur de ses yeux):* c'est ça, vieux camarade, c'est ça. (Schwarz-Bart 1987, 12)

It is in this strange land (one which is both *étrange* and *étranger*) that Wilnor will learn the painful news that Marie-Ange, the beloved wife he left in Haiti, has succumbed to the temptations of loneliness, betraying him with a vis-iting "friend". This invisible wife is both absent and present, physically removed from the action but nevertheless forcefully alive in the imagination of the audi-ence because of her voice, which, by cassette, "writes" a long and tortuous letter to her spouse. The interesting device of the cassette recorder which allows the husband and wife to attempt to bridge the waters between them gives rise to several striking phrases, such as Marie-Ange's reference to herself as "Ta femme en cassette" (Schwarz-Bart 1987, 20) and Wilnor's summation of the years of sep-aration as "Toutes ces années en cassette" (51). Such expressions combine to affirm, in this play, the primacy of the spoken word as well as the inventiveness of a people who will not be silenced.[2]

Nevertheless, this people is represented in the play as relatively powerless, marginal by reason of enforced exile. Marie-Ange expresses her concern for her husband's well-being in the first scene by linking it to what she has heard about the lamentable living conditions of "nos frères exilés en Guadeloupe" (Schwarz-Bart 1987, 15). And in a moving speech in which this solitary wife boldly defines herself as a sexual being (Schwarz-Bart, in this text, goes beyond the stereotype of the strong, consistently virtuous West Indian woman), referring to a recurring dream in which she holds her husband in her arms only to have him disintegrate into nothingness, she fuses her individual loneliness, her wish to hold her husband, with the larger longing of Haitians of the new diaspora, portrayed as a people apparently condemned to errancy and marginalization:

> Wilnor, je voudrais être un bateau qui s'en va vers la Guadeloupe. Là-bas j'arrive et tu montes à l'intérieur de moi, tu marches sur mon plancher, tu poses ta main sur mes membrures, tu me visites de la cale à la cime du mât. Et puis tu mets la voile et je t'emmène dans un pays loin, très loin. *(Pause)* A l'autre bout du monde, peut-être, où les gens vous regardent pas comme des moins que rien, des cocos secs. Wilnor, y a-t-il donc pas un pays sur la terre où nous Haïti on peut travailler, envoyer quelque argent chez soi, de temps en temps, sans se transformer en courant d'air? (19)

In the final scene of the play, which is a strange halfway house between monologue and dialogue – the audience might easily forget that in fact this is not a telephone conversation and that there is a *décalage* which means that Marie-Ange cannot respond directly to Wilnor's words – he confirms that her fears for his emotional safety are not baseless. For he too has been dreaming strange dreams: "des rêves qui m'entraînent dans des pays de plus en plus éloignés, de plus en plus étranges, étrangers, et j'ai peur un de ces quatre matins de ne plus retrouver le chemin du retour" (Schwarz-Bart 1987, 50).

A comparison of the two exracts just cited, both evoking journeys away from Haiti, amplifies the poignancy of this sense of estrangement from the homeland: return to the *pays natal* seems unimaginable, and the relatively insignificant distance between Haiti and Guadeloupe is blurred in the reader's mind as Haiti becomes a mythic country of origin, a pre-colonial Guinée, an imagined Ethiopia, repository of dreams and longings for dispossessed New World blacks. In fact, one hears in this tale of separation of husband and wife an interesting intertextual echo of a story within a story from Paule Marshall's *Praisesong for the Widow,* in which the African American protagonist is told by an old Carriacou inhabitant a "true" story which is a veritable allegory of displacement:

> "The Bongo? Have you heard of that one maybe? Is the one I like best, oui. The song to it tells what happened to a Carriacou man and his wife during the slave time. The smallest child home knows the story. They took and sold the husband – the chains on him, oui – to Trinidad and later the same day they put the wife on a schooner to Haiti and sell her separate. Their two children the people that owned them kept behind in Carriacou. Is a true thing, happen during the slave time. Both of them cry so that day we say it's their tears whenever there's a big rain." (Marshall 1983, 176)

Yet there is a difference between this legendary couple and Schwarz-Bart's pair: for the former, Haiti and Trinidad are equally alien, while the African motherland appears irremediably lost, as it certainly is for Médouze, the old storyteller in Zobel's classic plantation novel, who reminds the young protagonist that he has "ni maman, ni papa, ni frères et sœurs en Afrique" (Zobel 1974, 58). But Wilnor, the uprooted character of *Ton beau capitaine,* has intimate ties to his homeland. His belonging to a family and also to a community is underscored by Marie-Ange herself, as she tells of other Haitian travellers who will not return home, and specifically of the drowning of his friend Pétrus in an unsuccessful bid to reach the United States:

> Cependant, je dois te le dire, hélas seigneur: ton ami Pétrus s'est pour ainsi dire noyé, perdu corps et biens, avec une trentaine d'âmes qui essayaient de gagner les Amériques sur un radeau. Maman Pétrus quand elle a appris la nouvelle, la vieille, le sang lui a bouché les cordes vocales et elle est tombée par terre, soufflant comme un cachalot. (Schwarz-Bart 1987, 14)

It is worthy of note that even in relating this latest disaster involving would-be émigrés, Marie-Ange's voice holds sway, fluent and eloquent as if both the words themselves and the telling have the power to dilute the pain of the reality narrated. Furthermore, that the bereaved mother loses her voice in her distress is not, I think, gratuitous, since the text asserts, as did *Pluie et vent,* the association between language and power. The bold device of the cassette recorder clearly identifies the woman as speaking subject, and since about half of the text is dominated by "La voix", one may say that the two speakers have approximately the same "playing time". Because we cannot *see* Marie-Ange, and because there is no narrator to mediate her story, the disembodied voice demands careful listening, calling attention to itself, to its rhythms, to its every hesitation and to its occasional silences. In this context, one might usefully contrast the fluent outpouring of the beginning of the tape, where repetition simulates the unedited text of orality, to the end of the first scene, when Marie-Ange admits that even words cannot communicate the unspeakable. In the former section of the text, the illusion of intimacy is created by the so persuasive *voix:*

> Allô, allô, Wilnor Baptiste, dès que tu entendras cette voix, tu sauras que c'est Marie-Ange qui te parle. J'ai chassé tout mon monde de la case, y compris le coq, et maintenant nous sommes seuls, toi et moi, toi là-bas et moi ici, toi ici et moi là-bas, c'est pareil.
>
> Wilnor, comment vas-tu? Comment, *comment* vas-tu? J'ai tant de choses à te dire que ma langue en est toute sèche. (Schwarz-Bart 1987, 13)

While the emphasis on naming recalls an African tradition assertive of belonging and lineage, it soon becomes apparent that Marie-Ange is clutching at straws, throwing words into a void in full knowledge that the *real* words remain unspoken; a few pages later on, she admits that "il y a parfois certains mots qui vous stoppent, vous restent en travers de la gorge, comme des arêtes de poisson. J'essaierai encore demain, avec la grâce de Dieu" (20).

Yet, surprisingly given her generally penitent tone, after she has told Wilnor the unpalatable news, Marie-Ange seems impatient with what she assumes – correctly – to be his unwillingness to listen, as if the telling of the story has freed her, if not of guilt, at least of the meekness of the mute malefactor:

> *(L'homme secoue la tête sans comprendre; long silence, puis la voix de femme se fait à nouveau entendre)*
>
> LA VOIX
>
> Comprends-tu, Wilnor? . . .
> *Comprends-tu? (Pause)* Wilnor, je te connais, je sais combien tu as les oreilles délicates. Cependant arrête de secouer la tête et calcule, réfléchis:

en quel temps, en quel monde t'imagines-tu donc vivre, mon pauvre ami? (Schwarz-Bart 1987, 28–29)

What is perhaps more memorable than the story Schwarz-Bart tells in *Ton beau capitaine* is the way it is told, specifically the appeal to the "oreilles", delicate or not: the fact that there are no other characters and the starkness of the decor compel the audience to focus on and ultimately be seduced by these two voices reaching out for each other (if one were to compare *Ton beau capitaine* with another play with minimal props, such as Samuel Beckett's *En attendant Godot*, one would be struck by the even greater terseness of the former text). This valorization of speech is surely of particular importance in the Haitian context, where the majority is *créolophone* and not "literate" in the limited Western sense of the word – although the purists, in particular the theoreticians of *Créolité*, might scold Schwarz-Bart for not writing in Creole, seen by some as the defining element of Caribbean identity.

As I have suggested, there is hardly any *triomphalisme* in Schwarz-Bart's privileging of speech, since there are moments in the mono-/dialogue when words falter, and even fail; it is here that the playwright moves effortlessly from speech to dance, as at the end of scene 2, when Wilnor needs to escape a flow of words that is not a healing stream:

Assez vous dis-je, malpropre! Assez parlé, assez menti, assez dit la vérité! assez toutes choses! assez tout le monde! laissez-moi! laissez-moi!

(*L'homme arrête brutalement la cassette. Silence. Fait quelques pas en avant, chancelant, prononce:* assez, assez les dieux! *Puis le chancellement se transforme en danse (petits sauts par côté, comme dans le lérose), les bras se soulèvent comme pour planer:* assez les anges! *Et un tambour se met à battre . . . .*) (Schwarz-Bart 1987, 30–31)

While there is a certain irony in the majesty and harmony of the music, one may see this interlude not simply as a means of escape from unpleasant reality, but as the author's way of asserting continuity and coherence in the presence of apparent fragmentation, of asserting a *présence haïtienne* in this tale of absence, of asserting a Caribbean community in which music effortlessly transcends linguistic and other differences. This is even more striking in the later references to the highly structured quadrille, this European dance so seamlessly integrated into both francophone and anglophone Caribbean cultures, and finally, on the penultimate page, to the "ti-bois", the traditional drum rhythm of African origin found not only in Guadeloupe, Martinique and Haiti but also in St Lucia. The juxtaposition of these two music forms, one of European origin, the other African, is suggestive of the easy coexistence in the Caribbean of diverse cultural practices and even of the creative possibilities of such inclusiveness. Schwarz-Bart, perhaps deliberately, avoids the temptation of the overt allusion to *vaudou* here; instead, the audience is left free to interpret the dance from whatever religious or aesthetic perspective seems appropriate, so that a Jamaican reader or viewer might think of Pocomania instead of the purely Haitian tradition in which the text is apparently grounded. At this point, the music becomes not support but participant in the action, as Wilnor, who appears to be arriving at a difficult peace with his wife, first resists and then – "im ketch the spirit!" – gives in to the seduction of the dance. This final dance of the play is part spirit possession, a phenomenon of importance in several Caribbean religious practices; the dance becomes ritual, and even the painful solitude of this Haitian in exile cannot negate its potency as a reminder of the permanence and the cohesiveness of the community. In this context, a comment by Gordon Rohlehr on the role of possession as metaphor in the work of George Lamming seems pertinent: "Music is both the vehicle and the corridor by which one descends to the bottom of the ocean of consciousness, makes connection with hidden or suppressed areas of the Self, and begins the journey towards wholeness" (1992, 70). So Wilnor is transported, in more than one sense of the word.

Although the play ends with the abrupt cessation of the dance – perhaps a reminder that in this tragedy of loneliness and betrayal, a sudden serenity would be not only facile but in fact implausible – the story is open-ended, so that the *possibility* of reconciliation between this beleaguered couple, and of reintegration of the exile into the community, is not excluded. What is perhaps more important, and ultimately reassuring, is that this community, through its music, through the voice of Marie-Ange, through the symbolism of the child she carries (albeit reluctantly) and finally through the triumph of the cassette over poverty and non-literacy, is represented as vibrant, resilient and creative – need I add Caribbean?

Simone Schwarz-Bart's play, published in 1987, continues to have resonance for readers painfully aware of the ongoing upheavals and peregrinations of the people represented by the fictional Wilnor. At the end of the twentieth century,

Haitians continue to flee, mainly to North America but also to sometimes unfriendly "sister" islands of the Caribbean or to the Dominican Republic. Many of these journeys end brutally, either because of disasters at sea or because the unwelcome migrants are summarily returned to their port of origin. In the course of the prolonged dispute regarding the fate of the young Cuban refugee Elián González in the early months of the year 2000, the point was frequently made here in the Caribbean that had the unfortunate little boy been Haitian, it is doubtful whether he would have been the subject of so much attention. While this sort of hypothetical commentary may appear to be of limited value, the very fact of such a perception is a telling example of Haiti's continuing status as under-dog among Caribbean nations.

Libète: A Haiti Anthology, the 1999 anthology of writings on Haiti edited by Charles Arthur and J. Michael Dash, includes a lengthy chapter on "Refugees and the Diaspora", containing moving testimony on the flight of desperate people; the following extract from "Haïti Progrès" (1994) is a compelling example:

> From this past Friday to Monday, the US Coast Guard picked up some 2500 refugees from dozens of vessels. On June 27 [1994] alone, the US ships intercepted 1,486 people. . . . The latest surge of escapees from Haiti, which President Aristide has likened to people fleeing a house on fire, has kept the Coast Guard working overtime. (Arthur and Dash 1999, 198)

It is sad to note that much of the optimism generated by Aristide's triumphant return to Haiti – and to power – in October 1994 has been dissipated: at the end of the century, the Haitian "glory" of which David Rudder reminds us has still not been restored, as unrelenting poverty and political turmoil continue to attract attention in the international media. Yet one is also compelled by the power-ful voices of Haitian writers, by the resilience of so many Haitians who give "honour and respect" to the demeaning expression "travailler comme un Haïtien". Schwarz-Bart's play, too, with its open-ended form, with its tale of creativity and of survival, leaves the reader with hope for a valiant people, which, in the words of Edouard Glissant, "a résisté, . . . résiste encore" (1981, 267).

Notes

1. It seems to me that Cuba and Haiti have in common their "outsider" status within the Caribbean, both functioning as virtually closed spaces which feed the popular imagination. The difference, however, might be the association of Haiti

both with abject poverty and with *vaudou*, a belief system which has been
sensationalized and misrepresented in the West so that it is perceived by some
observers (West Indian and others) as the epitome of "backwardness".

2. When I presented the first version of this paper at the 1998 Conference on
Caribbean Women Writers, a member of the audience asked whether I saw any
similarity with the use of the cassette in Edwidge Danticat's *Breath, Eyes, Memory*
(1994). I subsequently gave thought to this and am grateful for the question that
was put to me because, indeed, Danticat's text also valorizes the spoken word
through the cassette, which serves as means of communication between the
protagonist's mother and her "illiterate" family back in Haiti.

References

Arthur, Charles, and J. Michael Dash, eds. 1999. *Libète: A Haitian Anthology.*
Princeton, NJ: Markus Wiener.

Césaire, Aimé. [1939] 1983. *Cahier d'un retour au pays natal.* Paris: Présence Africaine.

———. 1962. *Toussaint Louverture: la révolution française et le problème colonial.*
Paris: Présence Africaine.

———. [1963] 1970. *La Tragédie du roi Christophe.* Paris: Présence Africaine.

Condé, Maryse. 1995. *La Migration des cœurs.* Paris: Laffont.

Danticat, Edwidge. 1994. *Breath, Eyes, Memory.* New York: Soho.

———. 1995. "Haiti: A Bi-cultural Experience." In *Encuentros* 12. Washington, DC:
IDB Cultural Center.

Dash, J. Michael. 1997. *Haiti and the United States: National Stereotypes and the
Literary Imagination.* 2nd ed. New York: St. Martin's Press.

Glissant, Edouard. 1981. *Le Discours antillais.* Paris: Seuil.

Marshall, Paule. 1983. *Praisesong for the Widow.* New York: Penguin.

Pfaff, Françoise. 1996. *Conversations with Maryse Condé.* Lincoln: University of
Nebraska Press.

Rohlehr, Gordon. 1992. *The Shape of That Hurt and Other Essays.* Port-of-Spain,
Trinidad: Longman.

Rudder, David. 1993. "Haiti". *The Gilded Collection, 1985–1989.* Port-of-Spain,
Trinidad: Lypsoland.

Schwarz-Bart, Simone. 1972. *Pluie et vent sur Télumée Miracle.* Paris: Seuil.

———. 1987. *Ton beau capitaine.* Paris: Seuil.

Zobel, Joseph. 1974. *La Rue Cases-Nègres.* Paris: Présence Africaine.

9

The Martinican Writers of the *Créolité* Movement and History
Giving Back a Voice to the Disenfranchised

Marie-José N'Zengou-Tayo
University of the West Indies, Mona, Jamaica

. . . la vision intérieure et l'acceptation de notre créolité nous permettront d'investir *ces zones impénétrables du silence où le cri s'est dilué.* (Bernabé, Chamoiseau and Confiant 1993, 38)

In 1976, at a conference held at the University of the West Indies, Edward Baugh presented a paper entitled "The West Indian Writer and His Quarrel with History" in which he examined the sense of "historylessness" as a fear pervading the writings of many English-speaking Caribbean writers. He contended that

> behind the argument for historylessness is a basically determinist view of history, which would condemn us to being, indeed, forever, the slaves of history. The argument challenges us to examine or re-examine not only our idea of history, to look again at the question what is history, but also to examine our notions of what constitutes achievement. (Baugh 1977, 7)

Twenty years later, though most countries in the region, whether independent or not, have developed national historiographies and gathered a certain body of knowledge about their colonial past, history still remains an issue in the works of creative writers of the region, as noted by Barbara J. Webb in her study *Myth and History in Caribbean Fiction:* "Among Caribbean writers this issue [history=realism; rejection of historical representation in fiction in favor of mythic discourse] is related to the generally negative perception of New World history as a legacy of dispossession, exploitation, and betrayal" (1992, 3).

In the case of the French Antilles (Martinique and Guadeloupe), the Negritude writers were the first to make an attempt at reappropriating their past. In poetry and fiction, they confronted the reality of slavery and colonial exploitation. Contemporary writers, however, still complain about History. The issue is no longer a "sense of historylessness" but the meaninglessness of Caribbean history and the impossibility of ordinary people having their say in official history. This feeling has been consistently expressed by Martinican and Guadeloupean writers, even among those born after 1946 (the time of *départementalisation*) and who started to publish when regional power was granted to their islands (*décentralisation* in 1981). Martinican writers in particular have hard feelings towards history, as their reputation of assimilation (that is, alienation) continues to cling to them. The fiction of these contemporary writers gives the impression that the silence of history has created in their imagination a void that remains to be filled.

The relationship of French Caribbean writers with history is a recurrent theme in literary movements from Negritude to *Créolité*. Aimé Césaire strongly expressed this longing for history in *Cahier d'un retour au pays natal* and *La Tragédie du roi Christophe*. Césaire's exaltation of Africa and determined acceptance of the reality of slavery were an attempt at redeeming the Martinican population of African origin. Then the desire for History was a manner of reversing colonial history by giving positive values to a humiliating experience.

However, a younger generation was to take a stand against this compulsion to create for oneself "une histoire dont [on] n'ai[t] pas honte" (Condé 1976, 27). Guided by Maryse Condé's criticism of Negritude (1974, 1976), the gentle demythification of Africa by Simone Schwarz-Bart (*Ti Jean L'horizon*) and moreover by Edouard Glissant's reflections on *Antillanité* and Caribbean discourse in *Le Discours antillais* (1981, published in English as *Caribbean Discourse* in 1989), contemporary Martinican writers could examine their situation in the New World and assert themselves as the product of cross-cultural diversity. With this project in mind, they defined their relation to history in the following terms: "Notre Histoire (ou plus exactement nos histoires) est naufragée dans l'Histoire coloniale. La mémoire collective est notre urgence" (Bernabé, Chamoiseau and Confiant 1993, 36–37). These writers also define clearly their relationship with historians, as well as their right to undertake historical investigation of their people's past: "En ce qui nous concerne, l'histoire en tant que conscience à l'œuvre et l'histoire en tant que vécu ne sont donc pas l'affaire des seuls historiens. La littérature pour nous ne se répartira pas en genres mais impliquera toutes les approches des sciences humaines" (Glissant, 1981, 113).

This paper seeks to examine how two contemporary Martinican writers, Patrick Chamoiseau and Raphaël Confiant, leading figures of the *Créolité* movement, achieve in their fiction the goal (the search for collective memory) set out on their political agenda, *Eloge de la créolité* (1989). How does this choice affect their narrative techniques? Is it finally possible to give a voice to those forgotten by History? Or, to express it differently, how do Chamoiseau and Confiant inscribe within a text the life and the speech of the ordinary Martinican people whose culture is slowly disappearing due to the cultural blandishments resulting from being a French Department in the Americas?

These writers' fictions are developed from theoretical positions expressed in *Eloge de la créolité* in the wake of Glissant's ideas *(L'Intention poétique, Le Discours antillais)*: "Seule la connaissance poétique, la connaissance romanesque, la connaissance littéraire, bref, la connaissance artistique, pourra nous déceler, nous percevoir, nous ramener évanescents aux réanimations de la conscience" (Bernabé, Chamoiseau and Confiant 1993, 38). Chamoiseau and Confiant express their relationship with history by using similar strategies as for creative writing. The immediately noticeable feature is how they relate to Time. Both writers acknowledge the fact that the Western conception of time – the use of dates and chronology – is meaningless to the ordinary Caribbean person (middle class, working class, peasant). However, in *Texaco* Chamoiseau starts with a chronological table (1992, 13–15) and then divides his story into periods *("Temps"),* defined by the building material used by the city dwellers of the time. Nevertheless, he specifies the years which are encompassed for each period. Such a narrative structure bridges the gap between the Caribbean sense of time (cyclic and associated with events) and the Western requirement for a linear succession of time (chronology). Confiant, on the other hand, takes advantage of this attitude towards time by allowing his narratives to develop in "Circles" (for example, in *Le Nègre et l'Amiral,* [1988] 1993, and *Eau de café,* [1991] 1993). Paradoxically, he seems to accept some sort of chronology in *Eau de café,* where the circular sections end with the insertion of dated letters, going from one decade to the other, starting in 1937 (ten years after a violent uprising of sugar-cane workers, "la terrible révolte de 1927" [86]) and ending in 1977. However, these letters do not suggest any attempt at re-establishing a chronology. In addition, he creates an ambiguity concerning the exact period during which some events took place. For example in Eau de Café's account of her mother's story, one has the impression that the events told happened during slavery; it is therefore very surprising to discover that some events relating to life on the plantation occurred in the 1920s.

Rejecting chronological continuity affects the story in the sense that it makes any linear narration impossible. The authors adapt a "counterpoint" technique (the same event is told many times but with different narrators, focusing on different or even contradictory aspects of the event) or they use the technique of "l'histoire éclatée" (Glissant 1981, 142). These two techniques are used concurrently within the same text by Chamoiseau *(Solibo magnifique, Texaco)* and Confiant *(Le Nègre et l'Amiral)* in order to indicate the impossibility of recording and relying solely on one version of history, especially in the Caribbean. As a result, any attempt at writing history is undermined from the beginning. Consequently, they reject History and concentrate on stories. For instance, in *Le Nègre et l'Amiral*, Amédée Mauville, a would-be novelist (and Confiant's mouthpiece) records in his diary-novel, "Reniant tout cartésianisme, j'ai appris à l'instar de Philomène ou de Rigobert, à raconter, avec la véracité troublante de celui qui nie sur le bûcher, trente-douze mille versions d'un même événement. Une fois pris dans cette spirale, il n'y a plus qu'à croire en chacune d'elles successivement" (Confiant [1988] 1993, 347). Similarly, in Chamoiseau's *Texaco*, Esternome, the father of the main protagonist and narrator, rejects the single version of History:

Oh Sophie, . . . tu dis «l'Histoire», mais ça veut rien dire, il y a tellement de vies et tellement de destins, tellement de tracées pour faire notre seul chemin. Toi tu dis l'Histoire moi je dis les histoires. Celle que tu crois tige maîtresse de notre manioc n'est qu'une tige parmi charge d'autres. (Chamoiseau 1992, 102)

Chamoiseau's intention seems to be to record the attempts of Marie-Sophie Laborieux and her kin to "investir ces lieux qu'ils avaient créés, mais dont nul n'évaluait l'aptitude à leur Histoire en nos mille cent histoires" (1992, 66).

In these novels the history of the Martinican people is organized in order to "défaire" official history (*défaire* is used here with its military meaning, "to defeat", but also as "to undo" a piece of woven tapestry, the thread of which is pulled away in order to undo the work already done). In *Texaco*, longing for History is attributed to mulattos and is supposed to be the symbol of their alienation:

> C'est quoi, sermonnait le mulâtre politisé, c'est du papier ou de l'Histoire
> en marche? Il voulait qu'on réponde *C'est de l'Histoire en marche*, ce que
> tout le monde répondait sauf ce délirant de Théodorus qui juste avant
> l'ultime délire brailla: *Quelle Histoire, mais quelle Histoire? Où sont les nègres
> là-dedans?* (Chamoiseau 1992, 85)

Through the narrative voice one can clearly see an allusion to and then a dismissal of the Hegelian concept of history as well as of the nineteenth-century Romantic and twentieth-century Marxist ones (such as the belief in historical progress and the idea of a teleologic orientation in history).

Both Confiant and Chamoiseau oppose, on the one hand, "l'Histoire" (History) to "histoires" (stories). On the other hand, they consider "History" to be unique and exclusively appropriated by an educated (mulatto) elite versus multiple stories left to the "Others", the *nèg-en-terre* (bush Negroes) who are excluded from the historical field. This conception of History is equivalent to what we could call official history or history of the State. Paradoxically and maybe ironically, it is left to a "Petit-Blanc", Théodorus, to be the first to denounce this process of exclusion of the blacks at this moment when official history is being elaborated. I purposely use here historical concepts recently revived by Haitian historiography (see Trouillot 1995), because they seem useful to describe this period when Martinican mulattos are organizing themselves as a social class and taking the upper hand in colonial territory (civil service, political offices). Colonial Martinican official history is in fact that of the colonial structures of the territory (State); as a result, those left aside, the black majority, will constitute the Nation whose history is yet to be written.

Nevertheless, the two novelists do not simply seek a reversal of history ("righting" history) and to develop a "counter-History" (unique and with a capital H). On the contrary, they proclaim the uselessness of such an enterprise. What they try to do is to recapture these stories, which – because of their very diversity and scattered nature (referring to the notion of "rhizome" developed by Glissant in *Poétique de la relation*) – are the only ones that help the reader to understand the ordinary people of Martinique. In this attempt they are following Glissant, as the latter indicates in *Le Discours antillais* the desultory or illusory nature of any attempt at a chronological analysis of the Caribbean.[1]

> *Une fois ce tableau chronologique dressé, complété, tout reste à débrouiller de l'histoire martiniquaise.*
>
> *Tout reste à découvrir de l'histoire antillaise de la Martinique.* (Glissant 1981, 27)

Glissant, whose approach to history is based on the reconstitution of the past from a "prophetic vision" (see, for example, the preface to Glissant 1961), assigns to Caribbean writers the duty of "digging deep" into their memory in order to retrieve the signs of the ordinary world (1989, 64). This is the task Chamoiseau sets out to achieve in many novels, among them the widely acclaimed *Texaco*: "Je ne vais pas te refaire l'Histoire, mais le vieux nègre de la Doum révèle, dessous l'Histoire, des histoires dont aucun livre ne parle, et qui pour nous comprendre sont les plus essentiels" (Chamoiseau 1992, 45).

Though these writers want to pass on the history of their people (as a nation), they do not simply want to become their spokesmen, as they would run the risk of covering the voice of the disenfranchised with their own. For this reason Chamoiseau introduces himself in his novels as "le marqueur de paroles" ("the transcriber of words"). From this humble position, he sets out to capture the spoken words of the excluded, in the net of the "Written". We have to read the epigraph of *Texaco* in this light:

ÉPÎTRE DE TI-CIRIQUE AU MARQUEUR DE PAROLES HONTEUX: «A écrire, l'on m'eût vu le crayon noble, pointant moult élégantes, de dignes messieurs, l'olympe du sentiment; l'on m'eût vu *Universel,* élevé à l'oxygène des horizons, exaltant un français plus français que celui des Français, les profondeurs du pourquoi de l'homme, de la mort, de l'amour et de Dieu; mais nullement comme tu le fais, encossé dans les nègreries de ta Créolité, ou dans le fibrociment décrépi des murs de Texaco. Oiseau de Cham, excuse-moi, mais tu manques d'Humanisme – et surtout de grandeur.»

RÉPONSE DU LAMENTABLE: *Cher maître, la littérature au lieu vivant est un à-prendre vivant . . . .* (Chamoiseau 1992, 19)

In such an approach, the author is represented in his text as an investigator, but not necessarily as an omniscient narrator. In many cases he is just a witness, and in some cases he participates in a minor way in the action (see, for example, *Solibo magnifique, Chronique des sept misères, Eau de café*). What creates the difference between the *Créolité* writers and Glissant (in *La Lézarde,* written in 1956) or the French novelists of the beginning of the nineteenth century? Glissant's "Je" in *La Lézarde* was incidental, acknowledging that he witnessed the hopes raised by departmentalization. Concerning the device of first-person narration, the difference made by the writers of the *Créolité* movement comes from the fact that they use their presence in the text in order to reject the part of "Deus ex machina." They insist on their need to be humble, and even more on their precarious position in the community. They have to make themselves accepted by the community whose experience they intend to write about, and at the same time they are reminded every now and then that they are "tolerated" for the time being. The reader is also constantly reminded of the writer's presence (Chamoiseau/Solibo in *Solibo magnifique,* Confiant/Julien Thémistocle in *Eau de café*):

> Je l'avais connu [Solibo] durant mes fréquentations du marché en vue d'un travail sur la vie des djobeurs. A force de patience, j'avais fait admettre mes cahiers, mes crayons, mon petit magnétophone à piles qui ne fonctionnait jamais, mon appétence malsaine pour les paroles, toutes les paroles, même les plus inutiles. Pour me dissimuler, je rendais quelques menus services de-ci de-là. . . . Tout le marché me connaissait . . . si bien que les conversations ne s'éteignaient plus sur mon passage et que nul ne me posait plus en guise de bonjour: Alors Ti-Cham, écrire ça sert à quoi? . . . Prétendu ethnographe, je vivais sans plus de distance l'engourdissement des heures chaudes en m'affalant dans les brouettes comme les djobeurs. . . (Chamoiseau [1988] 1991, 43–44)

As a result, they modify the status of the character in their novels. Once more, we must underline the extent of these writers' debt to Glissant. With the objective of retrieving the collective memory of the Martinican people, Glissant in *La Case du commandeur* (1981) had experimented with the narrative voice, using the first-person plural "we" (see Webb 1992, 123). Such an experiment leads to a redefinition of the notion of character very similar to the death of the character in the French New Novel, since a central character is replaced by a group.

However (and this is a characteristic feature of Glissant's writing), he does not get rid of the central character as such: he simply changes its functions and uses it as a medium. For instance, in *La Case du commandeur,* Mycéa, the protagonist, is the medium that enables one to retrace the steps back to history and to collect the stories of the people. Similarly, Confiant and Chamoiseau emphasize the group (in *Texaco,* the community). To achieve this goal, they keep shifting the focus from one character to another. Each character introduces other ones, broadening the scope of the story. The result is a network through which the novelist is able to encompass the whole of Martinican society, with its contradictions and paradoxes (see, for example, *Le Nègre et l'Amiral,* 1988).

In addition, this quest for collective memory associated with the refusal to impose their personal interpretation on the events has some consequences in the use of language. These novelists set themselves the task of conveying the voice of Martinican people in their texts. They are successful in doing so by using the *parlure* (speech) of the poor urban dwellers and introducing the Creole language into their novels:

> Solibo Magnifique me disait: « . . . Oiseau de Cham, tu écris. Bon. Moi, Solibo, je parle. Tu vois la distance? Dans ton livre sur Manman Dlo, tu veux capturer la parole à l'écriture, je vois le rythme que tu veux donner, comment tu veux serrer les mots pour qu'ils sonnent à la langue. Tu me dis: Est-ce que j'ai raison, Papa? Moi, je dis: On n'écrit jamais la parole, mais des mots, tu aurais dû parler. Ecrire, c'est comme sortir le lambi de la mer pour dire: voici le lambi! La parole répond: où est la mer? Mais l'essentiel n'est pas là. Je pars, mais toi tu restes. Je parlais, mais toi tu écris en annonçant que tu viens de la parole. Tu me donnes la main par-dessus la distance. C'est bien, mais tu touches la distance . . . » (Chamoiseau [1988] 1991, 52–53)

It is not possible to embark on a detailed linguistic analysis of Chamoiseau and Confiant in this article (for such an analysis, see N'Zengou-Tayo 1996). The "authenticity" of their Creole has been discussed elswhere (see Desouza 1995; Perret 1995). Even if it is not exactly the one spoken in the streets of Fort-de-France, even if some of their words and expressions are totally made up, their morphological structure and their syntactic occurrences enable their "recognition" and acceptance as Creole,[2] for as they say in Haiti, "Kreyòl pale kreyòl konprann" ("Creole when spoken is understood"). One can question the presence of translations juxtaposed with Creole sentences or expressions in *Texaco;* this choice could be explained by the publisher's marketing requirements and their target audience (metropolitan French). Nevertheless, the juxtaposition of French and Creole carries an aesthetic and stylistic value, since having the translations as endnotes or footnotes would be easy and is practised by many writers (Haitian novelists, Condé, Dracius-Pinalie, and others; see Desouza 1995). Therefore, we must read their usage as a political statement: they proclaim Martinican diglossia in order better to claim their Creole language, as indicated in *Eloge de la créolité:* "La littérature créole d'expression française aura donc pour tâche urgente d'investir et de réhabiliter l'esthétique de notre langage. . . . Ce ne sera pas forcément du français créolisé ou réinventé, du créole francisé ou réinventé, mais notre parole retrouvée et finalement décidée (Bernabé, Chamoiseau and Confiant 1993, 46–47). It is not certain that this goal has been achieved yet, or even that it is possible to achieve. Nevertheless, it could be understood as an effort to make the "true" voice of Martinicans heard.[3] Through this linguistic choice we can see an attempt at bringing Martinicans an awareness of their own voice, as it will be the only way for them to become the "subjects" of their history.

Is the "prophetic vision of the past" that Glissant (1961) sought to achieve attained by these writers in their quest for collective memory? It does not seem so because the explosion of History into stories, as well as the breaking of chronological linearity, makes impossible any coherent version or logical order of the story and as a result makes a return to History impossible, even with a revisionist approach. Chamoiseau's and Confiant's fictions illustrate the attempt identified by Marc Ferro ([1981] 1995) at creating a "contre-histoire" or counter-history as they proceed to reconstitute the daily life and lore of ordinary Martinicans. This approach makes it impossible to write a unique and universal version of history. The notion of historical truth is also undermined, as they offer various versions of the past. As a result a new historical approach based on the social sciences (Ferro [1981] 1995) becomes absolutely necessary, one that needs to confront institutional history with oral and popular history. By gathering information on the everyday life of ordinary people through oral testimony, Chamoiseau and Confiant offer this non-institutional version of history.

At this point, however, the two writers diverge. While Chamoiseau tries to cover all aspects of Martinican society, Confiant prefers the lumpenproletariat of Fort-de-France and gives a negative description of the Martinican middle class in his stories. Only outcasts of this petit-bourgeois group are positively represented; the others remain in the background as if irremediably stained by the fact that they had shared colonial power (civil service and local institutions).

Nevertheless, by choosing to rewrite history through fiction, Chamoiseau and Confiant place their work deliberately on the fringe of academic historical discourse, with an ambiguous result. On the one hand, they contribute to giving back to the Martinican people their place in history according to the three capacities identified by Michel-Rolph Trouillot (1995): as "agents", as "actors" and as "subjects" of history.[4] On the other hand, they avoid the confrontation between oral history and official history. By refusing to identify "the necessary boundary between what happened and that which is said to have happened" (13), they refuse to address the issue of "historical credibility" (14) which is important for accessing "historicity" (23). This refusal undermines the historical project announced in *Eloge de la créolité*. In Confiant's novels, for instance, an objective analysis of the Martinican past obviously does not counterbalance his challenge of official history. Daniel-Henri Pageaux (1996) comments on these shortcomings and concludes that there is a discrepancy between the pugnacity of the pamphleteer and the weaknesses of historical and political analysis in the novels. Ironically, these very weaknesses may be the reason for their impact on the Martinican psyche and their literary success, because, as demonstrated by Trouillot, "the more important an issue for specific segments of civil society, the more subdued the interpretations of the facts offered by most professional historians" (1995, 21), and as a result, academic historical discourse seems "bland or irrelevant . . . to those to whom it matter[s] most [and they look] for historical interpretations on the fringes of academia when not altogether outside it" (21).

In addition, it is worth noting the systematic and explicit way in which Chamoiseau and Confiant present their fiction. Like a puppet master who takes his audience backstage, these writers invite the reader to witness the various stages of the writing process. The authors appear on stage, expressing their doubts and showing their rough work. In so doing, these writers play on postmodernism by offering versions of history to be read at a second level of understanding. Paradoxically, they end up practising a constructivist approach to history in which "the historical narrative [is viewed] as one fiction among others" (Trouillot 1995, 6). To this critic, such an approach heads dangerously toward the very opposite of the intentions originally professed in *Eloge de la créolité*, as "nowhere is history infinitely susceptible to invention" (Trouillot 1995, 8).

Notes

1. Glissant supports his analysis with a reference to Baugh: "History is irrelevant in the Caribbean" (Baugh 1977, 7).
2. A problem arises when Martinicans themselves have difficulties understanding these creolized texts. It might be a sign that the language is losing ground among educated middle-class Martinicans (see Perret 1995).
3. These comments are inspired by Trouillot's analysis of historical narrative. Taking the example of a meaningful description of a strike, he argues that "beyond dealing with the workers as actors, a competent narrative of a strike needs to claim access to the workers as purposeful subjects aware of their own voices. It needs their voice(s) in the first person or, at least, it needs to paraphrase that first person" (Trouillot 1995, 24).
4. "History as a social process involves people in three distinct capacities: 1) as *agents,* or occupants of structural position; 2) as *actors* in constant interface with a context; 3) as *subjects,* that is, as voices aware of their vocality" (Trouillot 1995, 23).

References

Baugh, Edward. 1977. "The West Indian Writer and His Quarrel with History". *Tapia* (20 February): 6–7; (27 February): 6–7, 11.

Bernabé, Jean, Patrick Chamoiseau and Raphaël Confiant. 1993. *Eloge de la créolité. In Praise of Creoleness.* Translated by Mohamed Taleb-Khyar. Paris: Gallimard.

Césaire, Aimé. [1939] 1971. *Cahier d'un retour au pays natal.* Bilingual ed., translated by Emile Snyder. Paris: Présence Africaine.

———. [1963] 1970. *La Tragédie du roi Christophe.* Paris: Présence Africaine.

Chamoiseau, Patrick. [1986] 1988. *Chronique des sept misères.* Folio 1965. Paris: Gallimard.

———. [1988] 1991. *Solibo magnifique.* (Folio 2277). Paris: Gallimard.

———. 1992. *Texaco.* Paris: Gallimard.

Condé, Maryse. 1974. "Négritude césairienne, Négritude senghorienne". *Revue de littérature comparée* 48, no. 3–4: 409–19.

———. 1976. *Heremakhonon.* Paris: UGE.

Confiant, Raphaël. [1988] 1993. *Le Nègre et l'Amiral.* Livre de poche 9643. Paris: Librairie Générale Française.

———. [1991] 1993. *Eau de café.* Livre de poche 9642. Paris: Librairie Générale Française.

Desouza, Pascale. 1995. "Inscription du créole dans les textes francophones: de la citation à la créolisation". In *Penser la créolité,* edited by Maryse Condé and Madeleine Cottenet-Hage, 173–90. Paris: Karthala.

Ferro, Marc. [1981] 1995. "Tentation et peur de l'histoire". *Manière de voir,* no. 26, "Leçons d'histoire", *Le Monde Diplomatique* special issue (May): 10–13.

Glissant, Edouard. 1958. *La Lézarde*. Paris: Seuil.

―――. 1961. Preface. *Monsieur Toussaint*. Paris: Seuil

―――. 1981a. *La case du commandeur*. Paris: Seuil.

―――. 1981b. *Le Discours antillais*. Paris: Seuil.

―――. 1989. *Caribbean Discourse*. Translation by J. Michael Dash. Charlottesville: University of Virginia Press.

―――. 1990. *Poétique de la relation*. Paris: Gallimard.

N'Zengou-Tayo, Marie-José. 1996. "Littérature et diglossie: créer une langue métisse ou la «chamoisification» du français dans *Texaco* de Patrick Chamoiseau". *TTR (Traduction, terminologie, rédaction)* 9, no. 1: 155–76.

Pageaux, Daniel-Henri. 1996. "Raphaël Confiant ou la traversée paradoxale d'une décennie". In *Portulan*, no. 1 (February 1996): 35–58.

Perret, Delphine. 1995. "Lire Chamoiseau". In *Penser la créolité*, edited by Maryse Condé and Madeleine Cottenet-Hage, 153–72. Paris: Karthala.

Schwarz-Bart, Simone. 1979. *Ti Jean L'horizon*. Paris: Seuil.

Trouillot, Michel-Rolph. 1995. *Silencing the Past: Power and the Production of History*. Boston: Beacon.

Webb, Barbara J. 1992. *Myth and History in Caribbean Fiction: Alejo Carpentier, Wilson Harris and Edouard Glissant*. Amherst: University of Massachusetts Press.

10

The Parent-Child Relationship in Gisèle Pineau's Work

Beverley Ormerod Noakes
University of Western Australia

In Guadeloupean literature, the dysfunctional family has often been used to represent, in microcosm, negative aspects of Caribbean society that stem from the psychological damage of past slavery. Simone Schwarz-Bart, for example, in *Pluie et vent sur Télumée Miracle* (1972) and *Ti Jean L'horizon* (1979), uses the theme of orphanhood to suggest the loss of stable kinship patterns among the descendants of slaves, and the motif of paternal deprivation as an underlying factor in a boy's search for the unknown village of his African forbears. In Michèle Lacrosil's first novel, *Sapotille et le serin d'argile* (1960), the bond between a black daughter and her white mother is undermined by stresses that echo the traditional colour discrimination of plantation life. Several of Maryse Condé's novels present a middle-class female protagonist who rejects parental values and engages in an ill-fated liaison with an outsider, a quasi-ancestral figure who seems to offer cultural identification with Africa: Sory in *Heremakhonon* (1976); Manuel in *La Vie scélérate* (1987); Spero in *Les Derniers rois mages* (1992); even Stanley in *Desirada* (1997). Gisèle Pineau, more explicitly concerned with parent-induced trauma and its repercussions on the child's future behaviour patterns, frequently portrays emotionally disturbed families that are also indirect reminders of the socio-economic ravages of slavery. The high incidence of neglect, betrayal, physical cruelty and desertion in her novels links present-day Guadeloupean society with those past centuries when the plantocracy's power over slaves was maintained through physical intimidation, financial deprivation and the undermining of emotional stability.

Pineau's interest in the parent-child relationship is apparent throughout a diverse oeuvre which ranges in genre from magical realism to autobiographical reminiscence, from an unflinching depiction of Caribbean ghetto life to a finely shaded study of late twentieth-century expatriates in France and the United States. *L'Exil selon Julia* (1996), described as a *récit,* is a tribute to her grandmother, celebrating an ideal rapport with a mother-figure whose emotional and moral influence shapes the narrator's sense of Caribbean identity. But this privileged affinity lies outside the sphere of Pineau's entirely fictional works, many of which show a childhood or adolescent crisis arising from the rupture of a formerly precious family tie. In some instances a new, quasi-parental relationship successfully replaces the one destroyed. However, while the role of a foster parent may be warmly positive, it may also be viciously negative. In extreme cases, the breakdown of the parental contract creates a socially ill-adapted character whose manner of relating to others is warped and self-destructive.

La Grande Drive des esprits (1993), Pineau's first full-length novel, is conceived in line with the precepts of *Créolité,* with characters drawn from a traditional peasant milieu who are keenly aware of the influence of the spirit world. Pineau exploits the lightly satirical tone of magical realism, associating the supernatural with exaggerated sexual feats while maintaining a note of scepticism through the device of a detached, town-bred outsider as narrator. Yet the supernatural also underscores some of the most serious aspects of the book, and dominates the fate of Léonce and Célestina, the father and daughter at the centre of the narrative. Through their responses to life, the novel highlights parental selfishness and inconsistency, the emotional dependency of childhood and the ways in which an individual's world view can be conditioned and restricted by a fatalistic belief in the power of the spirits.

A major function of the supernatural in the narrative is to call attention to the rejection of paternal responsibility. While the conditions of slavery made it impossible for most slaves to elect fidelity to a partner, a century and a half after abolition the restoration of free choice has made little impact on the phenomenon of infidelity in the Caribbean. In Guadeloupe, the proportion of single or deserted mothers is high within disadvantaged sections of the population (Gautier 1994, 162–66). The topic of male promiscuity has been treated by Pineau in a tragic vein in her short story "Les Enchaînés", in which a fifteen-year-old girl, readily seduced by a good-looking older boy who then abandons her, becomes an embittered single mother. After ten years of financial hardship she receives a letter from her former lover, offering a lame excuse for his desertion: he was "trop jeune" to make this commitment (Pineau 1998b, 134). In *La Grande Drive des esprits,* male sexuality appears in a lighter, more farcical context: a magic curse explains the compulsive infidelity of Léonce's father Sosthène – though the terms of the curse, "Tu seras l'esclave de ton grand long coco" (Pineau 1993, 168), also recall the condition of the slave as compulsory stud for the plantation. The lullaby sung by one of Sosthène's discarded mistresses sums up the situation of many Caribbean women without financial resources who must bear the brunt of family responsibilities:

> Pitit dodo
> Papa pa la
> Sé manman tou sèl
> Ki dan lanmizè
> (76)

In the narrative, these women take on a symbolic importance. Their deprivation is raised to the level of Caribbean society's past afflictions: they become a reminder of the helpless grief of slave mothers unable to protect their own offspring. These wounds deep in the folk psyche are also suggested by the desolation of Léonce's young wife Myrtha after a miscarriage, as she experiences "le désarmement de trois siècles de douleur . . . l'enfantement, l'attachement et l'enterrement" (105).

Léonce himself is shown not as a faithless man, but as a self-centred one who disregards the emotional claims of Myrtha (for whose miscarriage he is inadvertently responsible), and who lets his egoistic preoccupations ruin his relationship with his children. Like his father, he is the victim of supernatural forces. Although he is born with a club foot because of a jealous woman's spell, he also inherits the magic powers of his grandmother Octavie, and prospers on his hillside farm thanks to her goodwill. But angry and humiliated at being declared medically unfit to join the wartime resistance movement, he goes on a drunken binge and breaks the terms of his contract with Octavie's spirit. This rift with a ghostly matriarch has its ludicrous side, but it results in concrete disaster for Léonce. His prosperity disappears, he sinks into self-pity and his family falls apart.

For twelve years he totally withdraws from his four children. Their corresponding disturbance is variously expressed: mental delusions, physical violence, prostitution.

His eldest child, Célestina, appears to suffer the mildest disability, but her compulsive stammering condemns her to painful years of solitude since despite her beauty, no man has the patience to try to decipher her garbled words. Finally, it is the world of magic that resolves her dilemma: a stranger, promised to her in a dream, appears and lures her to a mysterious death by fire. Despite its comic overtones, this is also a tale of the vulnerability of childhood. Célestina relates her handicap directly to the loss of Léonce's love: "Et Papa Léonce qui s'était levé un beau matin sans plus la voir, sans plus l'entendre, sans plus l'aimer. Elle en avait perdu le fil des paroles" (Pineau 1993, 156). His defection at a crucial stage of her development inflicts spiritual damage that segregates her from her peer group. At the age of nine, feeling herself diminished, "transparente" (140), her sense of self-worth annihilated by Léonce's indifference, she responds to his emotional desertion by becoming fixated on his image. As she grows into adult life, the mysterious lover predicted in the dream becomes clearly recognizable in her imagination: handsome, loving and considerate, he is the exact replica of the father who abandoned her. This stranger who will cure her stammering but bring about her ruin has power over her because he promises not only the delights of passion, but also long-awaited consolation for the loss of paternal love.

It is interesting to contrast these parent-inflicted wounds with the different type of childhood susceptibility that preoccupies Pineau in her next book, *L'Exil selon Julia*. Here suffering arises from a social situation: that of the immigrant schoolgirl in France, subject to racial insults on the street and even in the classroom. Her salvation comes from within her family, as her grandmother, with a secure sense of Caribbean identity, inculcates in the child a firm pride in her racial and cultural origins. In this semi-autobiographical narrative, Man Ya, both grandmother and supplementary mother, deflects the external threat and enables the transition from vulnerability to self-confidence. Man Ya's stories of Guadeloupe are threaded through with references to the magic that also governs the events of *La Grande Drive des esprits,* but here that magic is presented not as destructive but simply as a dimension of Caribbean life – comparable to the knowledge of slavery, another hitherto denied part of the child narrator's heritage. In tracing the gradual development of a child's passionate attachment to a homeland which is spiritually longed for but not physically known, *L'Exil selon Julia* depicts the parent-child relationship in its most positive light, as a source of healing and wisdom.

L'Espérance-macadam (1995) gives a much more sombre account of that relationship, in which the fragility and ambiguity of family ties are illustrated among the marginalized inhabitants of a Caribbean ghetto, prey to physical danger and mental turmoil. The narrative's hidden structure, revealing itself only through the involuntary memories of the main protagonists, relates to the Cain-like figure of a single male ancestor, Ti-Cyclone, or "La Bête", who hides beneath a hat the stump of an amputated ear, the mark of his first sin. In fleeting appearances he is shown as the brutal rapist of his eight-year-old daughter, then as the "vieux macaque dessous son chapeau de cirque" who abandoned the son of his old age to the care of a cruel foster mother (Pineau 1995, 254). The raped child is Eliette, the principal narrator; the abandoned son is Rosan, Eliette's next-door neighbour and, unknown to her, her half-brother. As in a classical tragedy, the action is prepared in advance and the reader enters the drama at its point of explosion, when Rosan, who for years has blindly sought compensation for his childhood misery by sexually abusing his young daughter, has been denounced to the police for incest. The notion of original sin seems to loom over the terrible events, yet Ti-Cyclone's children, while responsible for their moral choices, are also clearly shown as the victims of paternal wrongdoing.

The legacy of Ti-Cyclone's actions is relentlessly demonstrated. Eliette suffers diminished maternal support, since her mother remains permanently disturbed after the trauma of stumbling upon the scene of rape. She has managed, however, to battle through a hurricane carrying her child in order to find a healer, who treats the girl's injuries and ensures that she will not remember what has happened. But Eliette is left sterile, and her own trauma is expressed by years of inability to speak. The subsequent good fortune of a loving stepfather helps her towards an apparently normal adult life. At the age of sixty, twice widowed, she lives alone in the humble district of Savane, a zone of increasing violence. With no conscious memory of her father's assault, she is nevertheless doubly crippled, by her barrenness and by her inability to form any close emotional relationship. Encased in an unnatural detachment, giving and receiving no warmth or affection, she avoids all involvement with her neighbours and turns a blind eye to the altercations of Savane, even when her intervention might have prevented physical harm.

An important aspect of the narrative is Eliette's gradual recovery of the memory of rape and, with it, her recapturing of the face of her father, the unknown assailant who in her flashes of recollection has appeared as "La Bête": the terrifying Beast identified in her child's imagination with the beam that was supposed to have injured her during the hurricane of 1928. As her memories become more precise, the Beast is identified with the hurricane itself, always referred to by her deranged mother as "Le Passage de La Bête". Wielding a cutlass, the figure of the rapist becomes the cyclone itself preparing to rip apart the earth as the child's body was torn open. Thus "La Bête" is fused with Ti-Cyclone: "C'est ainsi qu'apparut le visage de La Bête, bossuant d'abord la poutre de bois mol, et puis s'en détachant. . . . Tisons de désir, pépites de pacotille, ses yeux, tout lézardés aux remous de son âme, fouillaient déjà Eliette, la violentaient en songe" (Pineau 1995, 296). As the pattern is repeated with Rosan and his daughter Angela, allied images recur of phallic cutting weapons and plundering snakes, the "Bête" transmuted into a *bête longue*, the Creole equivalent of "serpent". Angela's suffering is represented as a long ordeal by fire. Following on these metaphorical evocations of sexual violence and betrayal, a second hurricane symbolically looms, not only a destroyer but a bringer of apocalyptic floods to erase the scenes of sin and offer redemption to Ti-Cyclone's descendants.

Pineau's narrative implies the repetition of dysfunctional patterns within successive generations of a disadvantaged society. Studies of sexually abusive fathers have suggested that many are emotionally dependent and immature, with a poor sense of their own worth, and that they themselves may have suffered abuse or abandonment in childhood (Porter 1984, 11–12, 20). Nothing is revealed to the reader about the background of Eliette's father, but her half-brother's early history corresponds to this profile of the future abuser. Rosan has grown up with the emotional pain of the unwanted child. His elderly father and his young mother have both abdicated responsibility for him, and he hates them. The grandmother who fosters him dislikes and physically abuses him, beating him with thorny sticks. His poor self-esteem, brooding resentment of his past and restless belief that happiness must lie elsewhere contribute to his first attempt at escape: he runs away with his sympathetic young neighbour, Rosette, and eventually establishes her and their three children in Savane, far from both their families. But the unresolved grief and anger of his childhood manifest themselves first in verbal aggression towards his wife and then in an obsessive conviction that the happiness which has always evaded him can be attained through union with his daughter. The ten-year-old Angela is his "angel", his "deliverance". He is irresistibly drawn by her loving, innocent gaiety, that of a child who has never known abuse. Although at one level he is conscious of harming her, his overriding preoccupation is with his own fierce need to lose himself in her body, that honeyed paradise that promises refuge from the demons of his childhood. And so his actions unconsciously reproduce those of his father towards his unknown half-sister, Eliette. Ti-Cyclone's motives, unlike Rosan's, are never examined, but the parallel between the two fathers is stressed, from the first apparently innocent game of tossing a little girl into the air and catching her plump, tender body to the escalation into violence: "Combien de fois s'était-il jeté pis qu'un cyclone sur le corps d'Angela. Bête sauvage!" (Pineau 1995, 252).

Through the figure of Rosette, Pineau studies the factors that can lead to a mother's neglect. Rosette seems to be as detached as Eliette from those surrounding her, but her psychological problems impact detrimentally upon her children. Cut off from her own family, as Rosan withdraws his love she looks for comfort to idealized parent-figures from the world beyond Savane: the woman leader of a group of Rasta fringe-dwellers, the Emperor Haile Selassie as gloriously depicted astride his white horse. She shuts out awareness of Rosan's emotional disintegration by losing herself in fantasies of the Rastas' African paradise and in the redemption songs of her hero, Bob Marley. This self-absorption also enables her to ignore the changes in Angela's behaviour, particularly the girl's morose taciturnity (a textual echo of Eliette's years of muteness after she is raped). "Rosette avait rien vu, rien entendu . . . dans l'extase de son paradis, occupée à suspendre des étoiles au ciel" (Pineau 1995, 247): this world of illusion is shattered only when Angela finally goes to the police. Then, rejecting any notion of personal responsibility, Rosette perceives her daughter as the cause of the family's ruin, beats her and casts her out. Her refusal of the truth is also a denial of compassion; yet beneath her aggression, she is as traumatized as Eliette's mother once was by the fact of incest. In horror, she gives herself up to the destructive onslaught of the cyclone, her fate a metaphorical parallel of that of Eliette and Angela, victims of the assaults of Ti-Cyclone and his son.

Angela, Ti-Cyclone's granddaughter, occupies less space in the narrative than Eliette, but the same patterns may be seen to affect both niece and aunt. Both are attacked by a trusted father; both lose their mothers, physically or mentally, through the fact of incest and the collapse of their family environment; both take refuge in silence rather than confront an unacceptable reality. Angela's silence reflects her impossible situation, caught between dread of her mother's displeasure and terror of her father, who seems to the child to be metamorphosed into a demon at nightfall. She eventually speaks out only through her greater fear that Rosan will turn his attentions to her younger sister. Her strongest wish is for the hurricane to kill her father and restore her to the protection of her mother's womb. But Eden cannot be recovered: Angela must live with the memory of her father's sin and her mother's repudiation. Yet out of tragedy comes a message of change and redress. In Eliette, Angela finds a foster mother uniquely prepared to understand her, and in equal need of redemption. Eliette's adoption of Angela signals the healing of old betrayals and release from a long reluctance to offer love. Of this much Eliette herself, as principal narrator, conveys her awareness. At a different level of the narrative, glimpsed through minor figures whose knowledge of the whole is fragmentary, the blood relationship between Angela and her aunt brings oblique fulfilment of a fortune-teller's prediction to Eliette that she, who knew herself to be barren, would one day have a daughter.

Although Eliette's maternal bonding with Angela reflects the patterns of hope and emotional consolation that characterize Pineau's denouements, the novel as a whole does not suggest the universality of happy endings. There is indeed something magical about the coincidence of Rosan's setting up house next door to Eliette, a hint of that drifting of the spirits which directed the events of *La Grande Drive des esprits*. But outside this nucleus of betrayal, suffering and ultimate reparation, the life of the ghetto continues, and for most of its inhabitants there is no salvation. Despite their nominal freedom, they are trapped in the same confines of poverty, social exclusion, fruitless labour, vain aspirations, bitterness and grief as were once imposed upon their ancestors.

This wider context of despair is reflected in the story of Glawdys, which forms a counterpoint to that of Angela. Glawdys is the foundling Eliette might once have adopted; her fate illustrates not only the long inhibition of Eliette's maternal impulses, but the general lack of compassion in Savane. Glawdys was an infant casually abandoned in an empty hut by her simple-minded mother. Her father might have been any one of seven butchers who, on Friday afternoons after work, used collectively to exploit Hermancia's goodwill and limited intelligence. At first, Glawdys seems to represent the potential for good in Savane. Despite their habitual mistrust, the ghetto dwellers welcome this pretty, smiling *chabine* baby whose green eyes offer hope. But no one intervenes when Glawdys is kept tied up on a rope for years by an incompetent foster mother, and the child's initial vivacity turns into savage dislike. Eliette, who yearned to take her in but was afraid of committing herself, observes in distress that Glawdys has lost the colours of hope, her bright hair and glances fading to a dull grey.

Eventually placed in an institution, the girl returns years later to Savane with her own fatherless baby. Again Eliette is divided between the impulse to succour this daughter-figure and her own dread of emotional commitment. The rest of Savane, less tender-hearted, is alienated by Glawdys's sullen vending of rotten chochos and ignores her underlying desperation. Penniless, she reverts to the only type of maternal behaviour she herself has experienced: cruelty and rejection. The bloody carcasses that framed her conception in an abattoir are horrifically recalled when she dashes out the brains of her baby against the rocks in a gully. Rosette, crazed by her own disasters, links this deed with the practice among early slave mothers of killing their infants so that they would be spared a life of servitude in the Rastas' Babylon. But the thrust of the narrative points to more immediate causes: a cruel foster mother, an impersonal institution, an unfriendly or indifferent community. When Angela is thrown out by her mother and her shadowy figure appears in the dark of the next-door yard, it is the figure of Glawdys that Eliette sees, the memory of Glawdys's accusing eyes that shames Eliette into overcoming her fear of involvement: "Alors, une voix que je ne connaissais pas sortit de mes entrailles pour crier Angela, qui s'en allait seule dans les bruits de la nuit" (Pineau 1995, 106). And so the tale of Glawdys plays its mysterious part among the strands that draw Eliette towards adult emotional commitment. Out of this narrative of maternal weakness and flawed paternal love, joy emerges as the intrinsic reward of parental responsibility.

In Pineau's most recent novel at the time of writing, *L'Ame prêtée aux oiseaux* (1998), parental cruelty and violence are replaced by desertion or deceit, physical harm by psychological damage. Moving away from the raw emotions and menacing atmosphere of the ghetto, the author explores the Caribbean need to escape from poverty and class oppression, and the spirit of adventure which spurred many throughout the twentieth century to seek their fortune abroad – in the wider West Indian region, in France and in North America. Some of her protagonists seize opportunities offered by wartime upheaval, or later by the possession of French citizenship, to join the voluntary Caribbean diaspora. In counterpoint, others accept the restrictions of plantation life or, as in *La Grande Drive des esprits,* are caught in the meshes of an ancient and deadly magic. The actions of all are traced back to formative early experiences which ultimately hold them within traditional ways or impel them to flee.

Although the novel's earliest events take place in the years before World War II, the pivotal character, Henry, initially seems a throwback to a more distant era. Linking past with present, Third World with First, he must negotiate a transition from the servility of plantation work to the contemporary track of emigration and financial advancement. The circumstances of his birth and upbringing echo the old slave days, as he is the product of a liaison between a white plantation owner and a servant girl. Slavery is long over in the English-speaking Caribbean where Henry grows up, but his parents' public relationship replicates the historical pattern of white autocracy and black subservience. Their private, passionate attachment excludes Henry and disregards his interests: his father never acknowledges or helps him, and his mother accepts this situation without protest. The boy is hostile towards his master, precociously aware of the exploitation of estate labourers and resentful of his mother's long hours in charge of the kitchen. Having been raised in the belief that he is the son of a dead groom, when the adolescent Henry learns the truth he repudiates both his parents, despising his mother for her humility and deceit. Shedding his old identity, he runs away to neighbouring Guadeloupe and later forges an independent life outside the Caribbean.

In tracing Henry's career, Pineau indulges her love of surprising the reader and plays with unexpected shifts of time and perspective. At various moments, he appears as a defiant boy, symbolically releasing rare birds from his employer's aviary; as a carefree soldier in Paris after the Liberation; as the affectionate lover of a French girl, Lila, who conceives his child but rejects it because of its colour; as a mature man who suspends judgement on Lila, takes his baby to the United States and brings it up himself. Henry's stability defies conventional wisdom, which predicts that a child deserted by its father and betrayed by its mother must necessarily go to the bad. He is portrayed not only as a survivor, but also as a warmhearted and understanding adult who is ultimately able to forgive both his mother and the fearful, defiant Lila. He refutes the Caribbean stereotype of paternal irresponsibility, effacing his own unhappy childhood experiences through his loving and communicative rapport with his son. He even turns to positive use his once-resented genetic inheritance, combining emotional fidelity and culinary talent, flourishing both as a restaurant owner and as a steadfast husband and father. The total assimilation of his son by Lila within his later

American family affirms the rebuttal of dysfunctional models that characterizes Henry's adult life.

The narrative represents maternity in conflicting ways. Henry's mother is caught in an irresistible passion that overrides the imperatives of class and colour, as it also ignores the claims of her son. Henry's mistress Lila enjoys his money but is unwilling to take responsibility for their child, who grows up devoted to Henry's American wife, the image of the good foster mother. Lila flirts with Caribbean commitments, but selfless maternity is not in her nature and she forms no genuine bond either with her real son or with his surrogate, Marcello, the illegitimate child of her Guadeloupean tenant Sybille. While the ageing Lila pampers Marcello as a substitute for her unacknowledged son, Sybille has a differently flawed relationship with the boy, seeing him almost as a reincarnation of her dead brother. In a replication of Henry's childhood situation, Sybille keeps Marcello ignorant of his father's identity. But her deception is not imposed by plantation custom; rather, it stems from unresolved anger over past unhappiness in the Caribbean, as much to do with her own parents' defection as with her faithless lover. As selfishly as Lila, she conspires to keep Marcello within the claustrophobic territory of their apartment in Paris, captive like the birds in Henry's father's aviary. But the boy learns accidentally who his father is, and breaks free of his twin mother-figures to seek out his birthright in Guadeloupe. His flight from France, like Henry's adolescent escape from the Caribbean, temporarily estranges him from his mother, but it also enables him to establish a cultural identity with which he is more at ease, and finally to develop a relationship with his father.

The portrait of the adult Sybille is almost subservient, in this narrative, to that of the child she was in the Caribbean. Lengthy flashbacks show her as the traumatized survivor of mysterious and sinister events. Her father, Robert, was enticed to his death by Clothilde, a girl with supernatural powers, an interpreter of dreams and maker of compelling perfumes. At one level, Clothilde is a witch, like her great-aunt who paid for her magic arts by never knowing human love; at another level, she is an ordinary girl whose gift for dream interpretation was lucrative to her family until she abandoned them for a life of casual prostitution in Basse-Terre, while waiting for the appearance of Robert, the lover predicted in her own dream. Clothilde's shadow falls over Sybille's life for long years afterwards, and her role and Robert's are obsessively re-enacted by Sybille and her best friend, the precocious Marie, herself a child of incest with a legacy of magic and of warped sexuality. Marie is Sybille's mainstay after her father's death, when her mother bears a stillborn son and loses her mind. After three years of wandering the countryside with the deranged woman, Sybille is left to foster parents and is parted from Marie, while her mother disappears forever.

The brutally unexpected loss of her parents and protectors shapes the course of Sybille's adolescence, which is marked by her insistent need to be loved, the need of an insecure child whose world is precariously held together by the frail strands of treacherous friendships. Like Célestina in *La Grande Drive des esprits,* Sybille unconsciously seeks out a lover who physically recalls her father – and who betrays her. The legacy of insecurity remains with her as she is reunited with Marie, only to discover that her own lover has been seduced by this former childhood ally. Marie is later the malicious agent of Sybille's estrangement from her son Marcello. Unsurprisingly, Sybille's adult life manifests a continuing suspicion of men and an emotional coolness towards other women. Even her maternal love is flawed by the impact of her own childhood trauma, since Marcello is above all a possessively guarded substitute for her stillborn brother, to whose birth she was a horrified witness. In the symbolic terms of the novel's title, she is a woman whose soul is lent to the birds, who does not truly know how to seek or accept love.

This emotional shortcoming is linked, as in the case of Eliette in *L'Espérance-macadam,* to the phenomenon of deeply troubled early family relationships of which the adult is still the psychological prisoner. Yet the narrative does not imply that all adult neurosis is the inevitable consequence of childhood trauma, nor, indeed, that every disturbed parent-child relationship is the fault of the parent. The mysterious, apparently arbitrary nature of some childhood responses to the adult world is suggested by an early episode in the life of Clothilde the witch, later the destroyer of Sybille's father, Robert. Already an established interpreter of dreams, one night she herself dreams that her father has drowned. The next evening, when he gathers his fisherman's nets and promises to bring back a fine catch for the family, she says nothing about her dream. Dislike does not appear to be her motive: she simply withholds her warning, whether through sheer curiosity or through an intoxicating sense of power. Her father does not return from the sea, and guilt over her filial betrayal warps the pattern of her adolescent sexuality. She reinvents his death with men picked up on the docks of Basse-Terre, driving them to a gasping, suffocating mime of drowning and then breathing life back into them: "Sept fois, oui, sept fois, elle avait eu le sentiment de serrer un noyé dans ses bras" (Pineau 1998a, 82). It is Robert's unmistakeable identity as a fisherman that impels her towards him; her death in his arms may be seen as an ultimate expiation. In the bizarre and supernatural case of Clothilde, it is the child who betrays the parent; but the motifs of trust, deception and disaster that are present in this childhood incident, as well as the subsequent obsessive quest for love, are all recognizable elements in Pineau's studies of family conflict and emotional damage.

These narratives all tend to identify major links between childhood experience and adult behaviour, whether the child reproduces undesirable parental models (like Rosan), suffers the consequences of them (like Célestina, Eliette and Sybille), or chooses (like Henry) to create their deliberate contrary. The situations which frame Pineau's characters range from the extremes of rape and madness to more unobtrusive zones of harm: indifference, neglect, rejection. The author does not suggest that parental influences, however powerful, necessarily account for the total psychological development of children. In these novels, other factors, some of them traceable to past slavery, are depicted as contributing factors. These include economic deprivation, racial inequality, ill fortune and the inexplicable domain of magic, whose role here is to shape the fiction of inevitability. Taken as a whole, however, Pineau's narrative world includes the basic premise that severe psychological damage can result from a breakdown in trust between the child and even one defecting parent. She is compassionately concerned with the devising of unexpected, even miraculous recoveries after parental wounding. Her novels ultimately illustrate an ideal type of emotional stability based on the successful establishment of a bond between parent (or benign foster parent) and child, one which enables the child's spiritual growth. This is the bond portrayed between Gisèle and Man Ya, between Eliette and her stepfather, between James-Lee and Henry, and – in embryo – between Angela and Eliette. This harmonious parent-child relationship is presented as an essential factor in the healing of Caribbean society.

References

Condé, Maryse. 1976. *Heremakhonon*. Paris: Union Générale.
———. 1987. *La Vie scélérate*. Paris: Seghers.
———. 1992. *Les Derniers rois mages*. Paris: Mercure de France.
———. 1997. *Desirada*. Paris: Robert Laffont.
Gautier, Arlette. 1994. "Guadeloupéennes et Martiniquaises". In *Les Antilles-Guyane*

au rendez-vous de l'Europe, edited by Richard Burton and Fred Réno, 153–75. Paris: Economica.

Lacrosil, Michèle. 1960. *Sapotille et le serin d'argile.* Paris: Gallimard.

Pineau, Gisèle. 1993. *La Grande Drive des esprits.* Paris: Le Serpent à Plumes.

———. 1995. *L'Espérance-macadam.* Paris: Stock.

———. 1996. *L'Exil selon Julia.* Paris: Stock.

———. 1998a. *L'Ame prêtée aux oiseaux.* Paris: Stock.

———. 1998b. "Les Enchaînés". *Ethiopiques* 61, no. 2: 129–34.

Porter, Ruth, ed. 1984. *Child Sexual Abuse within the Family.* London: Tavistock Publications.

Schwarz-Bart, Simone. 1972. *Pluie et vent sur Télumée Miracle.* Paris: Seuil.

———. 1979. *Ti Jean L'horizon.* Paris: Seuil.

11

"Une si belle enfant ne pouvait pas être maudite"
Polyphony in Maryse Condé's Novel
La Migration des cœurs

Carol Sanders
University of Surrey

From the vantage points provided by *pure* linguistics, it is impossible to detect in belleletristic literature any really essential differences between a monologic and a polyphonic use of discourse. In Dostoevsky's multi-voiced novels, for example, there is significantly less language differentiation, that is, fewer language styles, territorial and social dialects, professional jargons and so forth, than in the work of many writer-monologists. (Bakhtin [1963] 1984, 181–82)

According to Bakhtin, the essence of the polyphonic novel lies in the way in which it gives voice to a "plurality of equally valid consciousnesses" ([1963] 1984, 7). A fundamental feature of the evolution of the novel, he claims, is the move towards the erosion of the single authoritative narrator, a gradual erosion manifesting itself mainly in the ways in which characters' speech is reported and in the angles from which the story is narrated. Bakhtin presumably has in mind here linguistic analysis that does not go beyond the sentence. I shall argue that polyphony can best be analysed across long stretches of text and within the context of the novel as a whole. Indeed, Bakhtin's criticism of stylistics was that it was restricted to questions of detail ("bogged down in stylistic trivia" [(1934–35) 1981, 259]). Other Bakhtinian concepts related to polyphony that it may be appropriate to consider are dialogism, the idea that language is essentially interactive and creative, supposing more than one consciousness; heteroglossia, unofficial discourse which conducts a centrifugal struggle with "official", "monologic" discourse; the "chronotope", "the intrinsic connectedness of temporal and spatial relationships that are artistically expressed in literature" (Bakhtin [1937–38] 1981, 83); and the carnivalesque, allowing expression of centrifugal social forces which oppose the established order. It might be thought that concepts such as heteroglossia might apply particularly to the case of Caribbean literature, since the *Créolité* as defined by some contemporary writers (see, for example, Bernabé, Chamoiseau and Confiant 1989) entails an acceptance, indeed a celebration, of the diverse cultures and languages in the Caribbean and of the creative forces released by their mingling and mixing. As Chamoiseau comments on *créolisation* and *Créolité*, "Nous voulûmes préserver d'originelles puretés mais nous nous vîmes traversés les uns par les autres. L'Autre me change et je le change. . . . Chaque Autre devient une composante de moi tout en restant indistinct. Je deviens ce que je suis dans mon appui ouvert sur l'Autre" (1997, 202). These words chime with Bakhtin's idea that the author's freedom from a "unitary and singular language" opens up the possibility of "saying 'I am me' in someone else's language, and in my own language, 'I am other'" ([1934–35] 1981, 315).

Maryse Condé's *La Migration des cœurs* (1995) begins flamboyantly, with a carnivalesque Epiphany procession through the streets of Havana. The story subsequently spans the breadth of the West Indies, moving to Guadeloupe (its main anchor point), Marie-Galante and Dominica. The overarching "chronotope", that of a Creole society in a state of transition – or more precisely, the West Indies just after the abolition of slavery – contains within it various sub-chronotopes, most notably that of the family saga. Rather like Naga's spirit that flies back from Brazil to Africa in *Ségou* (Condé 1984), the reader is given a panorama of the whole Caribbean, with its shared history which manifests itself slightly differently in the different islands that are visited depending on which European power has colonized it. The story thus functions both at the narrowly local level and on a level which transcends this, giving the reader a disconcerting feeling of expansion and contraction, and of change of focus. On the one hand, this is a vast and undelimited world, open to the ocean over which so many influences have come; on the other, society is so compartmentalized on Cathy and Razyé's small "calebasse d'une île" (Césaire [1939] 1956, 44) that the characters are enclosed in a world every bit as claustrophobic as that of Emily Brontë's *Wuthering Heights* (1847) with its bleak mainland isolation. Families and communities are bound by strong bonds of love and hate, and uncompromising separateness exists alongside such striking examples of integration as Etiennise, an Indian who dances as well as any African ("On aura tout vu! *Mi Zindien ka dansé léwoz!*" [Condé 1995, 176]) and who celebrates a *noce barbare* with the dying, light-skinned Justin-Marie. It is an upside-down world, where black wants to be white but where some whites boast of being "black" ("Je mange comme un nègre; je charroie mon rhum comme un nègre" [182]), and where social and sexual identities are not always clear-cut. Lurking in this world is the threat of inbreeding, and even incest.

The family saga of *La Migration des cœurs* spans four generations in Guadeloupe but focuses particularly on two whose kinship relations are modelled on those of Emily Brontë's novel. Of the mulatto Hubert Gagneur's two orphaned children, the light-skinned brother, Justin, marries a rich *béké* who dies of tuberculosis soon after giving him a son, Justin-Marie. The darker-skinned and strong-willed Cathy marries an adoring and liberal *béké* landowner, Aymeric, but remains passionately linked to Razyé, the abandoned dark child that her father had adopted and preferred over Justin. Razyé, seeking revenge on his return from his self-imposed exile in Cuba, seduces Aymeric's sister, Irmine, and forces her to live in a ménage with the widowed and drunken Justin before moving her and their first child, Razyé/Premier-né, into a poor black area of town. Some months after Razyé's return, a distraught Cathy had died giving birth to a baby girl who is named after her. Aymeric becomes much attached to Justin-Marie, in whom he sees a likeness to his Cathy, and tries to cure him of his tuberculosis by having him cared for first at his own *domaine des Belles-Feuilles* and then by sending him to the care of his Indian servants on his property in a different part of the island. Justin-Marie dies, but not without first infecting Aymeric, whose estates are in difficulty because of the action being taken against landowners by militants such as Razyé. The orphaned younger Cathy takes up a post of schoolmistress in the little island of Marie-Galante, where she meets and falls in love with Premier-né, without at first suspecting whose son he is. The couple is forced to flee to Dominica, where Cathy dies giving birth to Anthuria; Premier-né returns home to live on L'Engoulvent, the crumbling estate where he had spent his childhood, and devotes himself to raising his daughter.

While this brief outline cannot do justice to the complexity of the relationships, licit and illicit, creative and destructive, that characterize the novel, it begins to show how they range from idealistic love (Aymeric's love for Cathy) to violence (Razyé and Irmine), and how they transgress racial and sexual boundaries (Aymeric's devotion to Justin-Marie, the intimacy between Lucinda Lucius and Cathy). In particular, the taboos normally associated with certain kinship relations in the dominant European culture are challenged. Razyé savours double revenge by forcing Irmine to be shared between himself and Justin, adding yet another strand to the unending web of stifling and tangled relationships: in the unlikely event of Premier-né not being Cathy's half-brother, he would still be her cousin. Defying any ideas of generational separateness or of the exclusivity of relationships, Premier-né/Razyé loses his virginity by sleeping with his father's prostitute. Such examples can be seen either as highly illicit or, alternatively, as a travestied version of practices which would not in themselves be unacceptable in another culture. In Condé's *Une saison à Rihata* (1981), for example, the West Indian narrator muses on the irony of being condemned for having an affair with her African husband's brother, when in the event of the husband's death he would have been assigned to look after her – or, according to some traditions, even to have taken her as his wife, as is the case for Nya in *Ségou* when her husband, Dousika, dies.

The family saga chronotope inevitably carries its own temporal span, the measured time of several generations, the human time of birth, love and death. However, in this respect also the novel functions on more than one level, ranging as widely in time as it does in space. Even within this chronotope, the generations point backwards to the ancestors whose voices are clearly heard and forwards to the new generation. At another level, "historical" time is represented in such a way that the past is constantly used as a springboard for the future. Thus, the initial setting of the novel in Cuba is not only a question of providing a pan-Caribbean perspective. Because slavery was abolished in Cuba some forty-two years after it was definitively abolished in Guadeloupe, Razyé's journey to Havana takes him back, as it were, to a society in its immediately post-emancipation days, as well as one in the throes of a civil war. It is not for nothing that we are privy to the governor of Havana's gloating thoughts of the dead freedom fighters José Martí and General Antonio Maceo. In a novel full of intertextual references, Martí's is the absent voice at the beginning of the novel; his prediction that to many generations of slaves would succeed many generations of martyrs gives the reader a yardstick against which to measure social change. Of social change, of course, there is all too little, a constant refrain of the servant-narrators of *La Migration des cœurs* being that nothing has improved for the poor and black of the islands ("Voilà bientôt cinquante ans que l'esclavage des nègres est soi-disant fini, et pourtant ils ne trouvent que la misère au fond du *kwi* de leur vie"; Condé 1995, 55). There is thus an implicit question mark hanging in the air over the fate of future generations. The birth of Cathy and Razyé's baby means that the end of the novel also looks towards the future, albeit an uncertain one. In any event, the succession from one generation to the next does not necessarily impose the chronologically linear form that we might assume; the question recurs whether the spirit of someone who dies enters into a baby. Cathy's mother died in childbirth, just as she herself will die in giving birth to Anthuria, but whether or not we should believe in some sort of transmigration is left uncertain, as are so many things in this novel. At the very least, however, one generation lives on and speaks to us through the next: there are strong resemblances and repeated patterns; the way in which the young Cathy and Razyé relive their parents' love for each other is just one of the cyclical loops that disturb the linear chronology of human lives.

As well as this earthly, chronological time, there is the time of the spirits. Razyé attempts to come into communion with Cathy's spirit, but each attempt is foiled until the one made by the seer Mahdi, who has seen past and future and who hears a voice without being sure if it is Cathy's. Besides the chronology of documented history, there is oral history, and there is the past of folklore, both African and European. The past in *La Migration des cœurs* is thus multilayered, and time is multidimensional. As well as the past of history and of folklore, of the forebears and the spirits, there is also the past of each individual, which is constructed out of his or her own experience and that of others, and woven into a narrative that advances, retreats and repeats. Time, it seems, is zigzag, spiral and circular as well as linear. Three questions recur, related but each appropriate to a different level of the novel. At the level of history, when will there be an improvement in the lot of the descendants of slaves? At the spiritual level, is there a life after death in which we shall be reunited with those we have loved? At the level of the story, is Anthuria the doomed fruit of an incestuous relationship, or can she look forward to a less benighted life than those of her parents? These questions are articulated by more than one speaker in the novel, and they make for an open ending which accords well with Bakhtin's idea of the polyphonic novel. Of Dostoevsky, Bakhtin wrote: "He heard both the loud, recognized, reigning voices of the epoch, that is, the reigning dominant ideas (official and unofficial), as well as voices still weak, ideas not yet fully emerged, latent ideas heard as yet by no one but himself, and ideas that were just beginning to ripen, embryos of future world-views" ([1963] 1984, 90).

Let us turn now to the various voices that are heard throughout this novel. The most obvious polyphony of voices comes from the changes of narrative perspective that are built into the structure and fabric of the novel. Developing further the division of narrative in *Wuthering Heights* between male observer (who, despite the veneer of the omniscient narrator, is an outsider) and lady housekeeper (the main narrator because of her inside knowledge), *La Migration des cœurs* is recounted by many different narrators. There are thirteen of these "officially" designated narrations, although, as in Brontë's novel, each does not necessarily occupy the whole chapter given that narrator's name as its title, nor does it exclude other perspectives. The vast majority of these narrators are black (of African or, in two cases, Indian descent), female and servants. The exceptions to this rule are of dubious social or sexual status, mostly dispossessed black males, such as Madhi, who claims to have been both male and female, and Roro the fisherman, an ambivalent figure who seems to be at one on the waves with his boat, *Marie, Mère de Dieu*. Irmine is allowed to speak and write letters, shorn as she is of her *béké* status, disavowed by her parents and living among poor black people, and Justin, a mulatto sunk in drunken depravity, narrates briefly. No white male holds the floor; nor do any of the main protagonists during their lifetimes; the only time that we hear from Cathy and Razyé is just after their deaths, before their spirits have completely left their bodies. In a speech defying conventions of temporality and logic, Cathy begins, "Je ne suis plus" (95), and thinks back on her life and forward to eternity, apparently negating any idea of lovers being joined in death. Those who usually monopolize speech are not heard, and the usually silent have the almost constant ear of the reader. There are other reasons for which the female servants are particularly well qualified to act as narrators. Illiterate and used to looking after children, they are gifted storytellers, and because of their "invisible" status, they have more to tell about the family than anyone. (The reader has the first confirmation of the Irmine-Rayzé relationship from Lucinda Lucius: "Elle avait des yeux pour voir"; Condé 1995, 71). They span the generations, often having stayed with the same family for many years – until they are sent away for knowing too much, as in the case of Nelly

Raboteur, who is dismissed by Aymeric for precisely this reason. Most important, they are the people in whom resides the lore of the minoritized cultures. It is only Man Victoire's herbal remedies that can cure Cathy, and it is to Lucinda Lucius that Cathy avows her realization that her problem stems from her rejection of the part of her that is African. These servant-narrators are thus substitutes for Mother Africa to the doubly orphaned characters. Motherlessness is a theme in many of Condé's novels; that it echoes the severance from Africa is made explicit towards the end of *La Migration des cœurs*. As Cathy senses that she will die in childbirth, she thinks of being rejoined with her mother: "Le cœur battant comme celui d'une esclave qui voit la côte de Guinée couchée sur l'horizon, elle imagina le moment de sa réunion avec sa maman" (300).

The novel is thus peopled with the voices of several continents and of many narrators. In one or two cases, a new narrator will be signalled by some sort of stylistic marking, such as the dramatic questions and exclamations of Nelly Raboteur ("Allez comprendre pourquoi!"; Condé 1995, 29) or the slightly child-like tones of Etiennise ("C'est jeudi et je n'ai pas d'école. Ma maman m'a recommandé de ne pas déranger M. Aymeric" [168]). Such markers as there are soon blend into the rest of the text, and there is certainly no crude dialectal stereotyping. Rather, we are aware of various consciousnesses at play (to use Bakhtinian terms). In part, this is because the narrator's voice often overlays the discourse of another. This may be the words of another character or a popular saying or the intrusion of another speech genre. It is not usually so strongly marked, or so subversive in intent, as to constitute parody; it is, however, very much part of the double-voicing which Bakhtin saw as one of the main features of the poly-phonic novel. On a number of occasions, for example, there is a shift from a *récit* or a passage in *style indirect libre* to what at first sight looks like an intervention by an omniscient narrator but which on closer inspection purports to draw on an "outside authority", in imitation of a textbook or history-book style. After the opening description of the procession at the start of the novel, the second paragraph switches to a passage some of which might have been imported from a *Guide bleu:* "Les neuf arcades et les dix colonnes de la façade occidentale du palais du gouverneur. C'est l'architecte Antonio Fernandez de Trevejo y Zaldinas" (12).

As we shall see, another type of double-voicing can be found in the paragraph that precedes this one, where the blurring of the distinction between apparently omniscient narration and *style indirect libre* means that the reader is not sure through whose eyes the scene is to be read. If the devices that produce this feeling of unease, the mild vertigo of having the ground removed from under one's feet, were explicitly signalled, they would be accounted for and would lose their power to disquiet. These devices are thus neither as blatantly self-referential nor as densely concentrated as in some postmodernist fiction, and for this reason they only become apparent, and amenable to analysis, when they are seen in the context of a long stretch of text.

The impression is created that some of the narration stems from the collective conscious. Sometimes there is the explicit use of the pronoun *on,* while at other times there is simply the weaving into the text of popular sayings and "accepted" wisdom. As in the striking opening of Jean Rhys's *Wide Sargasso Sea* ("They say when trouble comes close ranks, and so the white people did. But we were not in their ranks" [Rhys 1966, 17]), some narrative seems to express the opinion of the times or local gossip. For example, the reflections of Premier-né on his return to Guadeloupe consist of a mixture of information and popular opinion filtered through an individual consciousness:

> Les socialistes ne lâchaient pas la mairie de La Pointe et avaient pris celle des principales communes. Ils tenaient en plus le conseil général. N'empêche! la vie des nègres n'avait pas meilleur goût. Les champs de canne flambaient comme avant. Les anciens colporteurs libanais faisaient de l'or. Des Italiens débarqués des bateaux-vapeur ciselaient des bijoux au fond de leurs échoppes tandis que les Zindiens réclamaient le droit de voter.
>
> Bon Dieu! on aura tout vu dans ce pays-là! (Condé 1995, 332)

Sometimes attention may be drawn to a *locution* or a fixed form because it is modified to meet the circumstances: "Avant de manger, nous ferons le signe de croix et nous remercierons le bon Dieu pour ce qu'il ne nous a pas donné" (Condé 1995, 319).

As we have already mentioned, the narrators, characters and other voices may speak one of several languages, since the novel moves from the Spanish of Cuba to the French and French Creole of Guadeloupe and then to the French-based Creole and English of Dominica. Occasionally, the question of which language is being spoken is foregrounded to tell us more about a character or event. Just as Brontë's Heathcliff is characterized by his swearing, so Gagneur teaches Razyé both to swear and to use Creole. The younger Cathy, on the other hand, speaks

Creole with difficulty but forces herself to speak it with the local people on Marie-Galante, while insisting on her pupils speaking French and singing "J'aime la France, c'est mon pays" (244). As Bakhtin says, language is "populated – over-populated – with the intentions of others" ([1934–35] 1981, 294). Deprivation of the mother tongue is seen as another form of maternal loss through the eyes of Creole speakers:

> . . . malgré ses sourires et ses manières affables, les gens ne la portaient pas dans leur cœur. Est-ce que elle n'interdisait pas aux enfants de parler le créole? Le créole, c'est la langue de notre *manman,* ronchonnaient les gens. Qui l'empêche de sortir de la gorge d'un enfant le rend muet pour la vie. (Condé 1995, 235)

Here Aymeric, despite all his good intentions towards his workers, is despised for not being a carousing male and for not speaking Creole.

Of the smattering of Creole phrases in the text, some are used to denigrate the addressee, as when Justin turns Razyé out of his house after finding him with his sister: *"Dèro! Dèro, mwen di-w! Mache!"* (33). Others may be used to show that power is in the hands of the people, as when word gets around that the cane fields have been set on fire: *"kann-la ka brilé"* (155). Of the Creole language, Chamoiseau says, "Elle a vécu au cœur des génocides et des happées violentes. . . . Elle instituait le rapport entre les maîtres et les esclaves, dominants et dominés. C'était vraiment une langue de mise-sous-relations" (1997, 259). In the context of the flogging and hanging of slaves who had dared to anticipate on the basis of the rumour that emancipation was imminent, the Creole sentence *"A pwézen nèg lib"* (Condé 1995, 195) is certainly one that is "still warm from (social) struggle and hostility", to use Bakhtin's words ([1934–35] 1981, 331).

Creole is, of course, also the vehicle for ironic multi-voicing. The decree has come from the metropole in French, is translated by the French-speaking landowner into the language which the slaves will understand but in a phrase which denies them the credit for any active part in bringing about the ending of slavery. It is a phrase which, anyway, rings hollow in the mouth of *mabo* Sandrine, who recounts the past in order to lament how little "freedom" has brought to people like herself a generation later. Linguistic pluralism sometimes serves to divide people who should be making common cause; in Roseau, Cathy feels unable to communicate with anyone. Indeed, associated with speaking foreign tongues is the idea of irrational jabbering. Cathy's substitute

Dominican mother, Ada, cannot at first understand her: "Elle s'est arrêtée de pleurer et s'est mise à parler, ou plutôt à déparler en trois langues" (Condé 1995, 315). As well as the verb *déparler,* we shall find that the verbs *malparler* and *maudire* occur with some significance in the novel.

Creole – like most of the narrators in the novel – is associated with oral rather than written language. The artifice of the successive *récits,* told mostly by people who would not be capable of writing them down, implies that these are oral narratives which tap into the tradition of popular storytelling. This impression is reinforced by the presence of a number of letters, which are interspersed in the narrative but differentiated from it by being in italics. Oral narration, despite – or perhaps because of – the different versions given of the same event, may seem to be basically more reliable than its written counterpart. Letters fail to arrive at their destination (for example, Irmine's letter to Premier-né to tell him that he can come home because his father is dead). The *cahier* to which Cathy confides everything in Roseau, which would have ended Premier-né's doubts about whether or not Cathy realized that he might be her half-brother and which would have ensured the survival of her voice beyond the grave, is tossed into the sea by Premier-né on his return voyage to Guadeloupe. In view of the dubious status of the written language, it is interesting to compare *La Migration des cœurs* with *Les Derniers rois mages* (1992), in which the identity and raison d'être of the main character (a male West Indian this time, a drifter who is emasculated by his purposeful black American wife) are entirely defined by the *cahiers* which purportedly tell the story of his royal African ancestors. Although he has a written record on which to rely rather than a purely oral one, this fails to be authenticated after a French historian throws doubt on it, and an American publisher refuses it. The reader is of course alive to the irony that there are extracts from this "unpublished" work in front of his or her eyes, as it makes up a part of the novel. It is in any case no surprise that the relative status and reliability of oral and written language should be something to be explored by a Guadeloupean novelist – although we shall see that written language arguably has the last word in *La Migration des cœurs.*

As well as the voices of the narration, the isle is full of other voices and noises, from the strains of Mozart in Aymeric's *domaine des Belles-Feuilles* to the sound of distant drumming. The voices of the recently dead are heard: Aymeric hears his beloved Cathy's voice mocking him (Condé 1995, 183), and, hearing the voice of her dead father, the younger Cathy never ceases to forget the part that

Razyé played in Aymeric's downfall (225). By far the loudest cries come from the days of slavery, making Cathy acutely conscious of the history of Aymeric's estate. Flaubertian cadences and allusions ("Sous les chandeliers de cristal, elle valsait . . ." [56]) add an additional layer of associations to the passage into which several centuries of brutal history are condensed:

> [L]e domaine des Belles-Feuilles était rempli de soupirs et de peines de femmes noires, mulâtresses, blanches, unies dans la même sujétion. Esclaves violées par des planteurs sadiques. . . . Sœurs convoitées par leurs frères. Mères par leurs fils. Huit jours après ses noces, une épousée s'était jetée la tête en avant depuis la galerie circulaire du deuxième étage, et la tache de son sang coloriait les pavés de l'entrée. Pour la cacher, les servantes plaçaient dessus des anthuriums et des alpinias en pot. Après le rétablissement de l'eslavage par le fameux Richepance, des négresses mandingues s'étaient elles-mêmes serré le cou avec des garrots plutôt que de reprendre les fers. Et, discernant ces plaintes et ces soupirs sous les échos de la fête nuptiale, Cathy comprenait qu'elle prenait place de son plein gré dans une longue procession de victimes. (56)

Among the voices from the past, certain literary ones occupy a special place. Even if the precise reference is not recognized by every reader, these contribute further to the impression of a shared cultural heritage, to the impression of using words with a history. There are passing allusions which act as clues to the interpretation of particular parts of the book. The early (translated) snippet from Robert Louis Stevenson's *Treasure Island* ("ma mémoire a gardé le souvenir de ce temps-là comme s'il était d'hier", says Nelly, telling of the day on which Justin separates Razyé from Cathy [Condé 1995, 33]) refers us to a whole strand of literary tradition and suggestively puts Razyé in the role of Caliban/Man Friday, created by the white European for the black man. The chapter recounting the death of Razyé is – like Vigny's poem – entitled "La mort du loup", reminding us that Nelly said of him, "Je me demande à présent si je ne me suis trompée sur son compte et si, des deux, ce n'est pas lui la victime" (32).

The most pervasive intertextual reference, acknowledged in an initial dedication, is to *Wuthering Heights,* on which the family structure and much of the plot is modelled. However, Charlotte Brontë's *Jane Eyre* (and perhaps also by association *Wide Sargasso Sea*) is also an important point of reference. The two nineteenth-century novels, both published in 1847, the year before France abolished slavery for the second time, provide the basis for several incidents in Condé's novel, but these incidents are inevitably given additional layers of meaning by being transported to a West Indian setting. The scene in which Jane Eyre comforts and sleeps beside her dying friend Helen is mirrored by the scene in which the dying Justin-Marie is visited by Etiennise, but the gently implicit homoerotic undertones of the former are replaced by a violation of taboos of race and age in which the sex becomes brutal and explicit. Early on in *La Migration des cœurs,* the incident in which the children Justin and Cathy are asked what presents their father should bring them refers to a similar scene in *Wuthering Heights.* But in the latter, Cathy's choice of a whip is indicative only of her imperious nature, whereas in the West Indian context it is impossible not to think of slavery – indeed, one of the statues at Belles-Feuilles is of "une aïeule à tempérament qui donnait elle-même le fouet à ses esclaves quand cela lui faisait plaisir" (Condé 1995, 56). In addition, the whip is the ritual implement of the initiated who want to invoke the god Shango, with a reference to whom the novel opens. The choice of the violin by Cathy's brother is doubly marked in the West Indian context, being not only effeminate, but also European. Indeed, Justin blames Razyé's usurping of his family's attention on his choice of instrument: "Je ne savais ni chanter ni danser ni battre du tambour comme toi. Seulement jouer du violon, et le violon, c'est une musique de blanc qui ne fouette pas le sang!" (52).

The fact that Razyé speaks with the voice of the devil, to whom he is frequently compared in the narration, poses something of a problem to the reader. In the nineteenth century, Emily Brontë was criticized for portraying evil without sufficiently strong authorial condemnation. The author of the polyphonic novel, according to Bakhtin, passes no moral judgement, leaving that up to the reader ([1963] 1984). Moral condemnation is not absent from Condé's novel (it would be difficult for the narrators to say any good about slavery), but the character of Razyé is set before us in an ambivalent manner. Although it is hinted that he may be more sinned against than sinning, he is responsible for making other characters suffer, and he is constantly portrayed in a negative light. In the midst of the narratives by a series of servants who try to give their charges a sense of pride in their African ancestry, the association of his evil character with blackness sits uneasily. It inevitably reminds us of the way in which Heathcliff was characterized as "dark" and "gypsy-looking". Should we see Razyé as epitomizing the demonization of the native or the black man by the European colonizer? This demonization, or "calibanization", has to be assumed before it can be exorcized, as these extracts from a recent poem, "*All yours to exorcise*" by John Agard (1997, 43), remind us:

> Easy to lay your inner demons at the devil's door . . .
>
> And so it was when I rode into the white
> darkness, saddling the shoulders of the night.
> A grotesque icon of your imagination. . . .
>
> Well then folks I'm all yours to exorcise.

Enough of devilish talk. Let us return to the assertion that the polyphony of Condé's novel *can* be detected in linguistic markers but that these have to be viewed either over long stretches of text or over the work as a whole. We have already touched on the way the tone is set for the novel in the shifting perspectives and double-voicing of the opening chapters; let us now look further at this opening:

> Melchior marchait en tête de la procession et portait la bannière de son dieu: Chango. Il était habillé dans les couleurs que celui-ci affectionnait. *. . . [There follows a detailed description of Melchior's colourful costume]* En dessous de son sombrero blanc piqué de plumes rouges, il jetait des regards orgueilleux à la foule massée tout le long des rues jusqu'au palais du gouverneur récemment terminé. . . . Des curieux s'écrasaient aussi aux fenêtres. . . . Car la procession du jour des Rois était l'événement marquant du début de l'année. Tous les *cabildos* étaient présents. Derrière Melchior venaient les Congos et le Lucumis en bleu et noir. . . . Après les Mandingues, pourtant, le cortège se débandait. . . . De temps en temps, Melchior ne pouvait s'empêcher de se retourner et de jeter des regards de colère vers la queue de la procession. Personne n'y faisait attention et la bacchanale continuait. *[There follows a description of the palace]* Les neuf arcades et les dix colonnes ioniques. . . . (Condé 1995, 11–12)

The novel thus opens with a detailed description that is almost worthy of realist fiction. However, we soon realize that rather than being introduced to Melchior, we are being hurtled straight into the action with him: we seem to be among the marchers on the street, looking at the crowd, the swaggering cadences of the description making us part of Melchior's pride – or are we, rather, among the onlookers on the balcony? Yet again we feel as if we are kept in order by Melchior as he glares at the stragglers. The official-history/guide-book voice pipes up ("l'événement marquant du début de l'année") and then resurfaces in the second paragraph. The reader is thus pulled playfully from one angle to another, seeing the scene first through Melchior's eyes then through those of the crowd then through those of a more impersonal commentator. After the paragraph describing the architecture of the palace, a fleeting snatch of *style indirect libre* ("ce trublion José Martí . . . la soi-disant Armée de libéra-tion . . . la négraille" [13]) leaves us in no doubt that, for a moment at least, we are seeing things through the eyes of the governor, although a moment before, we were seeing the governor through the eyes of others ("il s'appuyait sur l'habit de velours de son conseiller . . . que l'on disait son amant" [13]). We learn that the governor respects Melchior's powers as a priest of *santería* and has consulted him ("En ces temps de confusion et de malheur, bienheureux celui qui pouvait arracher un signe à l'avenir!" [13]). We then follow Melchior through the cathe-dral where he prays (he both plays *mas* and goes to mass, and he will have a Christian burial), to a bodega, where we first see Razyé – an outsider in Cuba – through Melchior's eyes. Razyé tells him that he too wants Melchior's help to speak to the spirit world; we share in Melchior's thoughts as he makes his way home – only to find that the character with whom we had most identified in this first chapter, of whom we had some hopes that he might develop into our reliable narrator, is suddenly murdered. We have no inside knowledge, no choice but to share the surprise of the crowd, to listen to local gossip ("Chacun se posait la même question. . . . Est-ce que certains humains ne craignaient vrai-ment rien? . . . On ne pouvait plus distinguer entre assassinats politiques et assassinats crapuleux" [18]). The multiple reference of *on* adds to the confusion: it refers sometimes to the crowd, sometimes to the authorities ("On annonçait l'arrivée d'un général Blanco . . ." [18]). There follows narration and dialogue, between Razyé and his mistress, during which we begin to glean something of Razyé's own story, only for this to be discontinued and taken up again in the following chapter by Nelly Raboteur. Nelly's *récit* thus begins only in the third chapter; in the meantime, the plurality of perspectives that will characterize the novel has been established.

If the range of narrative perspectives is best seen in the context of the novel as a whole, so too is the imagery that runs like a slender thread through it. When we first meet Razyé through Melchior, we learn that his name is in itself a sort of metaphor, taken from the natural world: "je n'ai pas de pays. C'est en Guadeloupe qu'on m'a trouvé nu comme un ver et braillant plus fort qu'un cochon qu'on égorge, en plein milieu des *razyés*. Mon nom vient de là" (Condé 1995, 17). And when Melchior leaves him soon after this, he remains drinking alone "pareil à un rocher ou à un îlot déserté, perdu au mitan des vagues de l'océan" (17). These are just two images out of many linked to the natural world of the Caribbean which help to give the novel cohesion, a distinctive tone, and which are frequently responsible for the effect of double-voicing. All through the novel, regardless of who is supposed to be narrating, images are drawn from local vegetation, landscapes or seascapes. When Cathy spurns Razyé, it breaks the "calebasse de son cœur" (48). Nelly descibes Razyé's hand as "aussi rugueuse que la pelure d'une igname" (36), while in contrast, the baby born to Cathy and Premier-né is seen through her father's eyes in these terms: "Elle était belle! D'après les coquillages de ses oreilles ourlés et délicats, on voyait qu'elle ne serait pas claire, mais foncée comme père et mère. Très foncée. . . . Sa peau était veloutée comme celle d'un fruit cueilli juste au point sur la branche: sapotille, icaque, pomme café" (310).

In an interview with Gauvin, René Depestre remarks, "Le créole est mon vivier de métaphores" (Gauvin 1997, 90). Without necessarily coming from Creole, many of Condé's images give the impression that they do, and they anchor the novel firmly in the Caribbean. While they sound appropriate to the narrators of the story, they are manifestly not created by them, if only because they are consistent throughout. But they also have the feel of language which has been worked upon, whether wrought by artifice or having evolved naturally over successive generations of creative speakers. Each time one of these "home-grown" images is used, we hear both the specific reference made by the narrator's voice and the echo of the collective consciousness.

This double-voicing contributes to the expression of multiple points of view; often it leads to ambivalence. So it is at the end of the novel. Because the three main questions that have run through the novel cannot be resolved within the narrative, the ending opens out onto the future with the birth of Anthuria. The future is by definition pregnant with possibilities but uncertain; if we want any hint as to what the future holds for this baby, we have to look for clues in the last pages of the novel. Anthuria is motherless, just as her mother and grandmother were before her. However, she has a father who is determined to be a mother to her and who will not relinquish her to the *manman tout moun* who tries to claim her on the voyage back to Guadeloupe. Premier-né takes Anthuria back to live in the delapidated house where his parents lived, loved and were buried. At L'Engoulvent, there are reminders of a past that has to be confronted. There are the voices ("d'un côté s'élevaient des pleurs et des plaintes . . . tandis que de l'autre, c'était une voix d'homme . . . qui se lamentait ou rageait en prononçant des paroles ordurières" [334]). In addition, the linked names "Cathy de Linsseul-Razyé" on the graves seem to confirm his worst fears that his relationship with Anthuria's mother was incestuous. Evil gossip could have been disregarded, but not so an inscription in stone ("Ainsi les malparlants n'avaient pas fait que malparler" [336]). In his distress, Razyé lets himself go, becoming the butt of local jokes; however, the habitual reference to the devil seems to have lost its force in the ritual chants of children, and he remains unwavering in his devotion to his daughter:

> Premier-né n'écoutait pas la marmaille, prudemment retranchée derrière les palissades, qui chantait en le voyant, comme au temps de carnaval:
> - *Mi guib'là dero, kayiman!*
> Il s'absorbait dans la pensée d'Anthuria.
> Une si belle enfant ne pouvait pas être maudite. (337)

With this faint imitation of the carnival of the opening pages, and the reference to possible malediction, the book ends. Yet the status of this last sentence is ambiguous. Should it be read as following on from the previous sentence, that is, as a continuation of *style indirect libre* which expresses Razyé's attempts to be optimistic? Or as the final comment from a narrator who knows the future? Is it a vain hope, or a promise?

Because it is double-voiced, as so much of the novel has been, the signs are conflicting. But still, set in comparison to the tortured voices from the past, some of the signs from the present are promising. In some small way, Dominica seemed to show Cathy the future, a future where people would come to appreciate their own West Indian home, as Ada does hers ("Elle n'est pas grandiose, ma case. Mais je l'ai mise debout toute seule avec l'aide de mes garçons. A la Noël, les *six mois-six mois* devant la porte sont écarlates. En fin de carême, ce sont les flamboyants qui la couvrent de taches de couleur"; Condé 1995, 315). Razyé's return to Guadeloupe, entitled "Retour au pays natal", seems to imply that his may be the first generation to be content at home, without looking to Europe for an education or to Africa for communion with the ancestors. Cared for by him, his daughter seems untroubled by the spirits of the past: "L'enfant tenait bien droite sa tête et regardait sans ciller les oiseaux qui planaient" (335). Perhaps the most joyful sign is that despite her grandmother's attempts to powder her body and straighten her hair, this dark baby is considered beautiful. And perhaps, like the anthurium on the terrace of Belles-Feuilles which conceals a blood-stained history, Anthuria will draw her lifeblood from her past and transform it into a thing of beauty. If the most important questions in life are unresolvable, we are at least allowed some hope. In one of his last essays, "From Notes Made in 1970–71", Bakhtin wrote that any meaning "exists among other meanings as a link in the chain of meaning. . . . In historical life, this chain continues infinitely, and therefore each individual link in it is renewed again and again, as though it were being reborn" (1986, 146).

References

Agard, John. 1997. *From the Devil's Pulpit.* Newcastle upon Tyne, UK: Bloodaxe.

Bakhtin, M.M. (Mikhail). [1934–35] 1981. "Discourse in the Novel". In *The Dialogic Imagination: Four Essays,* edited by Michael Holquist, translated by Caryl Emerson and Michael Holquist. Austin: University of Texas Press.

———. [1937–38] 1981. "Forms of Time and Chronotope in the Novel". In *The Dialogic Imagination: Four Essays,* edited by Michael Holquist, translated by Caryl Emerson and Michael Holquist. Austin: University of Texas Press.

———. [1952–53] 1986. "The Problem of Speech Genres". In *Speech Genres and Other Late Essays,* edited by Caryl Emerson and Michael Holquist, translated by Vern W. McGee, 60–102. Austin: University of Texas Press.

———. [1963] 1984. *Problems of Dostoevsky's Poetics.* Translated by Caryl Emerson. Minneapolis: University of Minnesota Press.

———. [1970–71] 1986. "From Notes Made in 1970–71". In *Speech Genres and Other Late Essays,* edited by Caryl Emerson and Michael Holquist, translated by Vern W. McGee, 132–58. Austin: University of Texas Press.

Bernabé, Jean, Patrick Chamoiseau and Raphaël Confiant. 1989. *Eloge de la créolité.* Paris: Gallimard.

Brontë, Charlotte. 1847. *Jane Eyre: An Autobiography.* London.

Brontë, Emily. 1847. *Wuthering Heights: A Novel by Ellis Bell.* London

Césaire, Aimé. [1936] 1956. *Cahier d'un retour au pays natal.* Paris: Présence Africaine.

Chamoiseau, Patrick. 1997. *Ecrire en pays dominé.* Paris: Gallimard.

Condé, Maryse. 1981. *Une Saison à Rihata.* Paris: Robert Laffont.

———. 1984. *Ségou: les murailles de terre.* Paris: Robert Laffont.

————. 1992. *Les Derniers rois mages*. Paris: Mercure de France.

————. 1995. *La Migration des cœurs*. Paris: Robert Laffont.

Gauvin, L. 1997. *L'Ecrivain francophone à la croisée des langues: entretiens*. Paris: Karthala.

Rhys, Jean. 1966. *Wide Sargasso Sea*. London: André Deutsch.

Leur seule visite
Their only visit

Priska Degras

Translated by Gertrud Aub-Buscher

Quand ils sont entrés dans la pièce, nous avons tous senti l'odeur de feuilles mortes, de sel et de vent qui imprégnait leurs vêtements, leurs cheveux et même leur silence, car ils ne parlèrent pas. Jusqu'au bout ils sont restés silencieux et distants, tout enveloppés de leur silence dont l'odeur nous devenait peu à peu perceptible. Ces hommes ne ressemblaient à personne et personne ne pouvait leur ressembler. Personne ne pouvait, comme eux, être si massif et paraître si souple, être si démuni et rayonner d'une telle insupportable et infinie richesse. Depuis que je les ai vus, je cherche le mot qui pourrait décrire, rassembler les différentes et violentes impressions qu'ils produisirent sur nous. Si j'ai choisi de parler de richesse à leur propos, bien que ce soit un mot qui, sans doute, ne leur convient guère, c'est parce que tous les autres me semblent encore plus inexacts. Les mots *sérénité, plénitude* ou *tranquillité, indifférence, beauté, magnificence, puissance* me semblent faibles, mensongers. J'ai choisi le mot *richesse* car ces hommes étaient pauvres. La région d'où ils venaient est de celles que les voyageurs évitent, s'ils le peuvent. Ceux qui, par erreur, hasard ou sottise ont pénétré ces terres hostiles et ont pu en revenir disent tous la même chose : c'est une contrée désolée où rien ne pousse et où l'on sent partout la main du diable. C'est le diable qui fait briller d'un feu vif les yeux des rares enfants que l'on croise et qui, s'ils en ont la force, crachent sur votre passage. C'est le diable encore qui ferme les visages de toutes les femmes qui fixent, depuis le seuil de leurs misérables maisons, l'envahissante poussière et dont les yeux ne clignent pas. Tous les voyageurs – du moins ceux qui en sont revenus pour le dire – affirment que le diable est partout, même dans le corps fluet des jeunes filles qui se rassemblent sur les berges des maigres rivières. Les voyageurs disent encore que là-bas, ils sont tous maigres, tous fragiles, que leurs corps débiles sont entièrement marqués par la pauvreté et le malheur. Personne n'a jamais pu savoir comment ils arrivent à supporter la désolation qui les environne, comment ils parviennent, malgré tout le manque où ils vivent, à continuer à vivre. Certains voyageurs mystiques veulent croire que la main du diable et celle d'un dieu inconnu se livrent, là-bas, un combat étrange. Quand il sort victorieux de son incessant combat contre la force démoniaque, le dieu inconnu octroie ses bienfaits. Alors il pleut, pendant des jours et des jours. Les rivières se remplissent de poissons, des arbres qu'on croyait morts portent soudain des fruits et, de la terre, d'habitude sèche et ingrate, jaillissent de tendres légumes. Puis le diable gagne à nouveau et le dieu vaincu se retire quelque temps pour soigner ses blessures avant de se lancer dans une autre épuisante bataille. Personne, parmi nous, n'ajoutait foi à cette histoire trop simple et archaïque pour être vraie. Les trois hommes qui se tenaient devant nous n'étaient pas maigres mais, comme je l'ai déjà dit, massifs et déliés, lourds et souples, et leur grâce me semblait infinie. Je ne me souviens pas exactement de ce qu'ils portaient. Leurs vêtements semblaient, comme toute leur personne, participer d'un ordre qui n'avait rien à voir avec notre monde. Ces vêtements étaient peut-être bruns, noirs ou gris. Je me rappelle l'ampleur du tissu qui recouvrait leur corps, mais je ne saurais décrire la forme exacte de cette matière qui les enveloppait et donnait à leurs rares gestes une extraordinaire fluidité. D'ailleurs, ils bougèrent à peine, si l'on excepte le premier geste, par lequel ils saluèrent, et le dernier, dont je parlerai plus tard. Quand ils furent partis, nous parlâmes longuement sans qu'aucun d'entre nous pût trouver les mots qui auraient pu exprimer notre émotion. Depuis, chaque fois que le groupe se réunit, il en est toujours un, parmi nous, pour rappeler ce moment, quel que soit le sujet à l'ordre du jour.

Chaque fois, nos mots se pressent et s'affrontent, car chacun de nous croit être le seul à avoir compris ce qui s'est passé ce jour-là. Mais, chaque fois, nous arrivons à la même décevante conclusion et nous nous taisons alors un long moment, troublés, affolés par notre incapacité à accéder à une véritable connaissance de cet autre monde. Nous ne cesserons jamais, je pense, d'en parler.

Ce souvenir nous est, à tous, devenu plus cher que tout, et nous l'avons jalousement gardé pendant longtemps, même si, comme je le fais à présent, nous avons parfois tenté de raconter à d'autres ce qui s'est passé. Nous avons, pendant plusieurs années, observé une sorte de pacte tacite. Personne, à part nous, ne devait savoir. Puis, au fil du temps et la mémoire de certains s'affaiblissant, nous avons commencé à diffuser, oralement, autour de nous, cette histoire. Finalement, nous avons décidé de la répandre, le plus possible, autour de nous. Nous avons peur, en effet, d'atteindre ce moment – terrible – où nous ne pourrons plus nous souvenir. J'ai accepté de le faire tout en sachant que nos craintes étaient vaines car il est évident, il est sûr que nous n'oublierons jamais. Mais il est vrai, aussi, qu'un jour viendra où nous ne pourrons plus nous souvenir car nous aurons tous disparus.

Je vous raconte donc cette histoire, je tente de la raconter, et il est difficile – et horrible – d'extirper de soi une chose devenue si essentielle et si intime sans cesser, pour cela, d'être obscure. J'éprouve, en ce moment, l'incroyable souffrance d'un abandon. Je n'éprouve aucune joie à faire, à d'autres, ce récit informe. Le souvenir en est pourtant vif mais mon récit est maladroit, contraint, et mon cœur n'y est pas. C'est de mauvaise grâce que j'accomplis cette tâche car j'ai l'impression d'être dépossédé, ainsi, d'une profonde et indispensable partie de moi-même. Je ne dois pas parler de moi mais d'eux et je ne peux transcrire en mots le vertige de cette rencontre. C'est quand ils furent partis que le vertige nous saisit. Je me souviens que L., qui s'était tenu, comme nous tous, debout durant tout le temps que dura leur visite, commença, juste après leur départ, à chanceler, vaciller, et que M. eut juste le temps de lui approcher un siège avant qu'il ne s'écroule, terrassé par le poids d'une évidence qui nous étreignait tous. Je me rappelle aussi que l'air nous sembla soudain se raréfier comme s'ils avaient emporté, en même temps que leur odeur de feuilles mortes, de sel et de vent, tout l'air de cette pièce. L'un de nous dit, "Tout nous a quittés, même l'air". C'est à ce moment là que T. ouvrit toutes les fenêtres et se plaignit de l'odeur marécageuse et du bruit qui envahirent la pièce. Après le long silence qui nous avait enveloppés, ce bruit nous suffoqua. Comme je l'ai dit, ils ne prononcèrent pas un seul mot durant tout le temps qu'ils restèrent avec nous. Leur silence était puissant, inaltérable. Ils ne manifestèrent aucune impatience à écouter nos malheureuses paroles. Il me sembla que l'un d'entre eux – celui qui paraissait le plus jeune – sourit légèrement quand S. tenta, à grands renforts de gestes, de les faire parler. Je suis le seul à avoir vu ce sourire et les autres ont fini par me convaincre que je l'avais imaginé.

Chacun de nous, ce jour-là, prit la parole devant eux et j'ai honte, chaque fois que j'y repense. Nous devions avoir l'air, face à ces hommes au souverain silence, de petits animaux bavards et fébriles. Nos paroles tombaient dans leur silence, elles s'y noyaient. Ils contemplèrent, sans un geste, sans une parole, nos pitoyables tentatives de communication. Ils étaient au-delà de notre pauvre, si pauvre entendement.

Nous comprendrions aussi plus tard qu'ils avaient ouvert puis refermé les portes d'un univers dont nous garderions à jamais l'inépuisable nostalgie. Cet univers qu'ils nous montraient, par leur simple présence, nous était offert et refusé. Ne me demandez pas d'expliquer, car nous n'avons jamais compris, mais nous savons qu'il en était ainsi. Ils avaient apporté avec eux un lourd paquet, légèrement porté par celui qui semblait être le plus jeune. Il le garda dans ses bras durant tout le temps de leur visite. Il fallut trois d'entre nous pour le soulever après leur départ car l'objet pesait terriblement. Nous ne pouvions le savoir ni même le soupçonner étant donné l'aisance et la facilité avec lesquelles le plus jeune d'entre eux posa le paquet sur le sol. Ils défirent, tous trois, les multiples et complexes liens qui enserraient le tissu qui recouvrait l'objet. Quand ils se relevèrent, nous nous penchâmes pour voir: le tissu, entièrement développé, s'étalait, sombre et brillant, par terre; au milieu de toute cette splendeur, une pierre longue et plate, mate et sans ornements. Sur la pierre, on lisait trois mots, maladroitement tracés mais écrits dans notre langue. Notre surprise et notre gêne, quand nous les lûmes, ne provoqua en eux aucune réaction. Ils partirent sans nous saluer vraiment, avec un imperceptible hochement de tête. Cette pierre, nous la regardons longuement chaque fois que nous nous réunissons. Nous l'avons placée sur la table du fond, la seule dont le plateau permette de supporter un tel poids. Nous nous sommes interrogés pendant des années sur ces trois mots gravés dans la pierre et nous avons fini par en faire notre devise.

«Laissez-nous tranquilles» dit la pierre, mais c'est nous qui, depuis, n'avons jamais vraiment connu la paix. Nous n'avons jamais regretté non plus d'être ainsi projetés dans ce que nous croyons être le cœur vivant de leur mystère.

Their Only Visit

When they came into the room, we all became aware of the smell of dead leaves, salt and wind which permeated their clothes, their hair and even their silence, for they did not speak. Until the very end, they remained silent and distant, all wrapped in their silence, the smell of which gradually became perceptible to us. The men resembled no one and no one could resemble them. No one could be like them, so heavily built and yet seeming so supple, so destitute and yet radiating such an unbearable and infinite richness. Ever since I first saw them, I have been trying to find the word that could describe and bring together the different and violent impressions which they made on us. If I have decided to use the word *richness* when speaking of them, even though that is a word which no doubt is not really appropriate, it is because all the others seem even more inappropriate. The words *serenity, plenitude* or *tranquillity, indifference, beauty, magnificence, power* seem feeble and false to me. I have chosen the word *richness* because these men were poor. The region from which they came is one of those that travellers avoid, if they can. Those who, through error, chance or stupidity have entered these hostile lands and have managed to come away again all say the same thing: it is a desolate country where nothing grows and where you feel the hand of the devil wherever you go. It is the devil who puts a fiery brightness into the eyes of the few children you meet, who spit at you as you go by, if they have sufficient strength. And it is the devil who closes the faces of all the women who, from the doorsteps of their wretched houses, stare, unblinking, at the all-pervading dust. All the travellers – or at least those who have come back to tell about it – maintain that the devil is everywhere, even in the slight bodies of the girls who meet on the banks of the meagre rivers. Travellers also say that in that place they are all thin, all fragile, that their sickly bodies are marked all over by poverty and misfortune. Nobody has ever been able to find out how they manage to bear the desolation which surrounds them or how they can continue to survive in spite of all the deprivation in which they live. Certain mystical travellers claim that the hand of the devil and that of an unknown god are joined in a strange combat there. When the unknown god emerges as the winner from his endless fight against the demonic force, he grants his blessings. Then it rains, for days and days. The rivers fill up with fish, trees which were thought to be dead suddenly bear fruit, and tender vegetables sprout from the earth, which is usually dry and barren. And then the devil wins again and the vanquished god withdraws for a while to tend his wounds before going back into another exhausting battle. None of us believed this story, which was too simple and archaic to be true. The three men before us were not thin but, as I have already said, solidly built and agile, heavy and supple, and it seemed to me that they were infinitely graceful. I cannot remember exactly what they were wearing. Their clothes, like their whole appearance, seemed to belong to an order which had nothing in common with our world. Perhaps their clothes were brown, black or grey. I remember the fullness of the cloth that covered their bodies, but I cannot describe the exact shape of the material which enveloped them and gave a wonderful fluidity to their rare movements. It must be said that they hardly moved at all, apart from their first gesture of greeting and the last one, about which I shall speak later. When they had left, we spoke for a long time without any of us being able to find the words to express our emotion. Since then, every time the group meets, there is always one of us who brings up that moment, whatever the topic of the meeting.

On each occasion, our words rush out and confront one another, for each one of us thinks he is the only one to have understood what happened on that day. But every time we reach the same disappointing conclusion and we keep silent for a long while, disconcerted, appalled by our inability really to get to know this other world. I do not think that we shall ever stop talking about it. This memory has become more precious to all of us than anything else, and we have guarded it jealously for a long time, even if, as I am doing now, we have occasionally tried to tell others what happened. For several years we kept a sort of tacit pact. No one except us was to know. Then, as time went by and some people's memory began to fade, we began to spread the story around us by word of mouth. And then we decided to circulate it as widely as possible. Indeed, we are afraid that we shall reach the point – the terrible point – when we shall no longer be able to remember. I have agreed to do it, though I know that our fears were unfounded, for it is clear, it is certain that we shall never forget. But it is also true that the day will come when we shall no longer be able to remember for we shall all have gone.

And so I am telling you this story, I am trying to tell it to you, and it is difficult – and horrible – to tear out of oneself something which has become so essential and so intimate, without for all that ceasing to be obscure. At this moment, I am experiencing the incredible pain of relinquishment. Giving others this shapeless account affords me no pleasure. I have a vivid memory, and yet my telling of it is awkward and forced, and my heart is not in it. I fulfil the task with bad grace, for I feel as if by doing it I am being dispossessed of a deep and indispensable part of me. I must not speak of myself but of them, and I am incapable of transcribing in words the turmoil of that encounter. It was when they had left that the turmoil took hold of us. I remember that just after they had gone, L., who, like all of us, had stood throughout their visit, began to stagger and sway, and that M. just had time to move a chair towards him before he collapsed, overcome by the weight of a truth which held us all in its grip. I remember too that it suddenly seemed to us that the air had become rarified, as if, together with their smell of dead leaves, salt and wind, they had taken away with them all the air in the room. One of us said, "Everything has left us, even the air." It was at that moment that T. opened all the windows and complained of the marshy air and the noise which invaded the room. After the long silence that had enveloped us, this noise suffocated us. As I have said, they spoke not a single word all the time they were with us. Their silence was powerful and unchanging. They did not show any impatience while listening to our poor words. It seemed to me that one of them – the one who appeared to be the youngest – gave a slight smile when S. tried, with a great many gestures, to make them speak. I am the only one to have seen that smile, and the others finally convinced me that I had imagined it. On that day, each one of us spoke in their presence, and I am ashamed every time I think about it. Before those men with their supreme silence, we must have seemed like talkative and febrile little animals. Our words dropped into their silence and drowned. Without a movement, without a single word, they watched our pathetic attempts at communication. They were beyond our feeble, our very feeble, understanding.

We were also going to understand later that they had opened and then closed again the doors of a universe for which we would forever retain an inexhaustible nostalgia. We were being offered and then refused the universe which they showed us by their mere presence. Do not ask me to explain, for we have never understood, but we know that that is what happened. They had brought with them a heavy parcel, carried lightly by the one who seemed the youngest. He kept it in his arms throughout their visit. It took three of us to lift it once they had left, for the object was terribly heavy. We could not know or even guess that, given the ease and facility with which the youngest of them put the parcel down on the ground. All three of them undid the many complicated ties which tightly bound the cloth covering the object. When they stood up again, we leaned forward in order to see: the cloth, which had been fully opened out, was spread on the ground, dark and shiny; in the midst of all that splendour, there was a long, flat stone, unpolished and without any decorations. On the stone were written three words, awkwardly formed but in our language. The surprise and embarrassment we felt on reading them produced no reaction from them.

They left without really taking leave, with an imperceptible nod of their heads. We gaze at that stone every time we meet. We have put it on the table at the back of the room, the only one with a top strong enough to carry such a weight. For years we have wondered about the three words engraved on the stone, and we ended up making it our motto.

"Leave us alone", says the stone, but we are the ones who since that time have never really known peace. Nor have we ever regretted being projected in this way into what we think is the living heart of their mystery.

Appendix

Francophone Caribbean Fiction at the End of the Twentieth Century
A Select Bibliography of Texts
and Critical Material

Elizabeth A. (Betty) Wilson
University of the West Indies, Mona, Jamaica

Caribbean literature as a field of research has exploded in the past two decades. This brief bibliography concentrates on prose fiction written in French or French Creole and published between 1980 and 2000: novels, short stories, *récits*. It does not attempt or pretend to be an exhaustive list. The intention is to give an idea of the current production and publication of prose texts from Haiti and the French overseas *départements* in the Caribbean. Judging from the number of collections published since 1980, poetry too is alive and thriving in the French Caribbean. And theatre continues to flourish, as evidenced by Bridget Jones and Sita Dickson Littlewood's comprehensive *Paradoxes of French Caribbean Theatre: An Annotated Checklist of Dramatic Works – Guadeloupe, Guyane, Martinique – from 1900.*

Most writers from the region continue to be published by metropolitan publishing houses. There is still very little publishing in the DOM themselves, although there are some initiatives, Editions Desormeaux (Martinique), Editions Jasor (Guadeloupe) and Ibis Rouge (Guyane), for example. In the case of Haitian literature, readers owe a debt to local publishing houses: Editions Deschamps continues to be a main source of Haitian literature, together with other publishing enterprises, such as Fardin, Editions des Antilles and Editions Mémoire. Perhaps thanks to the large Caribbean populations in Canada who have contributed to the intellectual and artistic life of cultural centres such as Toronto, Ottawa and Montreal, Canadian presses increasingly publish Caribbean works.

Several contemporary francophone Caribbean writers now enjoy international recognition: Maryse Condé and Edouard Glissant come immediately to mind. New writers have emerged, both from the DOM (Patrick Chamoiseau and Raphaël Confiant have growing reputations) and from Haiti – writers such as Dany Laferrière, Emile Ollivier and Louis-Philippe Dalembert, whose most recent novel, *Le crayon du bon Dieu n'a pas de gomme* (1996), uses the French version of a Haitian Creole proverb for its title. A feature of any current bibliography is the increasing presence of texts by women. Many *écrivaines* have emerged in the past two decades. Moreover, writers such as Anne-Christine d'Adesky or Edwidge Danticat (classified as "Haitian American") point to the challenges inherent in attempting to identify or define "francophone Caribbean" writers, complexities and paradoxes which arise in any discussion of "Caribbean" writing. Danticat, for example, was born in Haiti, lives in the United States, speaks Creole, writes in English and treats of a reality which draws on her childhood experiences in Haiti and on the life of the Haitian community in the United States. Her work has been translated into French. As a Haitian writer (Danticat says she thinks and composes in Creole), Danticat's works and their translations have been included in this bibliography, as has d'Adesky's novel *Under the Bone* (1994), which grapples with the legacy of the Duvalier regime in Haiti. Genre too may be problematic: I have chosen to include Frankétienne's *spirales,* texts which include both "poetry" and "prose" and which are sometimes, but not always, *poèmes en prose.*

As English language translations of francophone and hispanophone writing become more and more available (there is still relatively little available in translation from the growing body of Dutch-language and Papiamentu literature), anglophone students and scholars, who hitherto had no access to these texts, increasingly refer to "Caribbean" rather than "West Indian" literature. The changing terminology is indicative of a shift in perspective: away from an insular fragmentation which tended to look at each of the four main linguistic groupings in isolation and without reference to the others, towards a more integrative approach in which the study of the literatures of the region no longer ignores common threads. Critical attention has established many connections. Some comparative approaches emphasize common themes or similar theoretical and aesthetic preoccupations. There are frequent cross-references, even where the concentration is on a single language area or national literature. In keeping with this trend and out of a desire to open up this corpus to readers from other language backgrounds, English translations of the works are included in the bibliography where available. Selected reference works which should prove useful to readers and students with an interest in francophone Caribbean fiction are also listed.

I would like to thank my colleague Marie-José N'Zengou-Tayo and the librarians of the Main Library, University of the West Indies, Mona, especially Pat Dunn, Charmaine Salmon (West Indies and Special Collections) and Paulette Kerr, for their patient and invaluable assistance.

This bibliography is dedicated to Bridget Jones, who did so much to encourage and promote the study of francophone Caribbean literature in the Caribbean, in the United Kingdom and elsewhere.

Texts Published since 1980
(Novels, Novellas, Short Stories, *récits*)

Haiti

Anglade, George. 2000. *Les blancs de mémoire*. Montreal: Boréal.
Apollon, Georges. 1995. *Anita Petithomme: roman*. Haiti: Imprimeur II.
Azor, Joseph D. (Joseph Dieffen). 1982. *Danielle Desormeaux: roman*. Port-au-Prince, Haiti: Henri Deschamps.
Bellande, Cuckita. 1996. *Porte-sauveur: récit = Pot sove*. Port-au-Prince, Haiti: Henri Deschamps.
Cazanove, Michèle. 1988. *Présumée Solitude, ou histoire d'une paysanne haïtienne: roman*. Paris: Julliard.
Charlier, Ghislaine Rey. 1989. *Mémoire d'une affranchie*. Montreal: Leméac.
Chauvet, Marie (Vieux). 1986. *Les Rapaces*. Port-au-Prince, Haiti: Henri Deschamps.
Clarck Parent, Jean Jacques. c1995. *Mi-dieu, mi-bête: roman*. Port-au-Prince, Haiti: J.J. Clarck Parent.
Clitandre, Pierre. 1980. *Cathédrale du mois d'août: roman*. Port-au-Prince, Haiti: Fardin.
———. 1982. *Cathédrale du mois d'août: roman*. Paris: Syros.
———. 1987. *Cathedral of the August Heat*. Translated by Bridget Jones. London: Readers International.
———. 2000. *Vins de soleil*. Port-au-Prince, Haiti: Editions Mémoire.

Dabel, Verly. n.d. *Histoires sur mesure: nouvelles.* Port-au-Prince, Haiti: Bibliothèque Nationale d'Haïti.

d'Adesky, Anne-Christine. 1994. *Under the Bone.* New York: Farrar, Straus and Giroux.

Dalembert, Louis-Philippe. 1993. *Le Songe d'une photo d'enfance: nouvelles.* Paris: Serpent à Plumes.

———. 1996. *Le Crayon du bon Dieu n'a pas de gomme: roman.* Paris: Stock.

Danticat, Edwidge. 1994. *Breath, Eyes, Memory.* New York: Soho Press

———. 1995. *Le Cri de l'oiseau rouge: roman.* Translated by Nicole Tessearnd. (Original title: *Breath, Eyes, Memory.*) Paris: Pygmalion.

———. 1996. *Krik? Krak!* New York: Random House.

———. 1996. *Krik? Krak!: récits.* Translated by Nicole Tesserand. Paris: Pygmalion.

———. 1998. *The Farming of Bones.* New York: Soho Press.

———. 1999. *La Récolte douce des larmes: roman.* Translated by Jacques Chabert. (Original title: *The Farming of Bones.*) Paris: Bernard Grasset.

Delmas, René. 1980. *Le Pont: roman.* Port-au-Prince, Haiti: Henri Deschamps.

———. 1983. *La Cannaie du diable: roman.* Port-au-Prince, Haiti: Fardin.

———. 1996. *Invitation au bal des zombis: roman.* Port-au-Prince, Haiti: Editions des Antilles.

Depestre, René. 1981. *Alléluia pour une femme-jardin: récits d'amour solaire.* Paris: Gallimard.

———. 1988. *Hadriana dans tous mes rêves: roman.* Paris: Gallimard.

———. 1990. *Eros dans un train chinois: neuf histoires d'amour et un conte de sorcier.* Paris: Gallimard.

Devieux, Liliane. 1988. "Piano-Bar". *Conjonction* 171, no. 18–19: 226–33.

———. 1991. "Piano-Bar". Translated by Lizabeth Paravisini. In *Green Cane and Juicy Flotsam: Short Stories by Caribbean Women,* edited by Carmen C. Esteves and Lizabeth Paravisini, 73–79. New Brunswick, NJ: Rutgers University Press.

Dominique, Jan J. 1984. *Mémoire d'une amnésique.* Port-au-Prince, Haiti: Henri Deschamps.

———. 1996. *Evasion: nouvelles.* Port-au-Prince, Haiti: Editions des Antilles.

———. 2000. *Inventer . . . la Célestine.* Port-au-Prince, Haiti: Editions des Antilles.

Fignolé, Jean Claude. 1990. *Aube tranquille: roman.* Paris: Seuil.

Frankétienne. 1986. *Fleurs d'insomnie: Spirales. (poèmes en prose).* Port-au- Prince: Henri Deschamps.

———. 1995. *L'Amérique saigne: gun blesse America: roman.* Port-au-Prince, Haiti: Frankétienne, C. Dambreville.

———. 1995. *Mur à crever: roman.* Port-au-Prince, Haiti: Editions Mémoire.

———. 1995. *Ultravocal.* Port-au-Prince, Haiti: Spirale.

———. 1996. *Une Etrange cathédrale dans la graisse des ténèbres.* Port-au-Prince, Haiti: Spirale.

———. 1996. *La Méduse orpheline*. Port-au-Prince, Haiti: Spirale.

———. 1996. *La Nocturne connivence des corps inverses*. Port-au-Prince, Haiti: Spirale.

———. 1996. *D'un pur silence inextinguible: spirale*. Port-au-Prince, Haiti: Frankétienne.

———. 1996. *D'une bouche ovale: spirale*. Port-au-Prince, Haiti: Frankétienne.

———. 1997. *Clavier de sel et d'ombre*. Port-au-Prince, Haiti: Spirale.

———. 1997. *Les Echos de l'abîme*. Port-au-Prince, Haiti: Spirale.

Gardiner, Madeleine. 1989. *Néna, ou la joie de vivre*. Port-au-Prince, Haiti: Henri Deschamps.

Laferrière, Dany. 1985. *Comment faire l'amour avec un Nègre sans se fatiguer*. Montreal, Que.: VLB.

———. 1987. *Eroshima*. Montreal, Que.: VLB.

———. 1987. *How to Make Love to a Negro: A Novel*. Translated by David Homel. Toronto, Ont.: Coach House.

———. 1991. *Eroshima*. Translated by David Homel. Toronto, Ont.: Coach House.

———. 1991. *L'Odeur du café*. Montreal, Que.: VLB,

———. 1992. *Le Goût des jeunes filles*. Montreal, Que.: VLB.

———. 1993. *An Aroma of Coffee*. Translated by David Homel. Toronto, Ont.: Coach House.

———. 1993. *Cette grenade dans la main du jeune Nègre est-elle une arme ou un fruit?* Montreal, Que.: VLB.

———. 1994. *Chronique de la dérive douce*. Montreal, Que.: VLB.

———. 1994. *Dining with the Dictator*. Translated by David Homel. (Original title: *Goût des jeunes filles*.) Toronto, Ont.: Coach House.

———. 1994. *Why Must a Black Writer Write about Sex?* Translated by David Homel. (Original title: *Cette grenade dans la main . . .*) Toronto, Ont.: Coach House.

———. 1996. *Pays sans chapeau: roman*. Outremont, Que.: Lanctôt.

———. 1997. *A Drifting Year*. Translated by David Homel. (Original title: *Chronique de la dérive douce*.) Toronto, Ont.: Douglas and McIntyre.

———. 1997. *Down among the Dead Men*. Translated by David Homel. (Original title: *Pays sans chapeau*.) Toronto, Ont.: Douglas and McIntyre.

———. 1997. *La Chair du maître*. Outrement, Que.: Lanctôt.

———. 1998. *Le Charme des après-midi sans fin*. Paris: Serpent à Plumes.

———. 2000. *Le Cri des oiseaux fous*. Paris: Serpent à Plumes.

Lahens, Yanick. 1994. *Tante Résia et les dieux: nouvelles*. Paris: L'Harmattan.

———. 1999. *La Petite Conception*. Port-au-Prince, Haiti: Edition Mémoire.

———. 2000. *Dans la maison du père*. Paris: Serpent à Plumes.

Lescouflair, Michel Georges. 1986, 1989. *Les femmes font la grève: roman*. 2 vols. Port-au-Prince, Haiti: Henri Deschamps.

Mathon, Alix. 1984. *La Relève de Charlemagne: les cacos de la plume: chronique romancée*. Port-au-Prince, Haiti: Editions Fardin.

Ollivier, Emile, 1983. *Mère Solitude: roman*. Paris: Albin Michel.

———. 1986. *La discorde aux cent voix: roman*. Paris: A. Michel.

———. 1989. *Mother Solitude*. Translated by David Lobdell. Ottawa, Ont.: Oberon.

———. 1991. *Passages: roman*. Montreal, Que.: Hexagone.

———. 1995. *Les Urnes scellées: roman*. Paris: A. Michel.

———. 1995. *Regarde, regarde les lions: nouvelle*. Paris: M. Solal.

Paul, Cauvin L. 1996. *Le Vieux Samuel: roman*. Port-au-Prince, Haiti: Henri Deschamps.

Philoctète, René. 1989. *Le Peuple des terres mêlées*. Port-au-Prince, Haiti: Henri Deschamps.

———. 1993. *Une saison de cigales: roman*. Haiti: Editions Conjonction/Institut Français d'Haïti.

Pierre, Romulus. 1984. *L'Arriviste: roman*. Port-au-Prince, Haiti: Fardin.

Poujol-Oriol, Paulette. 1980. *Le Creuset: roman*. Port-au-Prince, Haiti: Henri Deschamps; 2nd ed., 1985.

———. c1992. *La Fleur rouge: nouvelles*. Port-au-Prince, Haiti: Le Natal.

———. 1996. *Le Passage: roman*. Port-au-Prince, Haiti: Le Natal; Cambria Heights, NY: Haitiana Publications.

Raymond, Yvonne. 1985. *Une Raison d'espérer: roman*. Port-au-Prince, Haiti: Fardin.

Trouillot, Lyonel. 1996. *Rue des pas perdus: roman*. Port-au-Prince, Haiti: Editions Mémoire.

Victor, Gary. 1992. *Un Octobre d'Elyaniz: roman*. Haiti: G. Victor.

———. 1995. *Le Sorcier qui n'aimait pas la neige*. Montreal, Que.: CIDIHCA.

French Caribbean

Alante-Lima, Willy. c.1991. *Mémoires d'un bananier: (sur tous les tons): roman (polythème)*. Paris: N. Blandin.

Alcindor, Joscelyn. c.1995. *Cravache, ou, le nègre soubarou: roman antillais*. Paris: L'Harmattan.

Bazile, Gillette. 1993. *Trilogie noire: roman*. Steenvoorde, France: Foyer Culturel d'Houtland.

Bebel-Gisler, Dany. 1985. *Léonora: l'histoire enfouie de la Guadeloupe*. Paris: Seghers.

———. 1994. *Leonora: The Buried Story of Guadeloupe*, translated by Andrea Leskes. Charlottesville: University of Virginia Press.

Blanchard-Glass, Pascale. 1995. *Correspondance du Nouveau monde: nouvelles*. Paris: L'Harmattan.

Brival, Roland. 1996. *Le Dernier des Aloukous: roman*. Paris: Phébus.

Catalan, Sonia. 1992. *Clémentine: roman*. Paris: L'Harmattan.

Césaire, Ina. 1994. *Zonzon Tête Carrée*. Monaco: Editions du Rocher.

Chamoiseau, Patrick. 1986. *Chronique des sept misères*. Paris: Gallimard.

———. 1988. *Solibo Magnifique*. Paris: Gallimard.

———. 1992. *Texaco*. Paris: Gallimard.

———. 1997. *L'Esclave vieil homme et le molosse: roman*. Paris: Gallimard.

———. 1997. *Texaco*. Translated by Rose-Myriam Réjouis and Val Vinokurov. New York: Pantheon.

———. 1998. *Solibo Magnificent*. Translated by Rose-Myriam Réjouis and Val Vinokurov. New York: Pantheon

Charpentier, Josane. 1982. *La Dame des isles*. Paris: O. Orban.

———. 1984. *Tempête des isles*. Paris: O. Orban.

Condé, Maryse. 1981. *Une Saison à Rihata*. Paris: Robert Laffont.

———. 1982. *Heremakhonon: A Novel*. Translated by Richard Philcox. Washington, DC: Three Continents Press.

———. 1984. *Ségou I: les murailles de terre: roman*. Paris: Robert Laffont.

———. 1985. *Pays mêlé; suivi de Nanna-ya*. Paris: Hatier.

———. 1985. *Ségou II: la terre en miettes: roman*. Paris: Robert Laffont.

———. 1986. *Moi, Tituba, sorcière, noire de Salem: roman*. Paris: Mercure de France.

———. 1987. *La Vie scélérate: roman*. Paris: Seghers.

———. 1987. *Segu: A Novel*. Translated by Barbara Bray. New York: Viking.

———. 1988. *A Season in Rihata*. Translated by Richard Philcox. Oxford; Portsmouth, NH: Heinemann.

———. 1989. *The Children of Segu*. Translated by Linda Coverdale. New York: Viking.

———. 1989. *Traversée de la mangrove: roman*. Paris: Mercure de France.

———. 1992. *I, Tituba, Black Witch of Salem*. Translated by Richard Philcox. Charlottesville: University Press of Virginia.

———. 1992. *Les Derniers rois mages: roman*. Paris: Mercure de France.

———. 1992. *Tree of Life*. Translated by Victoria Reiter. (Original title: *La Vie scélérate*.) New York: Ballantine.

———. 1993. *La Colonie du nouveau monde: roman*. Paris: Robert Laffont.

———. 1995. *Crossing the Mangrove*. Translated by Richard Philcox. New York: Anchor Books/Doubleday.

———. 1995. *La Migration des cœurs: roman*. Paris: Robert Laffont.

———. 1997. *Désirada: roman*. Paris: Robert Laffont.

———. 1997. *The Last of the African Kings*. Translated by Richard Philcox. Lincoln: University of Nebraska Press.

———. 1998. *Windward Heights*. Translated by Richard Philcox. (Original title: *La migration des cœurs*.) London: Faber and Faber.

———. 1999. *Le Cœur à rire et à pleurer: contes vrais de mon enfance*. Paris: Robert Laffont.

————. 2000. *Célanire Cou-Coupé: roman fantastique.* Paris: Robert Laffont.

Confiant, Raphaël. 1991. *Eau de café: roman.* Paris: Grasset

————. 1993. *Ravines du devant-jour: récit.* Paris: Gallimard.

————. 1994. *L'Allée des soupirs: roman.* Paris: Grasset.

————. 1994. *Bassin des ouragans.* Paris: Mille et une nuits.

————. 1994. *Commandeur du sucre: récit.* Paris: Ecriture.

————. 1996. *La Vierge du Grand Retour: roman.* Paris: Grasset.

Delpech, Alice. 1990. *La Dame de Balata.* Martinique: Presses Universitaires Créoles; Paris: L'Harmattan.

Delsham, Tony. 1984. *Lapo Farine: roman antillais.* Fort-de-France, Martinique: MGG.

————. 1987. *L'Ababa.* Fort-de-France, Martinique: MGG.

Dracius-Pinalie, Suzanne. 1989. *L'Autre qui danse.* Paris: Seghers.

Glissant, Edouard. 1981. *La Case du commandeur.* Paris: Seuil.

————. 1985. *The Ripening.* Translated by Michael Dash. (Original title: *La Lézarde.*) London; Portsmouth, NH: Heinemann.

————. 1987. *Mahogany.* Paris: Seuil.

————. 1993. *Tout-monde: roman.* Paris: Gallimard.

Henry-Valmore, Simonne. 1998. *L'Autre bord.* Chateauneuf-le-Rouge, France: Vents des Iles.

Hospice, Marlène. 1984. *Chouval bwa = Le manège: un songe créole.* Paris: La Case-à-Vent.

————. 1984. *Pas de pitié pour Marny: une affaire martiniquaise.* Fort-de-France, Martinique: Desormeaux.

Hyvrard, Jeanne. 1984. *Auditions musicales certains soirs d'été: nouvelles.* Paris: Editions des Femmes.

Jaham, Marie-Reine de. 1989. *La Grande Béké.* Paris: Robert Laffont.

Jorif, Richard. 1987. *Le Navire Argo: roman.* Paris: François Bourin.

————. 1988. *Clownerie: roman.* Paris: François Bourin.

————. 1989. *Le Burelain: roman.* Paris: François Bourin.

————. 1990. *Les Persistants Lilas: roman.* Paris: François Bourin.

————. 2000. *Tohu-Bohu: roman.* Paris: Julliard.

Julia, Lucie. 1982. *Les Gens de Bonne Espérance.* Paris: Temps Actuels.

————. 1989. *Melody des faubourgs.* Paris: L'Harmattan.

Maximin, Daniel. 1987. *L'Isolé soleil: roman.* Paris: Seuil.

————. 1987. *Soufrières: roman.* Paris: Seuil.

————. 1989. *Lone sun.* Charlottesville: University Press of Virginia.

————. 1995. *L'Ile et une nuit: roman.* Paris: Seuil.

Orville, Xavier. 1993. *Cœur à vie: roman.* Paris: Stock.

————. 1994. *La Voie des cerfs-volants.* Paris: Stock.

Parsemain, Roger. 1992. *L'Absence du destin: nouvelles.* Paris: L'Harmattan.

Pépin, Ernest. 1992. *L'Homme-au-bâton: roman.* Paris: Gallimard.

———. 1995. *Coulée d'or.* Paris: Page Blanche/Gallimard.

———. 1996. *Tambour-Babel: roman.* Paris: Gallimard.

———. 2000. *Le Tango de la haine: roman.* Paris: Gallimard.

Pineau, Gisèle. 1993. *La Grande drive des esprits: roman.* Paris: Serpent à Plumes.

———. 1995. *L'Espérance-macadam: roman.* Paris: Stock.

———. 1996. *L'Exil selon Julia: récit.* Paris: Stock.

———. 1998. *L'Ame prêtée aux oiseaux: roman.* Paris: Stock.

Sae, Rosenberg. *c.*1983. *La Nuit pleurait: roman.* Fort-de-France, Martinique: Desormeaux.

Schwarz-Bart, Simone. 1981. *Between Two Worlds: A Novel.* Translated by Barbara Bray. (Original title: *Ti Jean L'horizon.*) New York: Harper and Row.

———. 1982. *The Bridge of Beyond,* translated by Barbara Bray. (Original title: *Pluie et vent sur Télumée Miracle.*) London: Heinemann.

Velayoudon-Faithful, Francesca. 1986. *Peau de banane.* Paris: Editions Caribéennes.

Warner-Vieyra, Myriam. 1980. *Le Quimboiseur l'avait dit: roman.* Paris: Présence Africaine.

———. 1982. *As the Sorcerer Said.* Translated by Dorothy S. Blair. Harlow, UK: Longman.

———. 1982. *Juletane: roman.* Paris: Présence Africaine.

———. 1987. *Juletane.* Translated by Betty Wilson. London: Heinemann.

———. 1988. *Femmes échouées: nouvelles.* Paris: Présence Africaine.

Zobel, Joseph. 1980. *Black Shack Alley.* Translated by Keith Q. Warner. (Original title: *La Rue Cases-Nègres.*) London: Heinemann.

Reference, Critical Works, Bibliographies

Antoine, Régis. 1992. *La Littérature franco-antillaise: Haïti, Guadeloupe et Martinique.* Paris: Karthala.

Arnold, A. James. 1994. *A History of Literature in the Caribbean.* Vol. 1, *Hispanic and Francophone Regions.* Amsterdam: John Benjamins.

Baudot, Alain. 1993. *Bibliographie annotée d'Edouard Glissant.* Toronto, Ont.: GREF.

Bernabé, Jean, Patrick Chamoiseau and Raphaël Confiant. 1989. *Eloge de la créolité.* Paris: Gallimard.

———. 1990. "In Praise of Creoleness". Translated by Mohamed B. Taleb-Kyan. *Callaloo* 13, no. 4: 896–909. Re-published in bilingual edition 1993, Paris: Gallimard.

Berrian, Brenda. 1989. *Bibliography of Women Writers from the Caribbean.* Washington, DC: Three Continents Press.

Bouchard, Monique. 1990. *Une Lecture de "Pluie et vent sur Telumée Miracle" de Simone Schwarz-Bart.* Fort-de-France, Martinique: Presses Universitaires

Créoles/GEREC; Paris: L'Harmattan.

Burton, Richard D.E. 1997. *Le Roman marron: études sur la littérature martiniquaise contemporaine*. Paris: L'Harmattan.

Burton, Richard D.E., and Fred Reno, eds. 1994. *Les Antilles-Guyane au rendez-vous de l'Europe: le grand tournant?*. Paris: Economica.

———. 1995. *French and West Indian: Martinique, Guadeloupe and French Guiana Today*. London: Macmillan.

Cailler, Bernadette. 1988. *Conquérants de la nuit nue: Edouard Glissant et l'H(h)istoire antillaise*. Tübingen, Ger.: G. Narr.

Case, Frederick Ivor. 1985. *The Crisis of Identity: Studies in the Guadeloupean and Martiniquan Novel*. Sherbrooke, Que.: Namaan.

Chamoiseau, Patrick. 1997. *Ecrire en pays dominé*. Paris: Gallimard.

Chancy, Myriam. 1996. *Framing Silence: Revolutionary Novels by Haitian Women*. New Brunswick, NJ: Rutgers University Press.

Collectif. 1996. *L'Œuvre de Maryse Condé: questions et réponses à propos d'une écrivaine politiquement incorrecte*. Paris: L'Harmattan.

Condé, Maryse, ed. 1992. *L'Héritage de Caliban*. Pointe-à-Pitre, Guadeloupe: Jasor.

Condé, Maryse, and Madeleine Cottenet-Hage, eds. 1995. *Penser la créolité*. Paris: Karthala.

Corzani, Jack, ed. 1992. *Encyclopédie antillaise*. 7 vols. Fort-de-France, Martinique: Desormeaux.

Cudjoe, Selwyn. R., ed. 1990. *Caribbean Women Writers: Essays from the First International Conference*. Wellesley, Mass.: Calaloux.

Dance, Daryl. 1986. *Fifty Caribbean Writers*. Westport, Conn.: Greenwood.

Dash, J. Michael. 1988. *Haiti and the United States: National Stereotypes and the Literary Imagination*. Basingstoke, UK: Macmillan; 2nd ed., 1997.

———. 1995. *Edouard Glissant*. Cambridge, UK: Cambridge University Press.

Davies, Carole Boyce, and Elaine Savory Fido, eds. 1990. *Out of the Kumbla: Caribbean Women's Literature*. Trenton, NJ: Africa World Press.

Dayan, Joan. 1995. *Haiti, History and the Gods*. Berkeley: University of California Press.

Fenwick, M.J. 1992. *Writers of the Caribbean and Central America: A Bibliography*. 2 vols. New York: Garland.

Gardiner, Madeleine. 1981. *Visages de femmes: portraits d'écrivains*. Port-au-Prince, Haiti: Henri Deschamps.

Glissant, Edouard. 1981. *Le discours antillais*. Paris: Seuil.

———. 1989. *Caribbean Discourse*. Translated by J. Michael Dash. Charlottesville: University of Virginia Press.

Green, Mary Jane, Karen Gould, Micheline Rice-Maximin, Keith L. Walker and Jack A.Yeager, eds. 1996. *Postcolonial Subjects: Francophone Women Writers*. Minneapolis: University of Minnesota Press.

Haigh, Sam. 1999. *An Introduction to Caribbean Francophone Writing.* Oxford: Berg.

Hoffmann, Léon-François. 1992. *Bibliographie des études littéraires haïtiennes 1804–1984.* Vanves, France: EDICEF.

Jonassaint, Jean. 1986. *Le Pouvoir des mots: les maux du pouvoir: des romanciers haïtiens de l'Exil.* Paris: L'Arcantère; Montreal: Presses de l'Université de Montréal.

Jones, Bridget, and Sita E. Dickson Littlewood. 1997. *Paradoxes of French Caribbean Theatre: An Annotated Checklist of Dramatic Works – Guadeloupe, Guyane, Martinique – from 1900.* London: Roehampton Institute.

Jouanny, Robert. 1996. *Espaces littéraires d'Afrique et d'Amérique: Tracées francophones.* Vol. 1. Paris: L'Harmattan.

Laroche, Maximilien. 1987. *Contributions à l'étude du réalisme merveilleux: essais, 2.* Quebec City: GRELCA, Université Laval.

———. 1991. *La Double scène de la représentation: oralité et littérature dans la Caraïbe.* Sainte-Foy, Que.: GRELCA.

Lionnet, Françoise. 1989. *Autobiographical Voices: Race, Gender, Self-Portraiture: Reading Women Writing.* Ithaca, NY: Cornell University Press.

Ludwig, Ralph, ed. 1994. *Ecrire la "parole de nuit": la nouvelle littérature antillaise.* Paris: Gallimard.

Maximin, Colette. 1996. *Littératures caribéennes comparées.* Pointe-à-Pitre, Guadeloupe: Jasor; Paris: Karthala.

Makward, Christiane, P. 1999. *Mayotte Capécia, ou l'aliénation selon Fanon.* Paris: Karthala.

Ormerod, Beverley. 1985. *An Introduction to the French Caribbean Novel.* London; Portsmouth, NH: Heinemann.

Paravisini-Gebert, Lizabeth, and Olga Torres-Seda, eds. 1993. *Caribbean Women Novelists: An Annotated Critical Bibliography.* Westport, Conn.: Greenwood.

Pfaff, Françoise. 1993. *Entretiens avec Maryse Condé: suivis d'une bibliographie complète.* Paris: Karthala.

———. 1996. *Conversations with Maryse Condé.* Lincoln: University of Nebraska Press.

Pyne-Timothy, Helen, ed. 1997. *The Woman, the Writer and Caribbean Society: Essays on Literature and Culture.* Los Angeles: UCLA Center for African American Studies.

Richardson, Michael, ed. 1996. *Refusal of the Shadow: Surrealism and the Caribbean.* London: Verso.

Rinne, Suzanne, and Joëlle Vitiello. 1997. *Elles écrivent des Antilles (Haïti, Guadeloupe, Martinique).* Paris: L'Harmattan.

Rosello, Mireille. 1992. *Littérature et identité créole aux Antilles.* Paris: Karthala.

Shelton, Marie-Denise. 1993. *Image de la société dans le roman haïtien.* Paris: L'Harmattan.

Taylor, Patrick. 1989. *The Narrative of Liberation: Perspectives on Afro-Caribbean Literature, Popular Culture and Politics*. Ithaca, NY: Cornell University Press.

Toumson, Roger. 1989. *La Transgression des couleurs: littérature et langage des Antilles*. 2 vols. Paris: Editions Caribéennes.

Toureh, Fanta. 1987. *L'Imaginaire dans l'œuvre de Simone Schwarz-Bart: approche d'une mythologie antillaise*. Paris: L'Harmattan.

Webb, Barbara J. 1992. *Myth and History in Caribbean Fiction*. Amherst: University of Massachusetts Press.

Contributors

Gertrud Aub-Buscher taught French at the University of the West Indies, Mona, Jamaica, from 1960 to 1979, and directed the language centre of the University of Hull from 1979 to 2000. She is the author of *Le parler rural de Ranrupt*, editor of *The Linguistic Challenge of the New Europe* as well as articles on Creole, and, now retired, is continuing to do research on French-lexifier Creoles.

Beverley Ormerod Noakes, a Jamaican, was until 2002 Associate Professor of French at the University of Western Australia. She previously lectured at the University of the West Indies, Mona, Jamaica, where, in 1967, she devised the first course in French Caribbean literature. She is the author of *An Introduction to the French Caribbean Novel* and co-author of a book on women writers from francophone Africa.

Pauline Christie taught linguistics at the University of the West Indies, Mona, Jamaica, until her retirement. She has worked and written on Creoles in general and that of Dominica in particular. She is the editor of *Caribbean Language Issues: Old and New* (1996) and *Due Respect: Papers in Honour of Professor Robert Le Page* (2001).

Michael Dash, born in Trinidad, has taught in the Caribbean, Africa and the United States and is currently Professor of French at New York University. His publications include *Literature and Ideology in Haiti* (1981), *Haiti and the United States* (1988), *Edouard Glissant* (1995), *The Other America: Caribbean Literature in a New World Context* (1998), as well as translations, notably of works by Glissant.

Priska Degras, born in Paris of Martinican parentage, teaches at the University of Aix-Marseille III and is working on the novel of the Americas. She has published numerous articles as well as novellas in journals and collections, such as *Présence Africaine, La Revue Noire* and *A peine plus qu'un cyclone aux Antilles.*

Mary Gallagher teaches French and francophone literature at University College, Dublin. She works principally on French Caribbean writing and her recent publications inlude *La Créolité de Saint-John Perse* (1998) and *Soundings in French Caribbean Writing since 1950: The Shock of Space and Time* (2002).

Sam Haigh is Senior Lecturer in French studies at the University of Warwick, where she teaches French and francophone literature. Her recent publications include *Mapping a Tradition: Francophone Women Writers from Guadeloupe* (2000) and an edited collection of essays, *An Introduction to Caribbean Francophone Writing* (1999).

Marie-Christine Hazaël-Massieux is Professor at the Université de Provence, docteur ès lettres (*doctorat d'état* on "The Creole of Guadeloupe: From Orality to Writing"), and in charge of the Groupe Européen de Recherches en Langues Créoles. The majority of her numerous publications (articles and books) deal with French-lexifier Creoles.

Bridget Jones taught French and francophone literature at the University of the West Indies, Mona, Jamaica, and the Roehampton Institute, and published widely, especially on topics of French Caribbean literature, but also on anglophone writing in the Caribbean. She died in 2000 and this book is dedicated to her memory.

Anthea Morrison, a former student of Bridget Jones, is Senior Lecturer at the University of the West Indies, Cave Hill, Barbados. Her research interests include post-Negritude francophone Caribbean literature and comparative literature, and she is currently working on a study of Maryse Condé.

Marie-José N'Zengou-Tayo, born in Haiti, teaches French language and literature and translation in the Department of Modern Languages and Literatures at the University of the West Indies, Mona. Her field of study includes Haitian literature and culture and comparative literature of the French-speaking Caribbean. She is currently working on the literary representation of Haitian labour migration.

Carol Sanders has published on the language and literature of the French-speaking world and on various aspects of French linguistics. She has taught at a number of universities in Britain, France, the West Indies and Australia, and she currently holds the chair of French at the University of Surrey.

Betty Wilson teaches anglophone and francophone literature and women's studies at the University of the West Indies, Mona, Jamaica. She co-edited the first anthology of prose writing by women from the Caribbean, *Her True-True Name* (1989) and has translated novels, short stories, and poetry from Africa and the Caribbean.